Extraordinary People
IN THE MOVIES

Judy L. Hasday, Ed. M.

Children's Press®
A Division of Scholastic Inc.
New York Toronto London Auckland Sydney
Mexico City New Delhi Hong Kong
Danbury, Connecticut

I'd like to express special thanks to friends Therese and Pam for their support and for cheerleading me along through this project. Love and thanks also to Mom, my biggest fan.

Interior design by Elizabeth Helmetsie

Library of Congress Cataloging-in-Publication Data

Hasday, Judy L., 1957–
    Extraordinary people in the movies / Judy L. Hasday.
      p. cm. – (Extraordinary people)
    Includes bibliographical references and index.
    ISBN 0-516-22348-8 (lib. bdg.)   0-516-27857-6 (pbk.)
    1. Motion picture actors and actresses—United States—Biographies [1. Actors and actresses.
    2. Motion picture producers and directors.] I. Title. II. Series.

PN1998.2.H44 2003
791.43'028'092273—dc21
[B]
2002011221

Contents

50

Greta Garbo
1905–1990
One of Hollywood's
Most Private Film Stars

66

Jimmy Stewart
1908–1997
One of America's
Best-Loved Actors

82

**Grandeur on
the Big Screen**

54

Katharine Hepburn
1907–
"Number One
Actress of All Time"

70

Ingrid Bergman
1915–1982
Costar of
Oscar-Winning
Film *Casablanca*

87

Paul Newman
1925–
Legendary Actor,
Entrepreneur, Activist,
and Humanitarian

58

Laurence Olivier
1907–1989
Greatest English-Speaking
Actor of the Twentieth
Century

74

Lauren Bacall
1924–
Award-Winning
Actress and Wife of
Humphrey Bogart

92

Peter Sellers
1925–1977
One of the
World's Greatest
Comedic Actors

62

Bette Davis
1908–1989
First Lady of the
American Screen

78

Marlon Brando
1924–
"Tough-Guy" Actor
Best Known for His
Performance in *The Godfather*

97

Marilyn Monroe
1926–1962
Film Star and
American Icon

101

Sidney Poitier
1927–
Influential Figure
in American Film

118

Elizabeth Taylor
1932–
English-Born Actress
and AIDS Activist

136

Jack Nicholson
1937–
One of America's Finest
and Most Unusual Actors

105

Audrey Hepburn
1929–1993
Actress and
Humanitarian

122

Shirley MacLaine
1934–
Award-Winning
Actress/Dancer and Author
of Best-Seller *Out on a Limb*

140

Robert Redford
1937–
Actor, Director, Creator
of Sundance Film Festival

110

Grace Kelly
1929–1982
Fairy-Tale Life of
Actress-Turned-Princess

127

Julie Andrews
1935–
Award-Winning Stage
and Screen Star

144

**"Lights! Camera!
Action!": Directors**

114

Sean Connery
1930–
First Actor to Portray
Spy-Hero James Bond

132

Dustin Hoffman
1937–
Award-Winning Leading
Man of Hollywood

150

Al Pacino
1940–
Multi-Award-Winning
Actor of Stage and Screen

154

Harrison Ford
1942–
Successful Actor and Star
of the *Star Wars* Trilogy

172

Sally Field
1946–
Actress Who Rose from
TV Stardom to Major
Motion Pictures

190

Robin Williams
1952–
The "Tasmanian
Devil of Comedy"

159

Barbra Streisand
1942–
Award-Winning
"Actress Who Sings"

176

Steven Spielberg
1946–
Influential Director
and Producer

194

Jackie Chan
1954–
International Martial
Arts Film Star

163

Robert De Niro
1943–
Regarded as One of
the Greatest Actors
in Modern Film

181

Glenn Close
1947–
Respected Stage
and Screen Actress

198

John Travolta
1954–
Acclaimed Actor
of His Generation

167

Cher
1946–
Multitalented
Singer and Actress

185

Meryl Streep
1949–
Acclaimed Actress
of Stage and Screen

202

Denzel Washington
1954–
Recipient of the 2002
Oscar for Best Actor

207

**Can Oscar
Become
Color-Blind?**

 224

Spike Lee
1957–
Influential African
American Director

 241

Halle Berry
1968–
First African American
Woman to Win the
Best Actress Oscar

212

Whoopi Goldberg
1955–
Multi-Award-Winning
Actress and Humanitarian

228

Tom Cruise
1962–
Acclaimed
Modern-Day Actor

245

Will Smith
1968–
Rapper and Actor

216

Bruce Willis
1955–
Regular Guy
Turned Actor

232

Jodie Foster
1962–
Multitalented Actor,
Producer, and Director

249

Gwyneth Paltrow
1972–
Highly Acclaimed
Award-Winning Actress

220

Tom Hanks
1956–
Versatile Actor
and Director

237

Julia Roberts
1967–
One of the Most Beloved
Actresses in Hollywood

253

Drew Barrymore
1975–
Former Child Star and
Current Day Popular
Film Actress

Charlie Chaplin

Silent Film Star
1889–1977

Even when I was in the orphanage, when I was roaming the street trying to find enough to eat, even then I thought of myself as the greatest actor in the world.

—CHARLIE CHAPLIN

Considered the most influential artist in the history of the motion picture industry, Charlie Chaplin achieved international recognition during the early days of the silent movie era. Almost 100 years since his film debut in *Making a Living,* the image of Chaplin's "Little Tramp"—toothbrush mustache, black bowler, baggy pants, oversized shoes, and waddle walk—is still instantly recognizable. The artistic expression Chaplin brought to the screen forever changed the way an audience related to the motion picture medium.

Charles Spencer Chaplin was born into poverty on April 16, 1889, in

London, England. Parents Charles and Hannah Chaplin barely eked out a living as music hall entertainers. Charles senior left the family when Charlie was still a baby, leaving Hannah to raise him and his older half brother, Sydney. When Hannah became mentally ill, Charlie and Sydney had to go out and work in order to eat. Hannah spent much of the rest of her life in and out of mental institutions, leaving Charlie to live in an orphanage.

Charlie had some experience entertaining and used that budding talent to make a living. At the tender age of eight Charlie appeared in a clog dance act called Eight Lancashire Lads. Charlie was good and was being noticed by people in the entertainment field. Sydney acted as his brother's agent and got Charlie an engagement at the London Hippodrome when he was just ten years old.

Charlie performed onstage in *Sherlock Holmes* from 1903 to 1906, playing the paperboy, Billy. He then joined the Casey Circus as a mime (acting without using words). When he became a teenager, Charlie returned to work in vaudeville, where he discovered he had a talent for comedic pantomime. In 1908 Charlie joined former music hall acrobat Fred Karno and his comedy troupe. Charlie was a quick study and soon became a principal player in the cast. In 1910 Charlie got a big break when Karno selected him to accompany the troupe on a touring engagement in America.

Chaplin performed with the Karno Troupe until 1913, when he signed a contract with Mack Sennett's Keystone Films. Silent films provided a great vehicle for Chaplin to showcase his comedic and acrobatic talents. He made his first film, *Making a Living,* in 1914. It was in his second film, *Kid Auto Races at Venice,* that Chaplin introduced his Tramp character—a little fellow wearing clothing from several other comics. The Tramp character remained virtually the same throughout the rest of Chaplin's career.

Not content to be just an actor, Chaplin wanted more control over his work and the filmmaking process. His silent comedy movies were making money, and he felt he was worth more money than he was being paid. When his contract was up at Keystone, he signed for an unprecedented salary of $1,250 a week, plus a $10,000 signing bonus, with another pioneering company, Essanay Films.

At Essanay, Chaplin further developed his Tramp character. Audiences around the country related to the downtrodden fellow, who despite adversity remained optimistic. *The Tramp* (1915), the first film devoted to the character, introduced the image of Chaplin traipsing off alone down a desolate road. Essanay enthusiastically promoted Chaplin's Tramp character. His image became a merchandiser's dream, appearing on collectors' cards, toys, and books.

The tremendous financial success of his films gave Chaplin more time to work on his writing, directing, and acting skills. When his contract with Essanay was up in 1915, Chaplin's brother, Sydney, worked out a deal with the Mutual Film Company that gave a half-million-dollar contract to a man who as a kid had to dance for his supper.

It was during his time at Mutual that Chaplin produced some of his greatest work, including films like *The Floorwalker* (1916) and *The Immigrant* (1917). Despite being well compensated at Mutual, Chaplin still yearned to have complete freedom and his own company. In 1919 Chaplin and colleagues Douglas Fairbanks, **Mary Pickford,*** and director D. W. Griffith founded United Artists Corporation (UA).

Before doing work exclusively for UA, Chaplin had a few more film obligations to fulfill at Mutual. His first full-length feature film, *The Kid,* was a masterpiece. Chaplin believed that in order for a film's comedy to fully come through, an element of sadness had to be present. In *The Kid* (1921), the Tramp takes in a small orphan boy. Ultimately *The Kid* grossed about $2.5 million dollars.

---

* There is a separate entry for names in bold type.

The 1923 *A Woman of Paris* was a terrible disappointment for Chaplin. It was the first UA film he directed; but it flopped at the box office, so Chaplin returned to the safety of his Tramp character and produced *The Gold Rush.* Perhaps Chaplin's best work, *The Gold Rush* (1925) focuses on the Tramp's search for gold and romance in the Klondike Mountains. Classic scenes from the film include Chaplin and two starving prospectors boiling and eating a shoe. The *Gold Rush* was Chaplin's most successful silent film, grossing more than $4 million dollars.

It was three years before Chaplin released his next film, called *The Circus,* in 1928. By now the sound era had come upon the film industry. Many, including Chaplin, were skeptical. He continued to make silent pictures throughout the 1930s. His film *Modern Times* (1936), though brilliantly conceived, caused controversy because of its socialist overtones. In 1940 Chaplin gave moviegoers their last look at the Tramp in his first talkie, *The Great Dictator.* In this satire of Adolf Hitler, Chaplin portrayed a Jewish barber whose resemblance to the Führer gets him into trouble. The film received several Oscar nominations and grossed $5 million at the box office.

No stranger to controversy in his personal life, Chaplin's first two wives, Mildred Harris and Lita Grey, were sixteen years old when he married them. His third wife, Paulette Goddard, was nineteen on her wedding day; Chaplin was forty-seven and already the father of two. Oona, the daughter of play-wright Eugene O'Neill, was just eighteen years old when she married a fifty-four-year-old Chaplin. Together they had eight children, the last of which was born when Chaplin was 73.

After Chaplin's release of *Limelight* (1952), he left for Europe with his family. Though he had lived in America for almost forty years, Chaplin never became a citizen. Once he was in England, the United States rescinded his reentry visa. Angry and bitter, Chaplin vowed never to return to America. He settled his family in Vevey, Switzerland, and made a few more unmemorable films before publishing his autobiography in 1964. His last film, *A Countess from Hong Kong*, was released in 1967.

At age eighty-three Chaplin did return to America to accept a special Oscar for his outstanding contributions to the film industry. In 1975 Chaplin was knighted by Queen Elizabeth II of England.

Mary Pickford

Silent Film Star and "America's Sweetheart"
1892–1979

My career was planned, there was never anything accidental about it. It was planned, it was painful, it was purposeful.

—MARY PICKFORD

At the turn of the twentieth century women had not yet attained the right to vote. Advanced education opportunities for women were the exception, not the norm. In industry there were perhaps a handful of women who owned their own businesses. The motion picture industry was in its infancy, and it was men who dominated both in front of, and behind, the camera—that is, until Mary Pickford came along. It is hard to imagine the magnitude of her celebrity and contribution, given the times.

Though she was dubbed "America's Sweetheart," Mary Pickford, née Gladys Louise Smith, was born in Toronto, Canada, on April 8, 1892. The oldest of three children, Mary did not have much of a childhood. When she was five, her father died, leaving Charlotte Pickford to raise Mary and her younger siblings, Lottie and Jack, alone. With little income, the widowed seamstress took in whatever work she could find, including working on theater costumes for the Cummings Stock Company. When the stage manager noticed little eight-year-old Mary, he thought she would be perfect for a part in a play being cast. The future star and family breadwinner made her acting debut at the Princess Theater in Toronto, in *The Silver King.* This brief appearance set Mary's career path for life.

Charlotte took on the role of stage mother and manager for her young daughter, overseeing every aspect of Mary's career. In 1902 the family left Toronto and moved to New York City. Mary spent several years touring with a number of road companies and was known as "Baby Gladys." Being on the road was hard work and a harsh way of life for such a young girl. When she wasn't traveling, Mary helped her mother by taking care of Lottie and Jack, as well as overseeing many household responsibilities, like preparing a budget, paying the bills, and watching expenses.

At fourteen Mary decided that she was ready for Broadway. She went to see theater producer David Belasco and charmed her way into getting a starring role in *The Warrens of Virginia* (1907). It was Belasco who insisted on the name change. Contrary to common belief that the name Mary Pickford was just made up, it was actually the name of her deceased great-aunt.

While the theater was enjoying popularity as an entertainment medium, the technology of moving pictures was also growing. Despite reservations about leaving the stage for work in the "flickers," Mary went to the Biograph Company to talk to its director, D. W. Griffith (the father of modern cinema). She used her persuasiveness to get Griffith to agree to sign her to a contract. She even negotiated the terms, which was unheard of at that time.

During the next two years Mary appeared in seventy-nine Biograph films. By 1910 Mary had become a huge star of the silent screen (movies did not yet have sound) and was sought after by other film companies. Though still only a teenager, she was an astute businesswoman. Mary knew she was in great demand and used that to her advantage. She began moving from studio to studio, so she could demand higher wages and more control over her films. As her popularity soared, so did her income.

By 1916 Mary's salary had climbed to $10,000 a week, plus a $30,000 bonus. That was the same money legendary star **Charlie Chaplin** was earning. Mary demanded to be treated equally with her male counterparts, and she was. She also got more involved with other aspects of filmmaking, from hiring the cast and crew, reviewing scripts, and overseeing the promotion of each film release.

In 1917, while on tour selling Liberty Bonds for the war effort (World War I), Mary met fellow actors Charlie Chaplin and Douglas Fairbanks. Two years later, in an era when most women didn't even work, she cofounded United Artists Corporation with partners D. W. Griffith, Chaplin, and Fairbanks. Mary Pickford had become the first female movie entrepreneur. In 1920 she and Douglas Fairbanks married. The couple was treated like Hollywood royalty. They played frequent hosts at their "Pickfair" estate to a wide variety of people, including the Duke of Alba; Lord and Lady Mountbatten; writers F. Scott Fitzgerald, Sir Arthur Conan Doyle, and H. G. Wells; physicist Albert Einstein; Amelia Earhart; and Helen Keller. It was an idyllic time in Mary's life.

With co-ownership of a film studio came more responsibilities. Mary was now more than a smiling face on the silent screen. Of that time she said, "There was none of this nonsense of nine to five in those days, believe me. When I finished on the set, I had to write all the checks and give the orders for the next day."

Ironically, by the time United Artists was formed, many of Mary's best films, like *Tess of the Storm Country* (1914), *Rebecca of Sunnybrook Farm* (1917), and *Poor Little Rich Girl* (1917), had already been made. She had stretched the "little girl" image as far as it would go. At age twenty-seven she just could not pull off looking like an adolescent any longer. To put an end to her girlish image, Mary finally cut her long angelic curls and had her hair fashioned into a new short "bob" look. To complete the transformation for the screen, Mary hired German director Ernst Lubitsch to work with her on the 1923 film *Rosita.* Even today, *Rosita* is considered one of the most beautiful films produced during the silent era. The film received rave reviews, and Mary had become a graceful woman of the screen.

The pinnacle of Mary Pickford's career came in 1929, when she won the Best Actress Academy Award for her role in her first film "talkie," *Coquette.* But within months everything took a downward spiral. The stock market crash in October threw the country into an economic depression. People no longer had money to spend on going to the movies. United Artists released just three more films over the next four years. Mary made her last film, *Secrets,* in 1933 and retired from the screen.

Mary's marriage to Fairbanks ended in 1936, and she and Chaplin bought out their partners in United Artists. The two continued to own the company until the mid-1950s. Mary turned her attention to other interests, including forming the Mary Pickford Cosmetics Company and writing several books, including her autobiography, *Sunshine and Shadow* (1955). On the charitable front, Mary helped establish the Motion Picture Country Home and Hospital, which provided aid to former film-industry stars and workers who were left without medical insurance or retirement benefits. In 1937 Mary married her third husband, actor Charles "Buddy" Rogers, with whom she remained for the rest of her life.

As she got older, Mary withdrew from the public eye and became reclusive. One highlight in her later years was when the Academy of Motion Picture Arts and Sciences honored Mary Pickford by presenting her with a Lifetime Achievement Award at the 1976 Oscars. For the next three years she remained behind the walls of Pickfair until her death from a cerebral hemorrhage on May 29, 1979.

Hattie McDaniel

First African American Oscar Winner
1895–1952

*I wanted to turn this stock role into a living,
breathing character.*

—HATTIE MCDANIEL

It was forty-seven years before Academy Award–winner Hattie McDaniel's last wish came close to being fulfilled. Before her death Hattie requested that she be buried at Hollywood Memorial Park Cemetery in California—the final resting place for many legends of the film industry, including Cecil B. DeMille, Douglas Fairbanks, Rudolph Valentino, and Peter Lorre. Her request was denied because the cemetery did not accept blacks.

Even in death the spunky star was subjected to the racism and segregation that permeated America during her lifetime. In 1998 Tyler Cassity bought Hollywood Memorial Park Cemetery, and on October 26, 1999—the forty-seventh anniversary of McDaniel's death—he unveiled a gray-and-pink granite monument dedicated to the actress. In the distance, on a hillside overlooking the cemetery, looms the enormous HOLLYWOOD sign. It is a fitting tribute to one of America's great character actresses.

The youngest of thirteen children, Hattie McDaniel was born on June 10, 1895, in Wichita, Kansas. Her father, Henry, was an ex-slave turned Baptist preacher; her mother, Susan Holbert McDaniel, sang in the church choir. In elementary school Hattie showed talent by singing and reciting poetry. As a teen, she performed in plays and musicals at Denver East High School. At an entertainment event sponsored by the Women's Christian Temperance Union, Hattie gave a stirring recitation of "Convict Joe," a poem by Alexander Murdoch detailing the horrors of alcohol abuse. The youngster finished with tears in her eyes, and the audience was moved to a standing ovation. Hattie earned the organization's gold medal for Best Performance.

Hattie dropped out of high school and joined family members in touring minstrel shows, traveling from Colorado to the West Coast. She enjoyed the three years on the road and wrote some songs as well. When her father retired, Hattie picked up odd jobs around Denver. Her break came in 1920 when she began touring with George Morrison and his Melody Hounds Orchestra. The band played in places like Portland, Salt Lake City, El Paso, and even Juárez, Mexico. Working with Morrison allowed Hattie to showcase her talents, even though widespread segregation prevented her from entertaining in white establishments. Undaunted, Hattie continued to perform with Morrison and made her singing debut on Denver radio station KOA in 1925.

When the Depression struck in 1929, Hattie was among the millions of Americans who were suddenly jobless. She traveled to Milwaukee for a shot as a performer at the Club Madrid—but she was hired as a ladies' washroom attendant instead. Working for a dollar a night plus tips, Hattie stood in the washroom doorway listening to the music and singing softly to herself. A white patron heard Hattie's beautiful voice and insisted that the club owner let her perform. She was such a hit that she earned ninety dollars in tips that night.

Hattie's growing popularity gave her the confidence to try her luck in Hollywood. Her brother Sam and sister Etta were already living in California, and each had earned several small film parts. Hattie arrived in Los Angeles in 1931 and immediately hit the studios, seeking work. She landed a job with her brother on the radio program "Optimistic Do-Nut Hour." Nicknamed Hi-Hat Hattie because of her fancy wardrobe and bossy but bubbly personality, she was an immediate hit. But because she earned just five dollars a week, she kept looking for better-paying jobs—and finally got a movie part.

At first Hattie was a film chorus singer. She received no screen credits and made just five dollars per movie. In 1932 she landed her first on-screen role as a beloved house servant in *The Golden West*. Hattie would reprise (replay) this same type of character in many other roles.

Slowly, McDaniel began receiving roles in films featuring Hollywood's biggest stars, including Mae West, Gary Cooper, and Will Rogers. In *Judge Priest* (1934), she was given a solo and performed a duet with Rogers. She gained a reputation for playing her trademark role, the take-charge, sometimes sassy, "boss" of the household. In *Gentle Julia* (1936), for example, Hattie is asked by the mistress of the house to wash the dog. "No ma'am, Miss Julia" replies her character. "I ain't playin' nurse to no dog." While some whites were unhappy with the screen image of a brash and independent black female, many blacks felt that McDaniel was being forced into stereotypical roles.

By the time producer David O. Selznick began casting for the film version of Margaret Mitchell's epic *Gone With the Wind* (1939), Hattie had many Hollywood supporters who wanted to see her cast as Scarlett O'Hara's "Mammy." Actor and singer Bing Crosby wrote to Selznick suggesting McDaniel. Selznick wanted an actress who could portray "a confidante, counselor, and manager of the O'Hara household." McDaniel's screen test proved she was perfect for the role.

Gone With the Wind was a blockbuster. It earned thirteen Academy Award nominations, including Best Picture, Best Actor, Best Actress, and two for Best Supporting Actress—Olivia de Havilland and Hattie McDaniel. On February 29, 1940, Hattie arrived at the Ambassador Hotel in Hollywood on the arm of longtime friend Wonderful Smith. Hollywood colleagues stood and applauded as she took her place in the Coconut Grove Ballroom, where the Academy Awards ceremony was being held.

When Hattie McDaniel was named winner of the Oscar for Best Supporting Actress, the audience went wild. "The ovation . . . will go down in history as one of the greatest ever accorded any performer in the annals of the industry," one audience member said. Hattie accepted her award with grace and humility. "[T]his is one of the happiest moments in my life," she said, "and I want to thank each of you who had a part in [it]. . . . I shall always hold it as a beacon for anything that I may be able to do in the future. I sincerely hope that I shall always be a credit to my race, and to the motion picture industry."

Hattie McDaniel had made history: she not only became the first black performer nominated for an award, but she was also the first to win one. In a country where segregation was rampant, Hattie's achievement was a spectacular triumph.

Hattie continued working in films, but was troubled by the continual criticism leveled against her for playing stereotypical or negative roles. She responded to the attacks by saying, "I'd rather play a maid and make $700 a week than be one for $7." McDaniel appeared in more than 300 movies in her sixteen-year career. In 1947 she left Hollywood to take the lead role on the radio program *The Beulah Show*. She made history once more, becoming the first black performer to gain a starring radio role. *Beulah* was a hit, drawing almost 20,000 listeners each week.

The Beulah Show went to television in 1950. Shortly after, however, Hattie was diagnosed with breast cancer. It was one challenge she could not overcome: she died on October 26, 1952.

Humphrey Bogart

Award-Winning Actor Best Known for Role in Casablanca
1899–1957

Acting is experience with something sweet behind it.

—HUMPHREY BOGART

Though immortalized on-screen for his honorable good-bye to the tearful **Ingrid Bergman** on the airport runway in *Casablanca,* Humphrey Bogart is also remembered for giving life to Sam Spade, the 1940s trench coat–wearing detective. Bogart, who appeared in more than seventy-five films in twenty-six years, was also seen as the tough romantic, learning how to whistle on-screen from **Lauren Bacall.**

While his well-off parents envisioned their son as a future Yale graduate and doctor, Humphrey DeForest Bogart showed himself ill fitted for that lifestyle. He was born in New York City on December 25, 1899, to the noted illustrator and artist Maud Humphrey, and the successful surgeon Belmont DeForest Bogart. They enrolled their son in the prestigious Trinity School and then Phillips Academy, but poor grades and an unfortunate incident with a teacher had him expelled from Phillips. In 1918 the young man who would become one of America's most celebrated on-screen tough guys proved his mettle in real life by joining the navy. While there are a few stories to explain how Bogart got his signature scarred lip, the most accepted version is that it occurred while he was in the service. A handcuffed prisoner Bogart was escorting smacked him in the mouth while trying to escape.

After several years in the navy, Bogart returned to civilian life. Looking for work, he approached family friend and theater producer William A. Brady. Brady gave him a job as an office boy, and the opportunity to be a stage manager. He also did some relatively menial work at Brady's New York film studio, World Film Corporation. In 1922 Alice Brady, the actress-daughter of William Brady, helped Bogart get his first shot at acting. He got a small part in *Drifting,* a play Alice was starring in. Through the 1920s Bogart worked in a number of shows, often being cast as a young thug or romantic second lead. Bogart's 1926 marriage to Helen Menken, a successful stage actress, was mostly motivated by the belief that it could help his career. It lasted only a year. In 1928 he married actress Mary Philips but headed to Hollywood, California, in 1930, hoping to find better acting opportunities for himself in a new location.

Bogart was awarded a contract with Fox Film Corporation in 1930, but after three poor films they released him. Despite the setback, Bogart did get other roles with other studios, but they were not parts that helped his career. In 1934 he returned to the New York stage after being enticed by a role as a heartless murderer in Robert Sherwood's *The Petrified Forest* (1936). The move paid off. Not only did Bogart get the part, but both the play and his performance were highly admired by critics and theatergoers alike. The role proved even more helpful when Warner Brothers acquired the rights to a film version of the play. *The Petrified Forest* lead actor, Leslie Howard, was cast to star in the film. He insisted that Bogart keep his stage part in the film as well. The studio agreed, gave Bogart a contract, and was highly rewarded by the film's great success.

From 1936 to 1940 Bogart worked in twenty-eight films. Even though he had proved himself a talented actor, Bogart found himself cast in weak roles, often as a gangster. Bogart's striking performance as Baby Face Martin in *Dead End* in 1937 was one of the few exceptions. Ironically, it was a Samuel Goldwyn Studio film that Bogart made while on loan from Warner Brothers. While struggling professionally, his personal life seemed in turmoil too. His long-distance marriage to Mary Phillips ended in divorce in 1938. Bogart then found himself duped into marrying the emotional actress Mayo Methot in August of the same year.

Bogart finally realized a sharp upswing in his career after two stars turned down the lead part in the film *High Sierra* (1941), directed by Raoul Walsh and written by John Huston. Warner Brothers begrudgingly handed the challenging part to Bogart, giving him the chance to show his excellence. His performance was highly praised, as was the film. Nearly the same thing happened later that year when screen star George Raft turned down the lead role in *The Maltese Falcon* (1941), a film in which John Huston made his directorial debut. In *The Maltese Falcon,* Bogart wasn't just a tough guy; for the first time his character had sex appeal and was involved in a full-fledged romance. He was a hit once again, and his performance finally placed him in the same category with other film star contemporaries like James Cagney and Errol Flynn.

By far, Bogart would be most remembered for his role as Rick Blaine in *Casablanca* (1942). The film had an excellent cast, director, and screenwriters. It brought Bogart his first Academy Award nomination, as well as a string of future roles as the sympathetic tough guy. His part in *To Have and Have Not* (1944) brought Bogart continuing strong recognition as well as an unforeseen opportunity to revitalize his personal life. It was on this set that he met the wry and funny beauty **Lauren Bacall.** When Bogart's wife finally agreed to a divorce in May of 1945, Bogart married Bacall eleven days later. The studio loved the added publicity of having two big stars as a real-life couple and rewrote Bogart's contract to authorize the first-of-its-kind annual $1 million salary for the following fifteen years. Bogie and Bacall appeared together in three more films, although none had the same impact of their first: *The Big Sleep* (1946), directed by Howard Hawks; *Dark Passage* (1947); and *Key Largo* (1948), another Huston film.

In 1947 Bogart formed his own production company, Santana Pictures Corporation, and starred in some of its productions for Columbia, including *In a Lonely Place* (1950). In 1948 Bogart played in *The Treasure of the Sierra Madre,* providing a powerful performance in a part that required much greater range than any of his previous roles. It received great attention from critics, although it made a poor showing at the box office. In 1949 Bogart's son, Stephen Humphrey, was born.

Bogart turned in another memorable performance opposite **Katharine Hepburn** in *The African Queen* (1951), for which he won his first Academy Award, in 1952. The same year, Bacall gave birth to a daughter, Leslie Howard. Bogart continued to take on a range of roles; most notable was his part in *The Caine Mutiny* (1954), for which he received his third Academy Award nomination. Bogart could also play a funny man and did so superbly in more comic roles, including *Sabrina* (1954) and *We're No Angels* (1955).

Bogart's last role was as a worn-out sportswriter in *The Harder They Fall,* which opened in 1956. Shortly after, Bogart, who had smoked cigarettes most of his life, was diagnosed with throat cancer. He underwent surgery but died on January 14, 1957.

Alfred Hitchcock

Director and "Master of Suspense"
1899–1980

There is no terror in the bang, only in the anticipation of it.

—ALFRED HITCHCOCK

K nown as the "Master of Suspense," director Alfred Hitchcock may have acquired his gift for creating films, as he put it, "to simply scare the hell out of people," from a rather chilling event in his own youth. When he was about four or five, Alfred committed some transgression that his father, William, felt needed more than the usual scolding.

William sent his son down to the police station with a note to give to the chief suggesting a punishment that would teach Alfred a lesson. The chief put Alfred in a cell and locked the door. The memory of "the sound and the solidity of that closing cell door and bolt," said Hitchcock, stayed with him forever. Though only behind bars for a few minutes, it must have seemed like an eternity to a five-year-old. Before letting Hitchcock depart, the chief punctuated his "visit" by telling him, "That's what we do to naughty boys."

The genius of the thriller film genre was born Alfred Joseph Hitchcock on August 13, 1899, in Leytonstone, London. His father was a poultry and produce dealer; his mother, the former Emma Whelan, a homemaker. Alfred, the youngest of three children, had a brother and sister who were several years older. Alfred often felt left out of things because of the age gap between himself and his siblings and had a rather lonely childhood.

Alfred was raised in a strict Irish-Catholic household. Strongly influenced by his Catholic upbringing, Alfred retained his fear of authority and punishment during his years as a student at St. Ignatius College, a Jesuit school. Corporal punishment was routinely doled out as a means of discipline there. A rap on the knuckles with a ruler was the usual method, and Alfred felt that such incidents were "like going to the gallows." As a rather shy, introverted child, he had few friends and preferred solitude to the companionship of his peers.

At an early age Hitchcock took solo rides on a London bus or wandered around the shipping docks and terminals. As a teen, he often found himself a spectator listening to a murder trial at the Old Bailey, a historic criminal court. He was also a frequent visitor to the Black Museum at Scotland Yard. Later in his life Alfred wrote, "I have always been fascinated by crime. . . . The British take a peculiar interest in the literature of crime."

Hitchcock's fascination with disturbing events and his fear of authority and reproach later emerged in many of his movies. He wove his fears into such films as *The Wrong Man* (1956) and *North by Northwest* (1959). A compelling feature of his filmmaking was that Hitchcock's characters were everyday people drawn into unexpected and often terrifying situations. The villain in one of his movies could very well be your next-door neighbor or someone you see at the market everyday.

Hitchcock began his film career after studying engineering and navigation at the University of London. He enjoyed drawing and drafting and collected maps and timetables as a hobby. His first job was as a technical clerk at the W. T. Henley Telegraph Company. His interest in drawing prompted him to take evening classes in art, and he attended the cinema and theater. Eventually

Hitchcock's interest shifted to filmmaking. In 1920 Famous Players-Lasky (later known as Paramount Studios) opened a studio in London and hired Hitchcock to create title cards for silent films.

Learning every aspect of filmmaking, Hitchcock worked his way up to assistant director in just three years. During that time he met freelance editor Alma Reville. They married in 1926, and she gave up her own career to work with Hitchcock on every phase of production. They had one child, a daughter named Pat, who would later be cast in minor roles in many of her father's films.

Hitchcock got his first big directorial break with the 1926 release of the silent film *The Lodger.* The film would become Hitchcock's trademark style—chock-full of intrigue and suspense. The plot revolves around a man falsely accused of a crime, who must find a way to prove his innocence. The film was also creative and unusual, another of Hitchcock's consistent film styles. In *The Lodger,* Hitchcock has an actor pace back and forth over a piece of glass upstairs where the heroine can hear him. The audience, on the other hand, gets to see the footprints.

Over the next several years Hitchcock released thirteen sound films, including *Murder!* (1930), *The Man Who Knew Too Much* (1934), *The 39 Steps* (1935), and *Sabotage* (1936). These films were quite successful in Europe, and Hitchcock had become one of Britain's top directors. Feeling he would have even more opportunities to produce his kinds of films in Hollywood, Hitchcock arrived in America in 1939. His instincts proved right. American producer David O. Selznick offered Hitchcock an unprecedented $800,000 to make five films. Hitchcock's first American film was *Rebecca,* made in 1940. The Academy of Motion Picture Arts and Sciences awarded the film the Best Picture Oscar.

With World War II raging in Europe and the Pacific, Hitchcock made a few films whose themes reflected the fears of the times—military espionage, terror, and sabotage, including the highly lauded *Foreign Correspondent* (1940) and the cross-country chase thriller *Saboteur* (1942). Inevitably a woman, preferably a blonde, was somehow woven into the story. Hitchcock would return to this style in later films like *Notorious* and *North by Northwest*.

In Hollywood, in addition to his works with a military theme, Hitchcock made many of the psychological thrillers he is most recognized for. In those films Hitchcock always included some dysfunctional dynamic—evil, criminal, or even voyeuristic. In Hitchcock's films evil didn't necessarily have to emerge in an act of physical violence; it could be psychological cruelty—the mere plotting and planning to drive someone mad.

All of Hitchcock's films had his signature elements, from **Jimmy Stewart**'s portrayal of a voyeuristic photographer who witnesses a murder in *Rear Window* (1954), to Anthony Perkins's knife-slashing scene with Janet Leigh in *Psycho* (1960). Beyond building the suspense, what made Hitchcock's films even more powerful was the way he chose to create the imagery to achieve that end. Charles Ramirez Berg explains in "Alfred Hitchcock: A Brief Biography" (*The Encyclopedia of Film,* 1996):

> *Psycho* (1960) is famed for its shower murder sequence, a classic model of shot selection and editing that was startling for its (apparent) nudity, graphic violence and its violation of the narrative convention that makes a protagonist invulnerable. Moreover, the progressive shots of eyes, beginning with an extreme close-up of the killer's peeping eye and ending with the open eye of the murder victim, subtly implied the presence of a third eye—the viewer's.

In all, Hitchcock made fifty-three full-length motion pictures, working with some of the biggest stars in the industry. He also hosted two successful television series—*Alfred Hitchcock Presents* (1955) and *The Alfred Hitchcock*

Hour. The show ran until 1965, offering Hitchcock-style intrigue through thirty-minute mystery-dramas. He drew the pencil-sketch profile of himself that appeared on screen at the beginning and ending of the shows.

Though a Best Director Oscar eluded him, the Academy of Motion Picture Arts and Sciences awarded Hitchcock an honorary statuette in 1968. In 1979 the American Film Institute honored Hitchcock with its Life Achievement Award. Just a few months before his death on August 13, 1980, Queen Elizabeth II knighted the English native son. He was the master of subtlety, surprise, and suspense. The next time you watch a Hitchcock movie, look for him to make a cameo appearance near the start of the film. He did so in all but his first two films.

Walt Disney

Creator of Mickey Mouse and Disney Theme Parks
1901–1966

Cartoon animation offers a medium of storytelling and visual entertainment which can bring pleasure and information to people of all ages everywhere in the world.

—WALT DISNEY

*M*ickey Mouse, the lovable rodent on which an entertainment empire was built, was a spur-of-the moment creation. The world-famous character, said creator Walter Elias Disney, "popped out of my mind . . . on a train ride from Manhattan to Hollywood, at a time when the business and fortunes of my brother Roy and myself were at lowest ebb and disaster seemed right around the corner." Working late one night in his Laugh-O-Gram office in Kansas City, twenty-year-old Walt had "adopted" a mouse that was foraging in his wastebasket. Remembering the mouse during the ride to Hollywood, he drew a cartoon character that made "Disney" one of the most recognized names of the twentieth century.

Born on December 5, 1901, in Chicago, Illinois, Walt was the fourth child of Elias and Flora Disney. He had three older brothers—Herbert, Raymond, and Roy—and a younger sister, Ruth. Though nine years apart in age, Roy and Walt were always very close.

When Walt was four, the Disneys moved to Marceline, Missouri. Walt loved observing animals in forests and on farms. He also loved to draw and often sold his sketches to neighbors. When Walt was sixteen, the Disneys moved to Chicago, where he attended McKinley High School. The school magazine published some of his cartoons, and Walt began taking evening drawing classes at the Academy of Fine Art.

When America entered World War I in 1917, sixteen-year-old Walt lied about his age and volunteered to drive emergency vehicles for the Red Cross's American Ambulance Corps in France. He decorated the interior of his ambulance with his sketches. After the war, he settled in Kansas City, where he worked first at a commercial art firm and then at a film company that produced commercials from "moving" drawings.

In 1923 Walt left Kansas City for Hollywood, California. With his brother Roy he formed a production company called Disney Brothers Studio. It was the first cartoon studio in Hollywood. The Disneys made "live animation" featurettes for a movie distributor. Business soon was so good that they hired more staff. One of Walt's new employees, Lillian Bounds, was hired to trace the animators' drawings onto sheets of clear acetate (cels) and paint the images in the appropriate colors. A romance developed between the two, and on July 13, 1925, they were married.

Problems with a movie distributor convinced Walt to become his own boss. Soon after, he developed his priceless cartoon character, Mickey Mouse. He originally planned to "debut" Mickey in a silent cartoon called *Plane Crazy* (1928), but by that time, sound technology had changed the motion picture industry for good. Walt instantly recognized the revolutionary importance of sound in film, and before long he created the world's first synchronized sound cartoon—*Steamboat Willie,* starring Mickey Mouse. *Willie* premiered on

November 18, 1928, in New York City and was an instant hit. The film, critics said, was "an ingenious piece of work with a good deal of fun. It growls, whines and squawks and makes various other sounds that add to its mirthful quality."

Walt produced dozens more Mickey Mouse sound cartoons. His next success was *Silly Symphonies,* a series of animated cartoons with no central character. In 1932 the film manufacturer Technicolor created the first color film process that reproduced the whole spectrum. Using the new technology, Walt's staff created *Flowers and Trees.* The cartoon earned Walt an Academy Award.

Disney wanted his characters to have distinct "personalities." The *Silly Symphonies* episode *Three Little Pigs* accomplished that—and earned Walt a second Oscar. In 1937 he released his first full-length animated film, *Snow White and the Seven Dwarfs.* The project cost an astronomical $1.5 million, but it was a huge success and is still considered a motion picture masterpiece. Walt earned a special Academy Award for *Snow White* (the award included seven miniature Oscars along with the regular statuette).

By 1940 Disney employed more than 1,000 people. He built a new studio on fifty-one acres in Burbank, California. The studio produced memorable full-length animated features, including *Pinocchio* (1940), *Dumbo* (1941), *Bambi* (1942), and the extravaganza *Fantasia* (1940). Set to the music of composers such as Bach, Beethoven, Tchaikovsky, and Stravinsky, *Fantasia* featured Mickey Mouse as the "sorcerer's apprentice."

Walt combined live action with animation in *The Three Caballeros* (1945), *Song of the South* (1946), and *Mary Poppins* (1964); he also produced completely live-action films like *Treasure Island* (1950). He strongly believed that a good education included knowledge of natural surroundings. "No one can have a well-rounded education without some knowledge of what goes on in the physical world around us," he said. This conviction led him to produce the award-winning nature series *True Life Adventures* in 1948. From films such as *The Living Desert, The Vanishing Prairie,* and *Seal Island,* audiences learned much about wild animals in their own habitats.

Disney made his debut on television with the premiere of *The Mickey Mouse Club* in 1955. Mickey Mouse himself introduced the show, but the twenty-four boys and girls nicknamed the "Mouseketeers" entertained millions of young viewers. The hour-long show also included many classic Disney cartoons.

Disney's crowning achievement was his grandest idea: the Disneyland theme park. "It will be a place . . . to find happiness and knowledge. It will be a place for parents and children to share pleasant times," Walt explained. "Disneyland will sometimes be a fair, an exhibition, a playground, a community center, a museum of living facts, and a showplace of beauty and magic."

Disneyland opened on July 17, 1955—complete with a fairy-tale castle and "themed" parks like Fantasyland, Tomorrowland, Frontierland, and Adventure-land. Each attraction was carefully placed to ensure easy navigation—and block out views of the outside world. In its first two months, Disneyland hosted more than 1 million people.

Disneyland's success prompted Walt to fulfill an even grander vision: construction of the Experimental Prototype Community of Tomorrow (EPCOT) on a parcel of central Florida land twice the size of Manhattan. "[EPCOT] will . . . always be introducing and teaching and demonstrating," said Walt. "[It] will be a showcase to the world for the ingenuity and imagination of American free enterprise." Today, the complex includes a Magic Kingdom (1971), EPCOT (1982), Disney/MGM Studios (1989), the Animal Kingdom (1998), and several luxurious hotels. It is one of the world's most popular tourist destinations.

The Disney Corporation has expanded into Japan (1983) and France (1992). But the Missouri boy who created an entertainment empire did not live to see this growth. A relentless worker and heavy smoker, Walter Elias Disney died of lung cancer on December 15, 1966.

Eighty-one Disney feature films were released during Walt's lifetime, including *Sleeping Beauty* (1959), *Cinderella* (1950), *Alice in Wonderland* (1950), *Peter Pan* (1953), *101 Dalmations* (1961), and *The Jungle Book* (1967). The empire that began in 1923 is now a thriving international corporation. Disney's newer feature animations, including *Aladdin, Beauty and the Beast, The Little Mermaid,* and *The Lion King,* have thrilled and amused fans of all ages.

Evolution of the Motion Picture

When Auguste and Louis Lumière debuted the Cinématographe in a Paris café in 1895, they could not have imagined its historical impact. The design combined a camera, an image printer, and a projector to form the basis for what would become one of the most extravagantly glamorous businesses in modern times—the motion picture industry.

The Cinématographe was not the only machine of its kind. Enterprising technicians in the United States and Europe built machines patterned on American inventor Thomas Edison's Kinetoscope, with a revolving shutter that allowed a single viewer to see sequential glimpses of moving images on celluloid film. The first Kinetoscope parlor opened on April 14, 1894, in New York City. The rows of Kinetoscope machines ran vaudeville performances, Wild West acts, and circus highlights. By year's end, Kinetoscope parlors dotted the United States and Europe.

In 1902 Frenchman Georges Melies produced *Le Voyage Dans la Lune (A Trip to the Moon)*. Melies introduced story lines, plots, scenes, and character

The Ford Film Company in 1914

development. He drew on his magician's background to create photographic "tricks," including hand-tinting film, adding "dissolves" and "wipes," double exposures, and slow motion. American director Edwin S. Porter was the first to shoot scenes out of sequence and edit them into proper order in *The Great Train Robbery* (1903).

Studios sprang up to meet the demand for new pictures. The "capital" of American film creation shifted from New York to Los Angeles, and the Nestor Company was the first to establish itself in a section of the city called Hollywood. By 1912 movies were available in theaters.

In the 1920s the studio system was born. Twentieth Century Fox, Metro-Goldwyn-Mayer (MGM), Paramount, United Artists, Universal, and Warner

Bros. were established. Studio owner-director Thomas H. Ince hired supervisors called "producers" to direct his films and introduced mass production by creating a rotation schedule for all films produced simultaneously. Warner Bros. produced the first "talking" film, *The Jazz Singer,* in 1927. The Movietone system allowed filmmakers to "photograph" sound onto the physical film. Movie attendance increased enormously—but the advent of talkies meant the end of silent films. Silent film stars who did not have voices suited to sound films faded from popularity; others, like husky-voiced **Greta Garbo,** achieved greater success.

The 1930s are often called the Golden Age of motion pictures. Hits included the lavish dance musicals *Top Hat* (1935) and *Swing Time* (1936), starring Fred Astaire and Ginger Rogers; gangster stories such as *The Public Enemy* (1931); slapstick comedies, such as the Marx Brothers' *Animal Crackers* (1930) and *A Night at the Opera* (1935); fantasy tales like the classic *The Wizard of Oz* (1939); and horror movies like *Dracula* (1931). By far the most popular film was *Gone With the Wind* (1939). The beloved epic was shot in three-strip Technicolor, a process named after the company that pioneered the method for adding color to film. *Gone With the Wind* broke box-office records and won eight regular Oscars and two honorary Oscars, one for "the use of color for the enhancement of dramatic mood."

Some of the best films of the 1940s had no live actors: they were produced by Walt Disney Studios, founded in 1923 by **Walt Disney** and his brother Roy. Among its early classics are *Pinocchio* (1940), *Fantasia* (1941), *Bambi* (1942), and *Cinderella* (1949). Later Disney films were live-action features and television programs with special effects. Among them were *Davy Crockett* (1954), *Mary Poppins* (1964), and *The Love Bug* (1968).

The movie industry underwent sweeping changes in the 1950s as it battled television's growing popularity. Innovations included enlarged screens and 3-D effects. CinemaScope debuted in Twentieth Century Fox's *The Robe*

(1953); the technique used a single lens with differing horizontal and vertical magnifications to create a wide-screen effect. The movie's success spawned other wide-screen techniques, including VistaVision (*White Christmas,* 1954) and Todd-AO (*Oklahoma!* 1955, and *South Pacific,* 1958). Other blockbusters were *The Ten Commandments* (1956), *Ben-Hur* (1959), and *El Cid* (1961).

Hollywood produced more extravagant epics in the 1960s, including the successful *Lawrence of Arabia* (1962) and the failed *Cleopatra* (1963), *The Sound of Music* and *Doctor Zhivago* (both 1965). Director Stanley Kubrick created one of the most popular films in Hollywood history, *2001: A Space Odyssey* (1968). A second golden age consumed Hollywood during the 1970s, as summer blockbusters drew huge audiences. Top hits included *Jaws* (1975), produced by twenty-seven-year-old **Steven Spielberg,** and George Lucas's *Star Wars* (1977).

Spielberg and Lucas represented a new generation of filmmakers who improved on older technical innovations and created their own. Lucas established Industrial Light and Magic, a postproduction company focused on computer-generated special effects. Film equipment became lighter and more portable, film quality improved, and production costs dropped as studios combined functions to save time and money.

The 1980s saw the introduction of Dolby stereo sound, Lucas's THX sound system, and Dolby SR. Such techniques helped create unexpected hits like *Amadeus* (1984) and *Batman* (1989). The latter inspired a 1992 sequel, *Batman Returns,* using an even newer sound technology, Dolby Digital. In 1993 DTS Digital Sound debuted in Spielberg's smash hit *Jurassic Park* (1993). Hollywood began garnering vast incomes from home-based movie technologies, including home videos, cable TV, and direct satellite broadcasts. "Premium" cable services such as HBO and Showtime began producing their own original films for television. Multiscreen theaters sprang up across the country to compete with the increasing demand for home-movie products.

The "multiplex" trend continued during the 1990s. Film budgets regularly topped $100 million and state-of-the-art technology spawned special effects such as CGI (computer-generated images). The first entirely computer-animated full-length film was *Toy Story* (1995), produced by pioneer John Lassiter. Film critic Roger Ebert hailed the movie as the "dawn of a new era of movie animation . . . where space not only bends, but snaps, crackles and pops." Steven Spielberg, former Disney executive Jeffrey Katzenberg, and music industry mogul David Geffen launched DreamWorks SKG, the first new Hollywood studio in decades. Among their Oscar-nominated productions was *Shrek* (2001).

Motion picture superstars commanded multi-million-dollar salaries; among them were **Tom Cruise, Harrison Ford, Jodie Foster, Tom Hanks, Julia Roberts, Will Smith, John Travolta,** and **Denzel Washington.** Award-winning films included *The Silence of the Lambs* (1991), *Schindler's List* (1993), *Forrest Gump* (1994), and *Dead Man Walking* (1995). Digital video discs (DVDs) hit the market in 1997, bringing better resolution and sound and greater durability than VHS, not to mention its bonus tracks of outtakes, games, and music.

What does the twenty-first century hold for Hollywood filmmakers? George Lucas believes that the concept of film will become obsolete as studios shift to digital format that does not require it. Lucas debuted the first film-free production in movie history with *Star Wars Episode II: Attack of the Clones* (2002). "We are in the digital age now," he told an interviewer, "and [it's impossible to] hold on to an old-fashioned technology that's cumbersome and expensive."

Clark Gable

Romantic and Popular Film Star Known for Role in
Gone With the Wind
1901–1960

*The only reason they come to see me is
that I know that life is great—and they
know I know it.*

—CLARK GABLE

With one line, "Frankly, my dear, I don't give a damn," Clark Gable immortalized his role as Rhett Butler in the historic Southern epic *Gone With the Wind (GWTW)*. Ruggedly handsome, manly, and magnetic, Gable was one of the most popular romantic stars Hollywood has ever seen. His brilliant performance in *GWTW* ensured him legendary star status.

Incredibly, Gable hadn't sought the part of the Southern gentleman from Charleston who tries to win over the beautiful, but often times insolent, Scarlett O'Hara. "I tried to duck that Rhett assignment, you know. I didn't want any part of it. . . . Everybody this side of Tibet had read the book, and everybody had different ideas about Rhett, and it was a cinch I couldn't please everybody," said Gable. He played the role well enough to earn a Best Actor Academy Award nomination, the third of his young career.

William Clark Gable was born on February 1, 1901, in Cadiz, Ohio, to Adeline and William H. Gable. His father worked as an oil rigger and later as a farmer. When Clark was just seven months old, Adeline died from epilepsy. Clarke's father remarried, and he was raised by his dad and stepmom, Jennie. Jennie was a devoted and loving mom, whom Clark called a "wonderful woman."

The family moved to Revena, Ohio, when Clark was sixteen. He quit school and took a job at an Akron tire factory. After seeing the play *The Bird of Paradise* at the local theater, Clark decided to become an actor. He kept his day job at the factory but worked for free as a stagehand for several stock companies. On his twenty-first birthday he took a $300 inheritance left to him by his grandfather and joined an acting troupe called the Jewell Players.

After a few months the troupe disbanded, and Clark took odd jobs until he could make it to Portland, Oregon, where he joined another theater troupe. He met actress Josephine Dillon, who began coaching Clark in acting techniques. When she decided to go to Hollywood, Clark went with her. They married in December 1934. He made his first film appearance as an extra in the silent movie *Forbidden Paradise*. Soon after, he started working under the name Clark Gable.

Gable continued to pick up work in some silent films and onstage. After being seen starring as Killer Mears in the stage production of *The Last Mile*, Gable was given a screen test. He was rejected because studio producers thought his ears were too big to play a leading man. But agent Minna Wallis (sister of Warner Brothers producer Hal Wallis) managed to get him a part in his first talkie, *The Painted Desert* (1931).

Metro-Goldwyn-Mayer (MGM) signed Gable to a two-year contract. For a while Gable was cast mostly in villain and gangster roles. Gable's performances were powerful enough to make him a star by 1932. After he complained about playing the same "rough 'em up" parts, Gable was "disciplined" by being loaned out to Columbia Pictures. His punishment, starring in Frank Capra's *It Happened One Night* (1934), backfired. The film was an enormous hit. It swept the 1934 Academy Awards, and Gable won an Oscar for his performance, as did his costar, Claudette Colbert.

Gable was now a viable film star, and was never loaned out to another studio again. He was cast in a wider range of roles, including an Oscar-nominated performance as Fletcher Christian in *Mutiny on the Bounty* (1935). Gable said it was one of his favorite films, noting that "it was history, a story about the struggle of real men, without the usual load of cinema romance." Gable could hardly go out anywhere without being mobbed by adoring fans. He was quite surprised by the reaction and was hard-pressed to explain it.

Though his professional life was soaring, Gable was in the midst of ending his second marriage (his marriage to Dillon had ended in 1930) to Ria Langham, whom he wed in 1931. While attending a formal Hollywood party, Gable and actress Carole Lombard got reacquainted. They had actually worked together on the film *No Man of Her Own* in 1932 (the only movie they appeared in together). The two began dating, fell in love, and were married in 1939.

Gable had become a superstar. The adulation of his adoring fans resulted in his being crowned the "King of Hollywood" when he was the overwhelming choice in a poll taken by entertainment readers. Incredibly, Gable almost passed up the opportunity to star in the role that would immortalize him on-screen— as Rhett Butler in the sweeping Civil War epic *Gone With the Wind* (1939). Years later, during an interview, Gable explained his initial reluctance: "Miss Mitchell had etched him in the minds of millions, each of whom knew exactly how Rhett would look and act. It would be impossible to satisfy them all, or even a majority. I knew that." He couldn't have been more wrong. Sixty-three years later *Gone With the Wind* is still considered one of the top-ten best films ever made.

Happily married and comfortable with his career, Gable seemed to be embracing life completely. In a "match made in heaven," Gable and Lombard were pretty much homebodies except for the occasional hunting or fishing trip. They named their twenty-acre estate "The House of Two Gables," and had close friends and family over for dinners.

Gable appeared in several movies over the next few years, including *Comrade X* (1940), *Strange Cargo* (1940), and *Honky Tonk* (1941). It seemed Gable couldn't make a bad picture. While he was working on the 1942 film *Somewhere I'll Find You,* Lombard went off on a war bond drive to raise money for World War II. Tragically, on January 16, 1942, the plane carrying Lombard, her mother, and twenty other people crashed outside Las Vegas, Nevada, while en route back to California. A grief-stricken Gable stopped work on the film but returned a few weeks later. Gable completed the picture; then as a tribute to Lombard, he enlisted in the service. He served courageously in the Army Air Corps, flying missions over Europe. He was awarded the Distinguished Flying Cross and the Air Medal.

He returned to the screen in 1945, opposite Greer Garson in *Adventure.* He consistently made a few pictures a year, earning respectable reviews, but never regained the box-office superstar draw he had before the war. When MGM did a remake of his 1932 film *Red Dust,* retitled *Mogambo,* Gable was tapped to reprise his role, with Ava Gardner and **Grace Kelly** as costars.

In 1954 Gable ventured out as a freelance actor, ending his twenty-two-year partnership with MGM. He became the highest paid nonstudio actor, formed his own production company, GABCO, and released his first project, *The King and Four Queens,* in 1956. In his next film he costarred in, and coproduced, the war drama *Run Silent, Run Deep* (1958) with Burt Lancaster.

Gable went to the altar two more times, though those who knew him said he mourned Lombard for the rest of his life. In 1955 Gable married Kay Spreckles. While he was working on his last film, *The Misfits* (1961) with Marilyn Monroe, Spreckles became pregnant. Gable was ecstatic about the news.

The Misfits was grueling for the fifty-nine-year-old who, portraying an aging cowboy, insisted on doing his own stunts. Sadly, shortly after completing the picture, Gable suffered a heart attack and died on November 16, 1960. He never knew he had a son, John Clark Gable, who was born on March 20, 1961.

Henry Fonda

Actor Known for Diverse Film Roles
1905–1982

I haven't ever done anything except be other people. I ain't really Henry Fonda! Nobody could be. Nobody could have that much integrity.

—HENRY FONDA

Ironically, Henry Fonda was a man who hated guns and wasn't keen on horses, but he provided excellent portrayals of heroes in numerous western films. Tall and handsome, he gained a devoted following not only from his roles in westerns but from his frequent parts as a quiet, sincere man who is undaunted in his quest to do what's right and who is highly respected as a result. While these may have been his most frequent roles, Fonda's deft skill and adaptability had such a broad scope that he was given many other diverse parts as well, proving himself much more than a soft-spoken hero.

Born on May 16, 1905, in Grand Island, Nebraska, Fonda pursued a degree in journalism at the University of Minnesota but then left and started working in an office. He recognized his acting gift when he took a role in an amateur production of the Omaha Community Players. From there he went on to act in summer performances and then joined with theater students in a group—called the Cape Cod University Players—that included Joshua Logan, who would become a famed director, and the budding actor and actress, respectively, **Jimmy Stewart** and Margaret Sullavan. Stewart would become Fonda's longtime close friend, and Sullavan would be his wife from 1931 to 1933. Stewart and Fonda made it to Broadway in the early 1930s, and relatively quickly Fonda proved his skill in the show *The Farmer Takes a Wife*. The fine performance brought him not only his first screen appearance in the show's movie version but also a contract with film producer Walter Wanger in 1934. In 1936 Fonda married Frances Brokaw, and the two would have two children, Jane and Peter, both of whom would become known in the film world as well.

By the end of the 1930s Fonda was already a key star. He acted in a number of the first Technicolor films: *The Trail of the Lonesome Pine* (1936), *The Wings of the Morning* (1938), and *Jesse James* (1938). He played in *Jezebel* (1938), which received notable attention and brought an Oscar for **Bette Davis.** It was in these still early years that Fonda started working with famed director John Ford, who cast him in the lead role in *Young Mr. Lincoln* (1939), which turned out to be one of Fonda's finest performances. It was followed in 1940 by yet another stunning Fonda portrayal, Tom Joad in *The Grapes of Wrath*. To get the part, Fonda had to sign a seven-year contract with Twentieth Century Fox, a move he didn't want to make because of his disappointment with many of the parts they had given him up until then. *The Grapes of Wrath* was also one of Ford's films and was masterfully directed and adapted from the John Steinbeck classic novel, with an all-around strong cast. It brought Fonda his first Oscar nomination, once again for an undaunted, albeit destitute, hero. Shortly after, he played successfully in comedies, then returned to a western with *The Ox-Box Incident* (1943), in which he turned in another of his most memorable performances.

Fonda's annoying contract with Fox was somewhat shortened by World War II. He served in the navy, garnering a Bronze Star and Presidential citation.

Upon returning to the States after his service, Fonda appeared in yet another powerful Ford western, *My Darling Clementine* (1946), as well as in a few more films. After the successful *Fort Apache* (1948), which was also directed by Ford and included actor John Wayne, Fonda turned his back on movieland for a number of years, returning to the East Coast's Broadway.

Fonda did well on the live stage once again, especially in his roles in *The Caine Mutiny Court Martial* and *Mister Roberts*. Seeing the success of the latter, Warner Brothers planned its movie version, and Ford convinced the studio executives that Fonda should play its lead as well. It appeared in 1955. Fonda stuck with films for a while, next starring in *War and Peace* (1956), an excessive extravaganza that was a near failure, although Fonda performed well. In 1957 he coproduced and starred in another film in a role that fans would remember him for in years to come—a key member of a disparate group of jurors in *Twelve Angry Men*. That same year he moved to a new genre with director **Alfred Hitchcock**, appearing in *The Wrong Man*. While a different type of movie for Fonda, his character still was one driven by a sense of justice.

From then on, Fonda stayed active both in film and on stage and did some television shows as well. The television work included a special on Clarence Darrow and a show that Fonda not only starred in but also produced, *The Deputy* (1959–1961). He was a guest star on dozens of shows and the narrator of many films and television shows.

In the 1960s Fonda gave exceptional performances in films that focused on politics, harkening back to his early Lincoln portrayal, *The Best Man* and *Fail Safe,* both released in 1964. He appeared in many other movies during this time, but most were either small parts or leads that offered little challenge. He said he took these parts to keep busy and make money. In 1974 the American Civil Liberties Union honored Henry Fonda, and he starred in the one-man show *Clarence Darrow.* The show was forced to close when he collapsed. Fonda was rushed to the hospital and given a pacemaker. Not to be deterred, the actor later performed the play in Los Angeles, where it was taped for television. Fonda's performance in the 1977 play *First Monday in October,* which opened in Los Angeles, was so appreciated that he also played the part on Broadway and in Chicago.

In 1978 Fonda received the American Film Institute's Life Achievement Award. He was also honored by the Kennedy Center for the Performing Arts in 1979 and was awarded an honorary Oscar in 1981 for his exceptional body of work. His autobiography appeared in the same year, but the actor was not ready to just look back on a career. In 1981 he appeared in the film *On Golden Pond* with his daughter, Jane, who was also its producer, and the two healed some wounds between them. For that performance Fonda won the Academy Award for Best Actor, at age seventy-six the oldest recipient in that category to date. Jane Fonda accepted the golden statue for her father, who was too sick to attend. He died in Los Angeles only a few months later, in August 1982.

Greta Garbo

One of Hollywood's Most Private Film Stars
1905–1990

*I feel like a criminal who is hunted. . . .
[W]hen photographers come, they draw
crowds. I am frightened beyond control.
When so many people stare, I feel almost
ashamed.*

—GRETA GARBO, ON FAME

While some say it was caused by her Swedish upbringing, others attributed it to her own conscious desire to perpetuate her mystique, and still others viewed it as intense shyness; what is known is that Greta Garbo, one of the hottest movie stars of her time, would live the most private of personal lives. She would be the highest paid actress in the mid-1930s and would enrapture fans at her films, many of these movies being saved from their mediocrity by her presence. Yet she would never live the Hollywood lifestyle, would give almost no interviews, and eventually would end her acting career at a young age and then live a near-reclusive life.

Born on September 18, 1905, in Stockholm, Sweden, as Greta Louisa Gustafsson, she was the youngest of three siblings in a family that was subjected to financial strife when Greta's father died when she was just fourteen. Being forced to work at a young age actually aided in the beginning of an acting career for the teenage Greta. Working as a clerk in a department store, she was asked to model for its catalog, and from there she garnered parts in two short advertising films, as well as a spot in another short film.

Stagestruck even before these opportunities, eighteen-year-old Greta received a scholarship to a renowned acting school in Sweden. It was here that the country's top film director, Mauritz Stiller, spotted her theatrical instinct and elegant looks and took her under his guidance. He cast her in his film *The Atonement of Gosta Berling,* which appeared in 1924 and became a silent-screen sensation, not just in Sweden but throughout Europe. Soon after, Greta received a lead role in *Joyless Street.* Directed by G. W. Pabst, the film and Greta's performance were critically acclaimed and achieved record-breaking box-office success. To this day the film is considered a treasure of German realism.

In the summer of 1925, Mauritz and Greta, now both with contracts from Metro-Goldwyn-Mayer in Hollywood, headed for California. There the still-young and adaptable Greta acted in *The Torrent,* but Mauritz had trouble adjusting to the new life and returned to Stockholm in 1928. Greta, though, was fast becoming Hollywood's biggest star. From 1925 to 1929 she was featured in eleven silent movies and proved her range by portraying an array of characters. She was beautiful and intelligent, and her screen persona captivated both men and women with its intense passion and independence. There had been no actress like her before, and she aided America in updating its view of women.

In 1927 Greta starred in *Flesh and the Devil* and *Love* with John Gilbert and started an intense romance with him that would last several years. Yet she would literally leave the famed actor at the altar, believing their marriage wouldn't work—in part because of the attention it would bring and in part because she thought John had too much of an interest in other women. While it lasted, their relationship created enormous attention and more money for the box office. Millions of female fans clamored to mimic Greta's looks—gluing on false eyelashes, donning cloche hats, and instructing salons to provide them with a Garbo hairstyle. While other marriage proposals would come to the "Swedish Sphinx," as some in the press would call Greta, she would never marry.

All actresses and actors at the time were confronted with the invention of the movie that was no longer silent, and Greta was one star that MGM was especially hesitant about transferring to the new medium because of her deep voice and foreign accent. In fact, she performed in the very last silent film the studio would produce, since its executives were intent on keeping her in that safe realm as long as possible. The executives' nervousness was imperceptible to the general public, however, which was barraged with "Garbo Talks!" headlines just prior to the opening of Greta's first sound picture. It opened in 1930, and to add anticipation, Greta did not come on-screen and speak until an half-hour into the film. The picture was *Anna Christie,* adapted from Eugene O'Neill's play, and it proved an exceptional success, to this day viewed as containing one of Greta's most engaging roles. Sound was anything but a deterrent for this star.

Greta's career continued unabated, and her broad skill is attested to by the fact that even today there are differing views as to which her strongest role was. She would star in more than a dozen sound movies, such as *Susan Lenox: Her Fall and Rise,* in which she costarred with Clark Gable in 1931; *Mata Hari* in 1931; and *As You Desire Me,* along with *Grand Hotel,* in 1932. Some that followed were *Queen Christina* in 1933, *Anna Karenina* in 1935, *Camille* in 1936, and *Conquest* in 1937. In 1939 she would experiment in another way, performing in her first comedy, *Ninotchka,* in which she once again wowed audiences.

Her second comic work, *Two-Faced Woman,* was a disappointment at the box office, although one of today's critics has described it as "better than its reputation." Greta looked into other roles after this, but none came through, partly because of World War II. In 1941 she moved into retirement, and while she lived a relatively isolated life, refusing any public appearances, it was one enriched by visits from an array of acquaintances and friends such as Jackie Kennedy, Winston Churchill, and Dag Hammarskjöld.

In 1951 Greta became a U.S. citizen, and in 1954 she was awarded a special Academy Award for "unforgettable screen performances," but did not attend the ceremonies. Although she traveled frequently, she moved into an apartment in New York City in 1953. The time away from the studio allowed the multifaceted, creative woman to enjoy painting, poetry, gardening, as well as designing clothing and furnishings—all without missing her rigorous daily exercise routine. She also spent much time acquiring artwork for what would become her internationally renowned collection. She died of natural causes in her New York home on April 15, 1990.

Katharine Hepburn

"Number One Actress of All Time"
1907–

It's life, isn't it? You plow ahead and make a hit. And you plow on and someone passes you. Then someone passes them. Time levels.

—KATHARINE HEPBURN

"I've just about done what I damn well wanted to," Katharine Hepburn once declared. Fiercely independent, defiant in a way that even today might raise eyebrows, Hepburn forged her own path without concerns over social approval. She wore trousers when it was almost scandalous for women to do so, always spoke her mind, and had a twenty-seven–year romance with a married man. The indomitable actress has earned twelve Academy Award nominations and is the only person to win four Oscars. For a woman who never intended to be an actress, her achievements seem even more extraordinary.

Born in Fenwick, Connecticut, on May 12, 1907, Katharine Houghton Hepburn was the second of six children of the socially prominent Dr. Thomas Hepburn and suffragette Katharine "Kit" Houghton. Kate enjoyed figure skating, swimming, tennis, and golf. Her parents raised their children to question and think for themselves. They also taught them to fear nothing—a lesson Kate always remembered.

The tomboyish Kate tagged after her adored older brother Tom. She played sports with him and his friends, and even learned how to wrestle. But when Kate was thirteen, Tom accidentally hanged himself. Devastated by the loss, Kate became withdrawn and sullen. To lift her spirits, her parents encouraged Kate to produce backyard plays. They took her out of school and hired private tutors. Kate devoted more time to sports than schoolwork, but by sixteen she was so well tutored that she applied to colleges. She was accepted at Bryn Mawr, a prestigious women's college outside Philadelphia, Pennsylvania.

After taking college drama courses and appearing in several plays, Kate decided—to her parents' dismay—to become an actress. After graduating in 1928, she headed to New York City, where she worked in summer stock productions before landing an understudy role on Broadway.

Cocky and confident, Kate believed she could tackle the starring role after the lead actress was fired. Her first professional stage appearance, however, was a disaster. Stricken with stage fright, she botched her lines and tripped over her feet. She was fired right after the performance.

Kate surprised everyone by marrying Ludlow Ogden Smith, an old family friend, on December 12, 1928. The marriage lasted less than a year. Hepburn hated being a homemaker and desperately missed her freedom. After the marriage ended, Hepburn worked hard to salvage her career. She had an unusual voice and a distinct New England accent. She was often ill-tempered and was unpolished. But she had an aristocratic look and demeanor that created a powerful stage presence. Nervousness was her worst enemy. Years later she explained the difficulty to biographer Charles Higham: "I could read a part without knowing what I was doing better than anyone in the whole world," she said. "I could always get a part quickly—but I couldn't keep it! I would lose my voice, fall down on lines, get red in the face, talk too fast, and I couldn't act. The sight of people out there just petrified me."

Undaunted, Hepburn kept at it, and in 1932 she earned the lead in *The*

Warrior's Husband. Her brilliant performance landed her a starring role in the RKO Pictures film *A Bill of Divorcement* (1932). For her third film, *Morning Glory* (1933), the twenty-six-year-old who "just wanted to be famous" won an Academy Award.

Although Hepburn's next picture, *Little Women* (1933), was a box-office smash, word of her brassy offscreen demeanor and nonconformity spread. Eventually Hepburn's brashness tarnished her public image. She made a few more good films in the 1930s, including *Alice Adams* (for which she received her second Oscar nomination) and *Stage Door* (1937). But her abrasive personality and a few unfortunate flops sent her career into a tailspin.

Hepburn retreated to New York in 1938, where she found a way to make a triumphant return to films with her starring role as pampered socialite Tracy Lord in the 1940 runaway hit *The Philadelphia Story.* She purchased the film rights, returned to Hollywood, and hired George Cukor to direct her, with costars Cary Grant and **Jimmy Stewart.** Hepburn's vitality hit a chord with female audiences. The film role brought her a third Oscar nomination.

Hepburn gained a fourth Academy Award nomination costarring with Spencer Tracy in *Woman of the Year* (1942). The chemistry between the two launched a series of successful screen pairings—and an offscreen love affair that lasted until Tracy's death. Tracy-Hepburn films such as *Adam's Rib, Pat and Mike,* and *Desk Set* showcased Hepburn's intelligence, athleticism, and independence.

In the 1950s Hepburn continued to shine, earning another Oscar nomination for *The African Queen,* in which she starred opposite **Humphrey Bogart.** She also garnered Oscar nods for *Summertime* (1955), *The Rainmaker* (1956), and *Suddenly, Last Summer* (1959). In 1962 she gave one of her most brilliant performances as Mary Tyrone in Eugene O'Neill's *Long Day's Journey Into Night.* The role bestowed on her an unprecedented ninth Academy Award nomination.

Hepburn took five years off to care full-time for an ailing Spencer Tracy, who suffered from heart problems and alcoholism. In 1966 director Stanley

Kramer approached the two to do another film, *Guess Who's Coming to Dinner?* with the controversial theme of interracial marriage. The film also featured **Sidney Poitier** and Hepburn's niece, Katharine Houghton.

The film would be Tracy and Hepburn's last together. Tracy did not live to see the film released: he died of heart failure on June 10, 1967, two weeks after filming ended. Hepburn did not attend Tracy's funeral out of respect for his estranged wife and children—but she grieved privately for months. She was in France on another film shoot when she learned the following spring that she'd won a second Oscar. "Did Mr. Tracy win too?" she asked. When told that he hadn't, she replied, "That's okay. I'm sure mine is for the two of us."

Hepburn won a third Oscar in 1968 for *The Lion in Winter* (tying with **Barbra Streisand** for *Funny Girl*). At sixty-one, she showed little sign of scaling back. She returned to Broadway for the hit show *Coco* (1969), based on the life of French designer Coco Chanel. Hepburn received a standing ovation after the closing performance in August 1970. "Well—I love you and you love me and that's that," she told the delighted audience.

Hepburn turned to television in 1973 with *The Glass Menagerie.* Two years later she turned in one of her best performances—and won an Emmy—in the TV movie *Love Among the Ruins.* Although in her seventies, with a neurological disorder that caused her hands and head to tremble slightly, Hepburn refused to slow down. In 1980 she turned in a solid role as **Henry Fonda**'s wife in *On Golden Pond.* The two major stars had never before costarred. Fonda won his first Oscar for the performance, while Hepburn got a twelfth nomination and her fourth Oscar.

Today, the American Film Institute's "Number One Best Actress of All Time" lives on her family's Connecticut estate. She has appeared in more than forty feature films, several television movies, and more than thirty stage performances. In 1990 Hepburn was chosen as a Kennedy Center Honoree for her contribution to the entertainment industry.

Laurence Olivier

Greatest English-Speaking Actor of the Twentieth Century
1907–1989

Art is a little bit larger than life—it's an exhalation of life and I think you probably need a little touch of madness.

—LAURENCE OLIVIER

*I*n a career that spanned more than six decades, Laurence Olivier appeared in more than 120 stage roles, almost 60 film roles, and more than 15 TV projects. He lived most of his life in England but was a Hollywood icon, earning eleven Academy Award nominations. He won two Oscars and received two honorary Oscars for special achievements. Olivier, said British playwright Charles Bennett, could speak the lines of Shakespeare's plays as though he were "actually thinking them." It is no wonder that he is widely viewed as the greatest English-speaking actor of the twentieth century.

Laurence Kerr Olivier was born in Dorking, Surrey, England, 1907. He was the third child of Agnes Louise Crookenden and Gerard Kerr Olivier, a stern prep-school master and Anglican minister. In 1910 Gerard moved his family to London, where he served at St. James's Church in Notting Hill.

Laurence was sent to the All Saints Choir School, an exclusive boys' academy in London's West End. In 1917 he made his stage debut as Brutus in a school performance of Shakespeare's *Julius Caesar.* In 1921 he enrolled at St. Edward's School at Oxford University, and after graduating in 1924, he attended the Central School of Speech and Drama in London.

At nineteen, Olivier joined the Birmingham Repertory Company. An impatient young man, Olivier was indifferent, even sloppy, when bored. Dissatisfied with the exaggerated mannerisms that were the norm in acting at the time, he believed that realistic, psychological intensity was more powerful.

When Olivier costarred with Jill Esmond in *Bird in Hand* at the Royalty Theatre, she suggested he dress more fashionably and take greater pride in his appearance. The two became engaged in 1929, and in 1930—after Olivier appeared in Noël Coward's *Private Lives*—they were married. The play went to Broadway, and Esmond joined the cast in 1931.

Despite his initial disdain of filmmaking, Olivier next landed a role in the British-German film *The Temporary Widow* and the British film *Too Many Crooks.* Soon after, Olivier was signed with RKO Pictures in Hollywood. But he was dissatisfied with his roles in *Friends and Lovers* and *The Yellow Ticket* (both 1931), and he got poor reviews. Discouraged, he returned to London and to relative anonymity on the British stage.

Olivier's fortunes changed when, in 1935, famed actor John Gielgud chose Olivier to alternate with him in playing both Romeo and Mercutio in *Romeo and Juliet.* Olivier received disappointing reviews as Romeo but was highly praised for his portrayal of Mercutio. Newcomer Vivien Leigh costarred with Olivier in *Fire Over England* (1936) and played Ophelia to Olivier's Hamlet at a special performance of *Hamlet* in Denmark. Olivier's performance was fueled by his growing interest in psychology; he had read a collection of psychoanalytic essays and decided to apply the principles to acting. Olivier delivered his lines in a clipped, anguished style suggesting the torment that Hamlet was experiencing. Audiences were thrilled.

Laurence Olivier was now a full-fledged star. He was also involved with Vivien Leigh. The year 1939 was a high point for both actors: Olivier's smoldering performance as Heathcliff in *Wuthering Heights* earned him an Oscar nomination; Vivien Leigh's Scarlett O'Hara in the epic *Gone With the Wind* brought her a Best Actress Oscar.

Olivier next applied his trademark intensity to a string of films: *Rebecca* (1940); *Pride and Prejudice* (1940); *That Hamilton Woman* (1941), and the war movie *Forty-Ninth Parallel* (1941). After *That Hamilton Woman* opened, Olivier and Leigh married one another.

While taking a break from his service in the British military during World War II, Olivier starred in, directed, and produced a film version of Shakespeare's *Henry V* (1944). It was a landmark in filmmaking: no one had ever made a serious—and successful—movie adaptation of a Shakespeare play. Olivier received both a Best Actor Oscar nomination and a special Oscar in recognition of his outstanding achievement.

After Olivier completed military service in 1944, he joined his friend and colleague Ralph Richardson at the famed Old Vic Theatre in London, where he turned in a stellar performance in *Richard III*. In 1948 he repeated his Hamlet role in a spectacular film adaptation that won a British Academy of Film and Television Arts (BAFTA) award (the British Oscar) and four American Academy Awards, including Best Picture and Best Actor. Olivier became the first in Oscar history to direct himself in an Academy Award–winning performance.

Olivier did not appear in another film until 1951 *(The Magic Box)*. In 1952 he costarred in *Carrie,* a screen version of Theodore Dreiser's novel *Sister Carrie,* while Leigh starred as Blanche DuBois in a film version of Tennessee Williams's *A Streetcar Named Desire.* Leigh's dramatic performance won her a second Best Actress Academy Award. By the late 1950s Leigh and Olivier's marriage was failing, in part because of Leigh's mental illness. They divorced in

1960. The following year Olivier married actress Joan Plowright, whom he met while performing in *The Entertainer* (1960).

From that time until the early 1970s, Olivier performed intermittently on stage and screen, preferring to dedicate himself to administrative work at London's St. James Theatre and as the first director of the National Theatre at the Old Vic. His screen persona as a romantic leading man shifted; he began playing "character" roles, often disguised under heavy makeup. His first such role was an Oscar-nominated performance as the washed-up vaudeville star Archie Rice in *The Entertainer* (1960). He also appeared in *Spartacus* (1960), *Khartoum* (1966), and *Nicholas and Alexandra* (1971). Olivier delighted audiences with leading roles in *Othello* (1965) and *Sleuth* (1972), both of which earned Oscar nominations. Among his more notable character roles was the vile Nazi dentist in *Marathon Man* (1976). He obtained his final Oscar nomination as Ezra Lieberman in *The Boys From Brazil* (1978).

Suffering from cancer and other health problems, Olivier resigned his post with the National Theatre in 1973. He made no further stage appearances, although he continued to work in films and on television. Some reviewers criticized his choice of roles during the 1970s and 1980s, but critic Richard Schickel saw Olivier's persistence differently. "To those of us who believe that the best kind of heroism is to be found in the relentless practice of one's profession . . . [Olivier] became a genuinely heroic figure," Schickel wrote.

Olivier won five Emmy Awards for his roles in television productions, including *Long Day's Journey Into Night* (1973), *Brideshead Revisited* (1982), and for his last TV performance, *King Lear* (1984). Despite his failing health, he also published an autobiography that year, *Confessions of an Actor*. On July 11, 1989, Sir Laurence Olivier died at his home in West Sussex, England.

Bette Davis

First Lady of the American Screen
1908–1989

Without wonder and insight, acting is just a trade. With it, it becomes creation.

—BETTE DAVIS

She has often been referred to as the First Lady of the American Screen. In a career that spanned six decades, Bette Davis was a strong, independent actress in an industry dominated by men. Immediately recognized by her strong, terse voice, Davis took on a multitude of difficult and assertive roles. Her battles with studio bosses were legendary. Yet through it all, Davis maintained a star appeal and longevity in an industry few can match.

The actress, who appeared in more than one hundred films, was born Ruth Elizabeth Davis on April 5, 1908, in Lowell, Massachusetts. Her father, Harlow, and her mother, Ruth, divorced in 1916, leaving young Ruth and her sister, Barbara, to be raised by their mother. Though her early interest was in dance, Ruth quickly turned her attention to acting once she discovered the stage in her freshman year in high school.

Upon graduation, Davis headed to New York, where she applied to the Eva LeGallienne Manhattan Civic Repertory Company. Judged not very serious about an acting career, Ruth's application was rejected. Undaunted, she instead enrolled in the John Murray Anderson Dramatic School. Her classmates, including a young redhead named Lucille Ball, thought Davis was remarkable.

After working in summer stock at the Lyceum Theater in Rochester, New York, with director George Cukor in 1928, Davis went directly to Broadway, starring in *Broken Dishes* and *Solid South.* She made a screen test for Universal Pictures and in 1930 headed to Hollywood as a contract actress. Davis had a dismal start in Hollywood. Upon her arrival at the train station in Los Angeles, the studio rep sent to meet her left without her because he didn't see anyone who looked like a movie star.

Davis didn't exactly set the film world on fire in her 1931 film debut, *Bad Sister.* A few more film appearances left studio executives unimpressed, and Davis's contract was not renewed. Undaunted, Davis got a call from Warner Brothers Studios and signed a seven-year contract. She turned in a strong performance in the 1932 film *The Man Who Played God,* but roles in Warner Brothers films were inconsistent. While she was on loan to RKO to appear in *Of Human Bondage* (1934), Davis gave her career breakthrough performance. She received a number of Academy Award write-in votes for her role in *Bondage.*

Her next film for Warner Brothers brought Davis the success she sought. In *Dangerous* (1935), Davis turned in a fantastic performance as the self-destructive actress Joyce Heath. Though Davis won the coveted golden statuette for the film, she continued to be cast in unsatisfactory roles. Daring to buck the mega-studio, Davis went to England to make films. The studio sued her, and she was forced to honor her contract.

Davis's act of defiance was enough to prod Warner's to offer the award-winning actress better roles. Their renewed partnership resulted in one of the most prolific periods in Davis's career. Her string of memorable roles started with her performance as the willful Southern belle Julie Marsden in the Civil

War–era film *Jezebel* (1938). Many agree that Davis's portrayal of Marsden comes closest to rivaling that of Scarlett O'Hara in *Gone With the Wind* (a role that almost went to Davis).

Nominated again for Best Actress, Davis walked away with her second Oscar in three years. Davis would never win another Academy Award, but she achieved four more of her remarkable ten Oscar nominations in the war-torn decade of the 1940s, including those for her roles as a timid spinster turned vibrant woman in *Now, Voyager* (1942) and as a spoiled socialite in *Mr. Skeffington* (1944).

Davis was among the many stars that contributed to the war effort during World War II. Turning an abandoned nightclub into a place where soldiers could enjoy an evening's entertainment, she helped to organize the Hollywood Canteen. In recognition of her contribution, Davis was awarded the Distinguished Civilian Service Medal in 1980, the highest civilian honor awarded by the United States Department of Defense.

Though her career began to take a downturn with mediocre roles in films after the war, Davis bounced back in 1950 with perhaps the role of a lifetime in Joseph Mankiewicz's *All About Eve*. Playing the stormy Broadway star Margo Channing, Davis gave audiences an intentionally cynical view of people in the theater. It is in *All About Eve* that Davis utters her most memorable line, "Fasten your seat belts, it's going to be a bumpy night."

Being a strong-willed, independent woman, Davis developed a reputation for being difficult. Though she never recouped the superstar status she attained in the 1940s, she was constantly reinventing herself. And she often did so while dealing with several serious health problems. In the 1950s Davis suffered from a bone disease that required part of her jawbone to be removed.

In 1962 Davis returned to top form in the dark drama *What Ever Happened to Baby Jane*. Playing a demented aging actress who tortures her wheelchair-bound sister (played by Joan Crawford), Davis earned her tenth

Academy Award nomination. Thus began a new career in horror films. She also found welcome opportunities to work in television, winning two Emmy Awards for her roles in *Mrs. Lincoln* (1954) and *Strangers: The Story of a Mother and Daughter* (1979). In 1987 Davis was named a Kennedy Center Honoree.

The list of Davis's credits and honors is almost as long as the list of her performance appearances. She was the first female president of the Academy of Motion Picture Arts and Sciences (1941) and the first female recipient of the American Film Institute's Lifetime Achievement Award (1977). In 1980, celebrating the fiftieth anniversary of her career, Davis starred in her eighty-fifth film, *The Watcher in the Woods.*

Despite suffering a stroke and a mastectomy due to breast cancer in 1983, Davis remained active. She wrote an autobiography entitled *This 'n That* during her recovery, and returned to acting. She appeared in the critically acclaimed TV movie *Murder with Mirrors* and made her final film in 1987 in *The Whales of August.*

Davis's personal life was as intense as her career. She always put her film career first but managed to marry four times, giving birth to a daughter, Barbara Davis Hyman, and adopting two more children, Margot and Michael. She died in Neuilly-sur-Seine, France, on October 6, 1989. In true Bette Davis style, her tombstone reads, "She did it the hard way."

Jimmy Stewart

One of America's Best-Loved Actors
1908–1997

I've had many people tell me that they remember certain little things that I did in pictures. I think it's wonderful to have been able to give people little pieces of time they can remember.

—JIMMY STEWART

On the corner of Eighth and Philadelphia Streets in the small town of Indiana, Pennsylvania, a hardware store once occupied space in a building constructed in 1853. The J. M. Stewart Hardware Store was owned and operated by Alexander Stewart. For years one of the store's windows was home to a gold statuette, better known as an Academy Award. Alex's son, actor Jimmy Stewart, took his Oscar home. That he shared his only Oscar with his parents and his community is testament to the importance of family and home to the shy Hollywood screen legend.

The Stewart family had been a part of Indiana County life from as far back as the mid-1800s, when Jimmy's great-grandfather fought in the Civil War. James Maitland Stewart was born at his parents' home on May 20, 1908. He was the only son of Alexander and Elizabeth Stewart. Two sisters, Virginia and Mary, came along later.

Jimmy grew up in a loving, middle-class family. He and his father were very close. Jimmy learned a lot about integrity and character building from Alex. Jimmy was a bright young man; he did well in his studies, was active in the Boy Scouts, attended church regularly, and played the accordion.

Upon graduating from the Mercerburg Academy prep school, Jimmy enrolled at Princeton University to study civil engineering and architecture. While at Princeton, he got involved with a small theater group called the Triangle Club. Jimmy played the accordion in some of their stage productions. When Jimmy graduated from Princeton with honors in 1932, America was in the middle of an economic depression, and jobs were difficult to find. However, on graduation day, a classmate asked Jimmy if he'd like to join the University Players, a summer stock theater company. One of the group's aspiring thespians was Margaret Sullavan. She and Jimmy later starred together in two Hollywood films, *Next Time We Love* and *The Shop Around the Corner.*

Jimmy worked with the Players all summer in Falmouth, Massachusetts. He made his professional stage debut in *Good-bye Again.* To his delight, the play moved on to Broadway in New York City, and he all but abandoned his architecture career. While working in New York, Jimmy roomed with another young aspiring actor, **Henry Fonda.**

Jimmy appeared in a few more plays, including *Yellow Jacket,* for which he received rave reviews. Shortly after that, the film studio Metro-Goldwyn-Mayer (MGM) cast him with Spencer Tracy in the 1935 film *Murder Man.* MGM signed Jimmy to a seven-year contract, and he appeared in numerous films, including his breakthrough role in *Next Time We Love.* Between the years 1935 and 1939, Jimmy made twenty-three films and worked with some of Hollywood's biggest stars, including Joan Crawford, Robert Taylor, **Clark Gable,** Jean Hersholt, Edward G. Robinson, and Oscar winner **Hattie McDaniel.**

The film that made Jimmy a bona fide film star was the 1939 release *Mr. Smith Goes to Washington.* His portrayal of an idealistic young man who takes on Washington's corrupt political world won Jimmy a New York Film Critic's Best Actor Award and his first Academy Award nomination. The following year, Jimmy starred in four films and hit gold with his performance in the classic romantic comedy *The Philadelphia Story,* costarring **Katharine Hepburn** and Cary Grant. Up against acting greats **Charlie Chaplin, Henry Fonda, Laurence Olivier,** and Raymond Massey, Jimmy walked away with the Best Actor Oscar.

The United States's entry into World War II in 1941 brought Jimmy's acting career to a halt. Having earned his commercial pilot's license in 1939, Jimmy joined the Army Air Corps. During the course of the war he flew twenty combat missions over Europe. Jimmy was awarded the Distinguished Flying Cross and the Air Medal for heroism while in aerial battle. Jimmy remained in the Air Force Reserves and was promoted to Brigadier General in 1959. He also received the Distinguished Service Medal (1968) and the Presidential Medal of Freedom (1985).

Jimmy's first film after the war was a heartwarming story about how an individual's life really can make a difference. Jimmy turned in one of his best performances as George Bailey in *It's a Wonderful Life* (1946). Though the film had a lukewarm response from audiences and critics, Jimmy received his third Best Actor Oscar nomination. *It's a Wonderful Life* was Jimmy's favorite film because, he explains, "It's what a true motion picture should be. It takes a tiny but very important idea—in this case, the idea that you're not born to be a failure—and developed it into a whole movie."

Jimmy's life saw many changes as the decade of the 1940s came to a close. At age forty-one he married Gloria McLean and became an instant father to Gloria's two sons from her previous marriage, Ronald and Michael. In 1951 the couple welcomed twin daughters, Judy and Kelly, into the Stewart family.

The 1950s probably saw Jimmy's best work. Wanting his career to take a different direction from his "aw shucks" screen image, Jimmy began starring in heavier film dramas like *Winchester 73, Rear Window,* and the **Alfred Hitchcock** thriller *Vertigo.* He also starred in memorable films like *Harvey* and *Anatomy of a Murder,* which earned Jimmy his fourth and fifth Academy Award nominations.

In his later years Jimmy found fewer good film roles and tried his hand at television. He appeared in two television series, *The Jimmy Stewart Show* (1971–1972) and *Hawkins* (1973–1974). He also appeared in a few made-for-television movies, including the 1983 film *Right of Way* with **Bette Davis.**

At age seventy-two Jimmy received the American Film Institute's Life Achievement Award, and five years later, in 1985, the Academy of Motion Picture Arts and Sciences honored Jimmy with a special Oscar for "his fifty years of memorable performances and for his high ideals on and off the screen." He was a frequent guest of Johnny Carson on *The Tonight Show,* sometimes reading poems from his book *Jimmy Stewart and His Poems,* published in 1989. Jimmy played his last film role as the voice of the gun-fighting dog Wylie Burb in the 1991 animated film *An American Tail: Fievel Goes West.* Gloria, Jimmy's beloved wife of forty-five years, died in 1994. His own health began to fail soon after, and he died in 1997 at the age of eighty-nine. Because of his heroic roles on and off the screen and his strong devotion to family and country, Jimmy Stewart is one of America's best-loved icons of the twentieth century.

Ingrid Bergman

Costar of Oscar-Winning Film Casablanca
1915–1982

*My whole life has been acting. I have had
my different husbands, my families. I am
fond of them all and I visit them all. But
deep inside me there is the feeling that I
belong to show business.*

—INGRID BERGMAN

As a girl in Stockholm, Sweden, Ingrid Bergman dreamed of being an actress. She wrote in her diary of her desire to star opposite Sweden's leading men. Five years later she was living that dream.

Bergman had a difficult childhood. Born on August 29, 1915, in Stockholm, Ingrid was the third child of Justus Bergman and Friedel Adler. Both of her siblings had died in infancy. When Ingrid was three, her mother died as well. Justus struggled to raise his daughter alone. The owner of a photography shop and a gifted painter, he introduced his daughter to art and accompanied her to the theater.

Ingrid had a stable, comfortable childhood with Justus. But when she was thirteen, her father died of cancer. Ingrid was sent to live with her Aunt Ellen, who died within six months of assuming care of her niece. Finally, Ingrid settled with her Uncle Otto and Aunt Hulda and their five children.

A lonely and intensely shy girl, Ingrid created imaginary playmates and dreamed of becoming an actress. "I had an enormous imagination. . . . I was even afraid of the youngsters in school. I couldn't express myself, I blushed all the time. . . . But at home I had all of the playmates I had invented, and I read plays out loud and felt very comfortable. . . . [T]he stage was my only protection."

When Ingrid turned eighteen, she used her inheritance money to begin studying at Stockholm's Royal Dramatic Theater School. Between school terms she took a screen test for Swedish director Gustav Molander at Svenskfilmindustri. Just a week later she debuted on film as a maid in *Munkbrogreven* (*The Bridge of Monks*). Ingrid never returned to school. Instead, she spent the next five years making films. Before long she was receiving starring roles. Her sixth film, *Intermezzo* (1936), thrust Ingrid into the spotlight. The love story, written and directed by Molander, found its way to Hollywood three years later.

Ingrid's personal life was also going well. In 1937 she married Dr. Petter Lindstrom, a dentist she met years earlier. On September 28, 1938, she gave birth to a baby girl, Friedel Pia Lindstrom. Although delighted with marriage and motherhood, Ingrid refused to give up her career. "If you took acting away from me," she told a friend, "I'd stop breathing."

In the United States, producer David O. Selznick *(Gone With the Wind, Spellbound)* had seen Ingrid in *Intermezzo* and wanted to produce an English-language version. Once Bergman arrived in America, Selznick set out to make her a Hollywood star. He planned to give her a screen name, have her teeth capped, persuade her to wear more makeup—but she would have none of it. She maintained this fiery independence throughout her life. "I never regretted anything I did," she said years later, "just the things I didn't do."

Most American filmgoers remember Bergman as the woman **Humphrey Bogart** toasted in the 1942 Oscar-winning film *Casablanca.* It is a scene in which Bogart spoke one of the most remembered lines in motion picture history: "Here's looking at you, kid." Bergman's and Bogart's performances ensured them film immortality. It catapulted Bogart from screen gangster to romantic lead and elevated Bergman to one of Hollywood's hottest female stars.

In 1943 Ingrid earned a Best Actress Academy Award nomination for her performance in *For Whom the Bell Tolls;* the next year she won her first Oscar for a riveting performance in *Gaslight.* Six more films followed, including *Spellbound, The Bells of St. Mary's* (1945, Oscar nominee), *Notorious* (1946), and *Joan of Arc* (1948, Oscar nominee).

By 1949 Ingrid Bergman was at the height of her popularity. Then her professional and personal life fell into a downward spiral. She was profoundly affected by Italian director Roberto Rossellini's film *Open City* and sought and got a role in his upcoming project, *Stromboli.* Ingrid flew to Rome to begin work on the picture—and stayed for seven years, abandoning her family and taking up with Rossellini.

Popular disapproval over Bergman's behavior was so vehement that when word reached America that she was pregnant with Rossellini's child, Senator Edwin Johnson berated her on the floor of the U.S. Senate. The actress, he said, was not worthy of "setting foot on American soil again." Stunned and hurt by the attacks, Ingrid nonetheless admitted years later that "the entire situation with Roberto Rossellini could have been handled with more discretion." She was shocked, she said, "to find that people would be so upset by my behavior."

Ingrid divorced Lindstrom and married Rossellini in 1950. The two made four films together, none successful. After Robertino was born in 1950, she had twin daughters, Isabella and Isotta, in 1952. Bergman and Rossellini separated in 1956, before she went to England to begin work on *Anastasia,* a Twentieth Century Fox picture. Her portrayal of an amnesia victim chosen to impersonate the only surviving member of the Romanoff dynasty landed her the New York Film Critics Best Actress award, a Golden Globe, and a second Best Actress Oscar. It seemed that America had fallen in love with Ingrid all over again.

Life in America the second time around felt like a warm homecoming. In 1958 Bergman's star status soared with her performances in *Indiscreet* opposite Cary Grant and *The Inn of the Sixth Happiness* with Robert Donat. That year she married theatrical producer Lars Schmidt, who convinced her to take on television and stage roles. She earned an Emmy in 1959 for her first TV appearance, in *The Turn of the Screw,* which she and Lars adapted from the book by Henry James.

Over the next few decades Bergman appeared in scores of TV productions, movies, and plays. She won a third Oscar in 1974 for a supporting role in *Murder on the Orient Express.* In her last film, *Höstsonaten (Autumn Sonata)* (1978), she teamed up with Ingmar Bergman, one of the most celebrated movie directors in the industry. In the only film the two Swedes collaborated on, Ingrid gathered yet another Oscar nomination.

Ingrid turned in an Emmy-winning portrayal of Israeli prime minister Golda Meir in the 1982 TV movie *A Woman Called Golda,* although the actress was extremely ill. Diagnosed with breast cancer nine years earlier, she had undergone two mastectomies but refused to let the disease slow her down. "Time is shortening," she said while filming *Golda.* "But every day that I challenge this cancer and survive is a victory for me."

On August 29, 1982, Ingrid Bergman died at her home in London. It was her sixty-seventh birthday. Bergman's radiant beauty, exotic accent, and superb talent had made her one of Hollywood's most alluring actresses.

Lauren Bacall

*Award-Winning Actress and Wife of Humphrey Bogart
1924–*

There should be room in this industry for reflecting the lives and dramas of people of all ages and relationships. Hopefully, we don't always have to have projects with guns going off and Bruce Willis hanging off the side of buildings.

—LAUREN BACALL

At age nineteen Lauren Bacall graced the cover of *Harper's Bazaar* magazine three months in a row. Barely twenty when she starred in her first Hollywood motion picture, her costar was none other than **Humphrey Bogart.** Though he was about twenty-five years her senior, Bogart and Bacall fell in love. Their impassioned romance, good looks, sophisticated style, and successful careers, personified the "Hollywood couple" image of the 1940s.

A child of divorce and raised by a working mother, Betty Joan Perske was born on September 16, 1924, in New York City. Her parents, William and Natalie, divorced when Betty was five years old. Betty and her mother moved in with her maternal grandmother, Sophie. She attended Highland Manor, an all-girls school where she excelled in dance and sports. Though dance was her first love, Betty was bitten by the acting bug at age fifteen and appeared in various school productions. After high school she attended the American Academy of Dramatic Arts. To help pay for school, Betty worked at various odd jobs, including ushering at Broadway theaters, selling theater guides in front of Sardi's restaurant, and as a garment district model.

Betty's big break came in 1942 at age eighteen when her striking good looks caught the attention of *Harper's Bazaar* editor Diana Vreeland. Betty was featured on the magazine's cover, and it wasn't long before Hollywood called. Socialite Nancy "Slim" Gross showed Betty's picture to her director husband, Howard Hawks. Hawks offered assurances to Natalie that her daughter would be looked after and invited Betty out to Hollywood.

Hawks was delighted with Betty's screen test and signed her to a seven-year contract with Warner Brother Studios. Before Betty made her first film appearance, Hawks molded and shaped his newest protégé into a Hollywood starlet. He changed Betty's name; from now on she would be known as Lauren Bacall. Of being "remade" by Hawks, Lauren said, "He Svengali-ed me and created me out of this terrified creature who had just arrived from the Big Apple. He was a great moviemaker, had tremendous variety in his career. But he had always wanted to create a star out of an unknown, and he succeeded with me."

When Hawks felt that Bacall was ready, he cast her in his 1944 film *To Have and Have Not* opposite screen star Humphrey Bogart (Bogie). The second time Bacall met with Bogie he said to her, "I just saw your test. We'll have a lot a fun together." He was true to his word. As the beautiful but naive Marie in *To Have and Have Not,* Bacall delivered perhaps the most memorable line of her career when she said to Bogie, "You know how to whistle, don't ya, Steve? You just put your lips together and blow." Bacall had a way of lowering her chin while glancing up at the camera that earned her the nickname "The Look." Her deep sultry voice and seductive glance made her an instant star.

Bacall's and Bogart's on-screen attraction to one another was not entirely an act. Though he was forty-four and she just nineteen, they fell passionately in love and married. Years later, when asked by a writer about her feelings for Humphrey Bogart, Bacall simply replied, "He was the love of my life. . . . I have to say . . . he was."

Bogie and Bacall made three more movies together: *The Big Sleep* (1946), *Dark Passage* (1947), and *Key Largo* (1948). With Bogart as a top-ten box-office draw, and Bacall in his shadow, her own career may never have fully blossomed. At the same time, the films they made together might not have had the same screen magic if Bogart had been cast with someone else. She did appear in her own films such as *Young Man with a Horn* (1950) and the very popular *How to Marry a Millionaire* (1953), in which she costarred with Betty Grable and **Marilyn Monroe**. But by the 1950s Bacall spent most of her time caring for her children—son Stephen Humphrey (born 1949) and daughter Leslie Howard (born 1952).

While filming *Designing Woman* (1957), Bacall learned that her husband had become very sick. A heavy smoker, Bogart was diagnosed with throat cancer. After undergoing a nine-hour surgery, Bogart recuperated at home with his wife and kids by his side. The surgery and subsequent medical treatments were to no avail, and **Humphrey Bogart** died on January 14, 1957. Bacall found herself a widow at the tender age of thirty-three.

After Bogie's death, Bacall finished *Designing Woman* and did one other film, *The Gift of Love*, before moving back to New York. Still grieving and having grown weary of the Hollywood scene, Bacall soon found her professional life reinvigorated by a new outlet for her talent—the theater. Even with her limited stage experience, Bacall wowed critics with her Broadway performance in *Goodbye Charlie*. She also found a new man to love, actor Jason Robards. The two were married in 1961 and had a son together, whom they named Sam. Bacall and Robard's notoriously turbulent marriage ended in divorce in 1969.

Lauren Bacall made a few more films in the 1960s, always searching for better roles for women. She returned to Broadway in the 1966 comedy *Cactus Flower*, having what *Newsweek* called "an achieved presence, the triumphant style of a real survivor." She reached the pinnacle of her theatrical career in 1970 with her starring role in the musical *Applause*. Critics and audiences alike raved over her performance. She was rewarded with her first Tony Award.

Through the 1970s and 1980s Bacall made a few more films, but she really felt most at home on the stage. In 1981, at age fifty-seven Bacall starred again in a Broadway show, *Woman of the Year,* an adaptation of the 1941 Hepburn and Tracy film of the same name. Bacall had another mega-hit on her hands, and was awarded her second Tony. The *New York Times* review said, "Her elegance is no charade. Her class begins where real class must. In her spirit. She is a natural musical-comedy star."

Just when Bacall thought movie opportunities had all but vanished for her, she found her film career reawakened. In the 1990s Bacall appeared in three films, the most important of which was *The Mirror Has Two Faces.* Offered the role as **Barbra Streisand's** mother, Hannah, the seventy-two-year old actress happily accepted. Having never worked with a woman director (Barbra) before, Bacall said, "The thought of working with Barbra was not only challenging but I felt it would be a fascinating experience, which it was." Bacall turned in what could have easily been an Academy Award performance. When Awards time came around, Bacall was nominated, but lost to Juliette Binoche. However, Bacall did not walk away empty-handed. She won her first-ever Golden Globe and a BAFTA award, the British equivalent of the Academy Award.

With almost sixty years in show business, Lauren Bacall's work has not gone unrecognized by her colleagues. In 1991 she received the Career Achievement Award from the National Board of Review. The following year she was awarded the Donostia Lifetime Achievement Award at the San Sebastian International Film Festival and the Cecil B. DeMille Award for Career Achievement. Perhaps one of her proudest moments came when she was named a Kennedy Center Honoree in 1997, joining other film greats like Jack Lemmon, **Sidney Poitier, Katharine Hepburn**, and **Bette Davis.**

Marlon Brando

*"Tough-Guy" Actor Best Known
for His Performance in* The Godfather
1924–

> *The more sensitive you are, the more likely
> you are to be brutalized, develop scabs and
> never evolve. Never allow yourself to feel
> anything because you always feel too much.*
> —MARLON BRANDO

When Marlon Brando played the seemingly dumb loser and mob's boy Terry Malloy in *On the Waterfront,* audiences quickly realized the character was much more than just that. They saw that Brando had enormous range and was not only outstanding in the sensitive scenes with the lovely Eva Marie Saint but in the many that followed, showing Malloy's growth into a man ready to fight for what is right, putting himself at risk of death. When Malloy rides in the backseat of a car with his older brother, not knowing he is on his way to his own death, he gives one of the most remembered and earnest speeches in all of golden Hollywood history: "I could've had class. I could have been a contender; I could've been somebody . . . instead of a bum." So heartfelt are the words, that Terry's brother cancels Terry's killing, at great risk to himself, and audiences were completely won over.

A tough guy who was born in Omaha, Nebraska, on April 3, 1924, Marlon Brando had a rough childhood. He grew up in Libertyville, Illinois, with two older siblings and parents, Marlon and Dorothy, who drank excessively and frequently paid him little attention. He was expelled from schools, including the Shattuck Military School, and finally decided to follow his sisters to New York City, where he studied under the famous Lee Strasberg at the Actors Studio. In 1944 he performed on Broadway in *I Remember Mama;* then in 1946 did such a stunning job in *Truckline Café* that New York theater critics voted him Broadway's Most Promising Actor. It was not long after that he gave his outstanding stage performance in the intense and complex role of Stanley Kowalski in Tennessee Williams's *A Streetcar Named Desire* (1947).

Ready for the challenges of film, Brando headed to Hollywood and was given his first role in *The Men* (1950). To prepare for his part as a paraplegic, Brando stayed in a veterans' hospital for a month. In 1951 he played his Kowalski part again, this time for film, and earned magnificent critical response and his first Academy Award nomination. He received the next three nominations for movies that closely followed—*Viva Zapata!* in 1952, *Julius Caesar* in 1953, and *On the Waterfront* in 1954. His portrayal of the lost young man turned hero in *On the Waterfront* won him not just the nomination but his first Academy Award for Best Actor. In the same year that the film was released, Brando also played the bitterly angry and misunderstood motorcycle gang leader in *The Wild One,* a cinematic landmark role that ushered in similar undaunted characters in other biker films and movies such as *Rebel Without a Cause* and *Easy Rider.* Already, however, Brando had a reputation for being difficult to work with.

Through the 1950s Brando appeared in some films that were unsuccessful. But he unleashed his acting scope, working in a diversity of parts such as Napoleon in *Desirée* (1954), a singing and dancing role as a gambler in *Guys and Dolls* (1955), and as a Japanese interpreter who may be homosexual (a most risky part in light of Brando's previously established film image) in *The Teahouse of the August Moon* (1956). His role in *Sayonara* as an American airman who becomes romantically involved with a Japanese actress won him yet another Oscar nomination in 1957. From 1957 to 1959 he was in a difficult marriage with actress Anna Kashfi. With her he had a son, Christian. In 1960 he married Mexican actress Movita Casteñada, with whom he had two children, Miko and Rebecca, before they split up.

The actor made his first attempt at directing when he took over from Stanley Kubrick midway through the production of *One-Eyed Jacks.* He also acted in that 1961 film, which some critics consider a gem of a western. Soon after came Brando's role in MGM's remake of *Mutiny on the Bounty* in 1962, a failed production that not only was grossly overbudget but that drew few to the box office. By now the rambunctious actor had himself lost much control, having tantrums on the set and attempting too many improvisations. In his personal life he was overindulging in women and food (in the mid-1990s he would weigh more than 300 pounds). In 1966 he purchased the Polynesian atoll of thirteen islands known as Tetiaroa. He lived there with his third wife, Tarita Teripaia, the actress he worked with in *Mutinty on the Bounty.* They had a son, Tehotu, and a daughter, Cheyenne. While information about Brando's relationships with women is limited, it is believed that he also had two or three children with his Guatemalan housekeeper, Christina Ruiz, and that he had three other children from affairs as well. The 1960s also was a time when Brando failed upon experimenting with a new venue—comedy. His roles in two comedies nearly ruined him.

The actor's resurrection occurred in 1972, when he gave an outstanding performance in Francis Ford Coppola's film *The Godfather,* winning him another Oscar. Brando did not attend the award ceremonies but instead sent an actress depicting a Native American to the stage to decline the award as a protest against the Native American plight. The following year, he appeared in

Last Tango in Paris, the highly controversial film that initially was X-rated and that brought him another Oscar nomination. From there, Brando slowed down.

He appeared in the intense *Apocalypse Now* in 1979 and years later was nominated for an Academy Award for Best Supporting Actor for *A Dry White Season* (1989). He also took small parts if directors offered him an excessive salary. He costarred with Johnny Depp in *Don Juan DeMarco* in 1995, giving a strong performance. When he worked on *The Island of Dr. Moreau* (1996), he reportedly told others on the set that they should just go home because the film would be poor, a prediction that unfortunately would hit the mark.

In 2001 Brando costarred in *The Score*, along with **Robert De Niro,** Edward Norton, and Angela Bassett; on the set he was said to have been a thorn in the side of director Frank Oz. He lives a rather reclusive life at his home in Beverly Hills, California.

Grandeur on the Big Screen

They are grand, sweeping visions of families, villages, nations, cultures and whole planets at crossroads, when every human fate depends on a decision some solitary soul must make.

—Mary Shaffer and Jerry Bunin, "more than just long movies," *Telegram-Tribune*

*E*pics. Motion picture films that are so enormous in scope and intensity that they almost seem to spill out beyond the parameters of the movie screen. The epic film blends the elements of action, grandeur, romance, and drama, woven around a single event such as the sinking of the ocean liner *Titanic* (1997) or a period saga such as *The Ten Commandments* (1956). The subject matter of an epic can range from treatment of war or medieval history to biography or fantasy. They usually run longer than most films, employ casts of thousands, use massive sets or vast on-location sites to frame the story, require hundreds of pieces of equipment, and are often accompanied by an extensive musical score. In the movie *First Knight* (1995), more than 200 horses and 250 stuntmen were employed to appear in the film's many battle and celebration scenes. Epics often carry underlying messages—how one person can change the fate of a people (*Gandhi*, 1982) or how good ultimately triumphs over evil (*Gladiator*, 2000).

Epic motion pictures often focus on one character's personal journey. The audience should be drawn into the crisis the character may be faced with along that journey while he/she looks for strength or wisdom to get through the situation. The difficulty should arouse our emotions and make us want to pull for the protagonist whatever the crisis—men battling one another to defend their beliefs (*Gettysburg,* 1993), the emergence of an individual willing to take up the cause (*Lawrence of Arabia*, 1962), or a realization that alters the course of a character's destiny (*Schindler's List,* 1993).

An epic may follow a story or event accurately, or it may be infused with some fictitious elements deemed necessary to make the film more interesting for the audience. Despite the fact that an epic by definition runs longer than the average film, sometimes even an epic tale must condense its timeline, causing some parts of the story to be eliminated. Often, too, the focus of an epic revolves around a few main characters—Rose and Jack's love affair in *Titanic* made the disaster more personal; the war raging in Europe became the backdrop in **Tom Hanks**'s mission to find a soldier in *Saving Private Ryan* (1998). Whatever elements are employed in producing an epic film, most of the time the final result is an encompassing visual, as well as entertaining, experience for the viewer.

The subject matter of an epic can be limitless. It can revolve around an historical event or time (*Cleopatra,* 1963), a war or conflict (*Braveheart,* 1995), a medieval story (*First Knight,* 1995), or total fantasy (*Lord of the Rings,* 2001). Epic movies can take months and months to shoot and are very expensive to produce—the cost of hiring crews, casts, extras, on-location travel, and the creation of period costumes and sets requires an enormous budget. For example, in *First Knight,* 300 suits of full body armor and armor worn by 200 horses were made in six weeks. Despite the advancements in special-effects technology, its use does not necessarily diminish costs, for the technology itself is expensive.

A scene from the epic motion picture The Ten Commandments

The evolution of the epic began with silent films. Director D. W. Griffith probably produced the first commercial epic with his release of the controversial Civil War film *Birth of a Nation* in 1915. It was the longest film of its time, running three hours, and made about $18 million. In 1926 MGM released its $4 million silent version of the biblical tale *Ben-Hur*. In the famous chariot race scene, forty-two cameras filmed the action, in which five horses are killed in the ensuing chariot wreck. Several other silent epics graced the screen in the 1920s, including *The Ten Commandments* (1923), *The Thief of Bagdad* (1924), and *King of Kings* (1927).

The sound era ushered in a whole new wave of epic films, including *Sign of the Cross* (1933) and *Samson and Delilah* (1950). Cecil B. DeMille's remake of *The Ten Commandments* (1956) was a lot more elaborate than his 1923 version. The famous parting of the Red Sea sequence required 600 extras and a 32-foot-high dam directing tens of thousands of gallons of water.

As the motion picture industry's technology evolved, so did the epic. The use of special effects brought a whole new way of making epics look even more realistic or made fantasy more fantastic. In 1977 George Lucas released *Star Wars,* the first installment of his space-age heroism tale. The film had a modest budget ($11 million) and used computerized and digitally timed special effects not known before in motion picture history. It was a mega-blockbuster hit, breaking box-office records and grossing almost $514 million in its original release. Lucas went on to produce two other films in the trilogy and has continued to add other chapters to his space epic.

In terms of the business end of the motion picture industry, epic movies are no different from any other films released except for the higher cost to produce them. And though studios are in business to entertain, they are in business to make money, too. Just like any film project, an epic can be a success or it can bomb at the box office. To date, the most expensive movie ever made was James Cameron's 1997 *Titanic.* With a staggering budget of $200 million, the movie cost more to make than the actual ocean liner ($7.5 million at the time and about $120 to $150 million in 1997 dollars). However, *Titanic* was a huge box-office hit, grossing over $600 million in the United States alone. The biggest box-office bomb was the 1963 version of *Cleopatra,* despite a star-studded cast that included **Elizabeth Taylor,** Richard Burton, and Rex Harrison. This epic was ill-fated from the start, with Taylor becoming gravely ill and director Rouben Mamoulian being fired during filming. The movie cost an unbelievable $44 million (translating to $270 million today) and almost bankrupted Twentieth Century Fox studio.

Though some of these films, such as *Ishtar* (1987), lost money (grossing only $14 million; budget, $40 million), additional revenue is possible through international distribution, cable television, home-video rentals and sales, and commercial television, so most films do recoup their costs. With countless stories to be told and countless others to be written for everyone's particular tastes, special effects dazzlers, such as *Harry Potter and the Chamber of Secrets* (2002), will continue to bring audiences to theaters in droves.

Paul Newman

Legendary Actor, Entrepreneur, Activist,
and Humanitarian
1925–

Acting is a question of absorbing other
people's personalities and adding some of
your own experience.

—PAUL NEWMAN

The legendary screen actor with the most famous blue eyes in the motion picture industry is also a loving family man, a successful entrepreneur, a political activist, and a generous humanitarian. Never one to take himself seriously, Paul Newman has often quipped that it's a bit embarrassing that sales of his Newman's Own famous salad dressing is outgrossing his films. An intensely private man, Newman prefers to talk about his charitable endeavors—the Scott Newman Foundation for drug rehabilitation or the Hole in the Wall Gang camps for kids with life-threatening diseases.

Life for Paul Leonard Newman began in the comfortable Cleveland suburb of Shaker Heights, Ohio, on January 26, 1925. The second son of Arthur and Theresa Newman, Paul and his older brother, Arthur, enjoyed a middle-class upbringing, thanks to the success of his father's sporting goods store. Paul acted in plays in Shaker Heights High School before enlisting in the navy in 1943. Though he hoped to become an aviator, doctors discovered that Paul was color-blind, so he served as a radio operator aboard torpedo bombers in the South Pacific during World War II.

After his discharge from the navy in 1946, Newman returned to Ohio, where he enrolled in Kenyon College. He played football, ran a campus laundry service, and embraced his passion for acting. Paul graduated from Kenyon in 1949 and spent a year in Chicago working in local theater, but he had to return home when his father died.

By then Newman was married to actress Jacqueline Witte, who was pregnant with their first child. Newman took over running the sporting goods store, but his aptitude wasn't retail sales work. He sold the business a year later and returned to acting.

Newman studied at the Yale Drama School before moving to New York City to attend the famed Actors Studio. He made his Broadway debut in William Inge's 1953 production *Picnic.* It was during that time that Newman met southern actress Joanne Woodward. In 1958, after a difficult and painful divorce for Newman, he and Woodward wed. They have been together ever since, raising three daughters, Nell, Melissa, and Clea, along the way. (Newman also had three children by Witte—Scott, Susan, and Stephanie.)

Newman's classically handsome features and mesmerizing blue eyes only added to his appeal. He was also a bit lucky, for he came into acting at a time when live television dramas were aired on shows like *Playhouse 90.* The small-screen medium opened up many opportunities for actors beyond the theater stage. It was not long before Warner Brothers Studio signed him to a film contract.

His first film, the ridiculous biblical saga *The Silver Chalice* (1954), was so bad it might well have been his last. He fared much better in his next role, portraying boxing great Rocky Graziano in *Somebody Up There Likes Me*

(1956). The critics applauded Newman's terrific performance, and his acting career was well on its way.

Over the next decade Newman became one of the biggest box-office draws, starring in such acclaimed films as *Cat on a Hot Tin Roof* (1958), *The Hustler* (1961), *Hud* (1963), *Cool Hand Luke* (1967), and *Butch Cassidy and the Sundance Kid* (1969). He also appeared in several films with Woodward, including *The Long Hot Summer* (1958), *From the Terrace* (1960), *Paris Blues* (1961), and *A New Kind of Love* (1963). He made his directorial debut with *Rachel, Rachel* in 1968. The film received an Academy Award nomination for Best Picture.

In 1969 Newman cofounded First Artists' Production Company with colleagues **Sidney Poitier** and **Barbra Streisand.** In the 1970s Newman appeared in some forgettable films such as *Buffalo Bill and the Indians* and the disaster epic *The Towering Inferno,* but he wowed audiences once again when he reteamed with his Butch Cassidy costar **Robert Redford** in *The Sting.* The film walked away with seven Oscars, including Best Picture. In the 1980s and 1990s, a maturing Newman was still as charismatic as ever. He continued to select challenging projects to star in and direct. He turned in great performances in *Absence of Malice* (1981), *The Verdict* (1982), *Message in a Bottle* (1999), and *Where the Money Is* (2000). He also directed wife Woodward in *The Glass Menagerie* (1987).

Newman has appeared in more than fifty films and has earned eight Academy Award nominations (the last for the 1994 film *Nobody's Fool*). The Oscar eluded him until he reprised his role as pool hustler Eddie Felson in the 1986 film *The Color of Money* (1986). In response to his win, Newman quipped, "I'm on a roll. Maybe I can get a job."

Though well into his seventies, Newman is more active now than when he was making three motion pictures a year. When tragedy struck the Newman family in 1978, when his son, Scott, died of a drug overdose, Newman founded the Scott Newman Foundation. Since its inception in 1980, the foundation has helped thousands of children, families, and communities to overcome the dangers of alcohol and other drugs through its many education programs. Each summer the Rowdy Ridge Gang Camp in California opens its grounds to hundreds of families, mothers, and children recovering from the effects of alcohol and drug abuse as well as those whose lives have been affected by domestic violence.

A longtime kitchen aficionado, Newman used to give out bottles of his specially mixed salad dressing as Christmas presents. The dressing became so popular that Newman and his friend A. E. Hotchner founded Newman's Own food company in 1982. The first product they marketed was Newman's Olive Oil and Vinegar dressing. At the end of the first year Newman gave away approximately $1 million dollars to charity. Today the product line includes several salad dressings, pasta sauces, a steak sauce, two types of lemonade, four kinds of salsa, ice cream, and gourmet popcorn. All profits from the sale of his products goes to educational and charitable organizations. To date, Newman's Own has donated over $125 million dollars.

Newman's Own gives its founder a creative outlet very different from acting. With the help of Hotchner and his wife, Ursula, and with funds from Newman's Own, Newman founded the Hole in the Wall Gang camps, located in Ashford, Connecticut, in 1986. Another passion is auto racing. While preparing for his role in the 1968 film *Winning,* Newman went to a racing school to learn how to drive. He was a born natural and began competing. In 1979 Newman finished in second place in the Le Mans twenty-four-hour race.

In recent years Newman has been recognized more for his life's work than any single project. The Academy of Motion Picture Arts and Sciences awarded Newman two honorary Oscars—one for recognition of his many memorable screen performances and professional integrity, the other, the Jean Hersholt

Humanitarian Award, for his tireless charity work. In 1992 Paul and Joanne shared the Kennedy Center Honors with Lionel Hampton, Ginger Rogers, Mstislav Rostropovich, and Paul Taylor.

What is so refreshing about this multitalented actor, director, entrepreneur, philanthropist, and fearless race-car driver is his unabashed humbleness. When asked what he would like his epitaph to say, the quick-witted Newman responded, "Here lies Paul Newman, who died a flop because his eyes turned brown." Turning serious for a moment when asked how he would like to be remembered, Newman quietly replied, "Just that I was part of my times. That's all."

Peter Sellers

One of the World's Greatest Comedic Actors
1925–1977

There is no me. I do not exist. There used to be a me, but I had it surgically removed.

—PETER SELLERS

Acclaimed as one of the world's greatest comedians, Peter Sellers's performances in *Dr. Strangelove,* the Pink Panther series, and *Being There* continue to delight audiences decades after their release. He amassed more than eighty film and voice-over credits; wrote, directed, and produced numerous films; and earned three Academy Award nominations. Yet throughout his life Sellers suffered from intense loneliness and unhappiness. At times a difficult and self-indulgent man, Sellers always feared that under the multitude of hilarious characters he portrayed, he did not have a personality of his own.

Richard Henry Sellers was born on September 8, 1925, in Southsea, England. His parents, vaudeville performers Agnes (Peg) and Bill Sellers, doted on their son from the start. (They began calling him Peter in memory of their first child, who had died at birth.) He made his first stage appearance at two days old, when his parents proudly introduced him to the King's Theatre audience.

Peter spent his childhood on the road with his parents, and before long he was infatuated by the excitement of the stage. His mother sent him to dance schools in Southsea and London before he was enrolled in a boarding school for boys. As a teen, he played the drums with jazz bands, and he learned to play the banjo and ukelele.

When Sellers turned eighteen, he was drafted into the British Royal Air Force (RAF). He became an official entertainer for the military, and until 1946 he performed humorous sketches and played drums for the troops. He became a master of mimicry. Following several unsuccessful auditions at the British Broadcasting Company (BBC) after World War II ended, he applied his gift for impersonation to land a "real" show business job. Pretending to be a popular radio star, he telephoned BBC producer Roy Speer and recommended himself.

Sellers later admitted his deception, but Speer was so delighted with the impersonation that he hired him. Before long the young man was starring in the BBC radio show *Crazy People,* which premiered in May 1951. Retitled *The Goon Show* in 1952, the variety show costarred Sellers's wartime buddies Michael Bentine, Harry Secombe, and Spike Milligan (who himself would become a legendary comic). Sellers created a menagerie of characters, including the high-spoken cad Hercules Grytpype-Thynne, the cowardly Major Denis Bloodnok, and the forgetful inventor Henry Crun. *The Goon Show* was a smash hit; by the time it ended its run in January 1960, Peter Sellers was a star in England.

On *The Goon Show,* Sellers also dubbed voices for many actors, including Hollywood icon **Humphrey Bogart** in *Beat the Devil* (1954). Among his most masterful achievements was in the minor film *Malaga* (1954), in which he recorded the voices of fourteen male and female cast members. In one scene, eleven of these characters are involved in the same conversation!

Peter's vocal talents landed him on-screen roles in a number of British movies, including *Penny Points to Paradise* (1951), *The Ladykillers* (1955, starring Alec Guinness), and *Your Past Is Showing* (1957). Sellers got his "big break" in 1959, when he played labor leader Fred Kite in *I'm All Right, Jack.* His performance earned him the BAFTA Best Actor Award in 1960 (the equivalent of the American Oscar). Sellers also received his first American Academy Award nomination for the short piece *The Running, Jumping, and Standing-Still Film* (1959), which he wrote, produced, directed, and edited. In his first film to achieve success in America, Sellers played three raucously funny roles in *The Mouse That Roared* (1959).

Sellers was also an accomplished singer. In 1960 he recorded the duet "Goodness Gracious Me" with Italian actress Sophia Loren. The song reached number four on the British charts. The following year, another Sellers-Loren duet, "Bangers and Mash" (sausages and mashed potatoes), made the British Top 25. His cover of the Beatles tune "A Hard Day's Night" was fourteenth on the British pop charts in 1965.

Though Sellers appeared in, or dubbed, fourteen movie and TV projects from 1960 to 1963, only one, *The Pink Panther* (1963), was successful. He introduced perhaps his most memorable and best-loved character in *The Pink Panther:* the determined but hilariously inept French detective Jacques Clouseau. In 1964 Sellers hit it big again when he starred in director Stanley Kubrick's *Dr. Strangelove: Or, How I Learned to Stop Worrying and Love the Bomb.* In addition to the title role (a mutant German scientist), Sellers played two other characters: British captain Lionel Mandrake and Milquetoast U.S. president Merkin Muffley. His spectacular performance earned him his first Academy Award Best Actor Oscar nomination. Many critics still regard *Dr. Strangelove* as Sellers's best film.

In 1964 the comic actor replayed his Inspector Clouseau role in *A Shot in the Dark,* but audiences would not see the popular character again for a decade. By then, he had made a string of unremarkable TV and film appearances, including a costarring role in Woody Allen's screenwriting debut, *What's New, Pussycat?* The third Pink Panther film (1974), *The Return of the Pink Panther,* revived Sellers's flagging career. The actor followed with two more sequels, *The Pink Panther Strikes Again* (1976) and *Revenge of the Pink Panther* (1978), but his other 1970s films were not as successful.

In 1979 Sellers starred in the screen adaptation of the novel *Being There* by Jerzy Kosinski. The movie was a longtime ambition of the actor's—ever since he had read the novel years earlier, he had been determined to bring it to the screen. Sellers played Chauncey Gardener, a childlike gardener whose silence and simplicity lead him to be mistaken for an economic guru. His subtle performance won critical acclaim and brought Sellers a second Best Actor Academy Award nomination. Sellers's last film role was in the 1980 movie *The Fiendish Plot of Dr. Fu Manchu.* The actor had experienced heart problems for many years. He suffered a fatal heart attack on July 24, 1980, just one year after *Being There* premiered.

Peter Sellers's personal life was rocky. Pampered by an overbearing mother through childhood, the adult Sellers often behaved childishly and was known to throw tantrums. He demanded undivided attention from family and friends. His first marriage, to Anne Howe, lasted from 1951 to 1961; the couple had two children, Michael (1954) and Sarah (1957). In 1964 he married actress Britt Ekland; they had one child, actress Victoria Sellers (1965), and divorced in 1968. His third marriage, to Miranda Quarry in 1970, lasted just two years. He was married to fourth wife actress Lynne Frederick (1977) when he died.

Despite his volatile personality, Sellers is fondly remembered by many of his colleagues, including **Shirley MacLaine,** Maggie Smith, Goldie Hawn, and

Elke Sommer. In addition to Stanley Kubrick and Blake Edwards, he also worked with directorial greats Billy Wilder and Roman Polanski. In a tribute to Sellers, Edwards assembled outtakes of the actor's performances in "Pink Panther" films and combined them with new footage of other cast members, releasing the film as *Trail of the Pink Panther* in 1982.

Sellers requested that the song "In the Mood," which he hated, be played at his funeral. According to biographer Roger Lewis, Sellers told his son, Michael, that the tune was "wonderfully inappropriate—hence, wonderfully appropriate—for solemn occasions." It was a final display of the convoluted humor of a lonely, complex man.

Marilyn Monroe

Film Star and American Icon
1926–1962

I knew I belonged to the public and to the world, not because I was talented or even beautiful, but because I had never belonged to anything or anyone else.

—MARILYN MONROE

All it took was a well-placed slight breeze to create a visual image that would become imprinted on moviegoers for decades. In the film *The Seven Year Itch* (1955), Marilyn Monroe steps innocently onto a subway grate in hopes of achieving some relief from the day's wilting heat. A breeze blows from below, just enough to playfully swoosh under her full skirt. Indeed, while it appears playful, the scene is much more; for the skirt is pushed quite high above Marilyn's knees, revealing much of her curvy legs, elongated by high heels. While trying to push the dress down with her arms, her joyous smile and beautiful face are framed by her thick tousled white-blond curls.

While the final edited version of this scene was very short in the movie, its incredible sex appeal proved so powerful that it would be replayed, imitated, and marveled over for generations. Those few moments seemingly captured what Marilyn Monroe had become for America—immensely sexy, yet innocent and vulnerable. That combination, as well as her humility, honesty, and wit, helped Monroe create a love affair with the public that would make her not just a star but an icon in film history.

Even icons struggle, though. In Marilyn's case, that struggle occurred right from the start. For years she claimed she was an orphan. It was true that she never knew her father, but she did know her mother, Gladys Baker Mortenson. The two did not live together very long, however, because of her mother's mental illness. Born on June 1, 1926, in Los Angeles, Marilyn was first named Norma Jeane Mortenson (later baptized as Norma Jeane Baker). She spent most of her early years in orphanages and foster homes, where she was emotionally neglected and sexually abused.

On June 19, 1942, Norma Jeane married Jimmy Dougherty, and they were happy until he joined the merchant marines and was sent to the South Pacific in 1944. Since Norma Jeane had dropped out of high school when she was fifteen, she started working on the assembly line at the Radio Plane munitions factory. Several months after she started there, photographer David Conover, who was taking pictures for a story on the war effort, became enchanted with her looks and demeanor and used her in his photo shoot. Norma Jeane enrolled in a three-month modeling course, and Conover helped her win a modeling contract. Within two years she appeared on many popular magazine covers, enrolled in drama classes, and decided to become a film star. Since marriage didn't fit into the new life she envisioned and she was bored with her husband, Norma Jeane divorced Jimmy shortly after he returned home in June 1946.

By August, Norma Jeane had signed her first studio contract with Twentieth Century Fox. She changed her name to Marilyn Monroe and dyed her brown hair blond. She had small roles in a few movies, then gained some attention for her part in John Huston's *The Asphalt Jungle* in 1950. That same year she attracted more attention for her role in *All About Eve,* starring **Bette Davis.** Between 1950 and 1952 Monroe appeared in more than a dozen films. But in 1953 Monroe achieved the star status she had longed for, garnering the lead female roles in *Niagara,* the intensely popular *Gentlemen Prefer Blondes,* and *How to Marry a Millionaire.* Fan mail was flooding in for Hollywood's newest sex symbol.

On January 14, 1954, Monroe married the legendary baseball superstar Joe DiMaggio, twelve years her senior, at San Francisco's City Hall. While they had dated for two years, the marriage lasted only nine months because of Monroe's career ambitions and DiMaggio's continued discomfort with her sexy screen persona. Still, the pair would remain close for the rest of Monroe's life.

While Monroe had achieved stardom with her sexy, dumb-blonde image, she was intent on becoming a serious actress. She left Hollywood in 1955 and started studying at the Actors Studio in New York City with Lee Strasberg, who had also helped such celebrated actors as Montgomery Clift and **Marlon Brando.** Since the studios wouldn't give her the chance she wanted, Monroe decided to do it her own way. In 1955 she opened the motion picture company Marilyn Monroe Productions in hope of giving herself the opportunity to play more demanding and versatile roles. The company produced *Bus Stop* (1956) and *The Prince and the Showgirl* (1957), which costarred **Laurence Olivier,** who also directed the film.

Monroe began dating famed playwright Arthur Miller and married him on June 29, 1956. He would remark about her years later that she had "so much promise . . . was endlessly fascinating, full of original observations. . . . [T]here wasn't a conventional bone in her body."

Returning to work for the Hollywood studios, Monroe accepted the starring role in *Some Like It Hot,* which appeared in 1959 and for which she earned a Golden Globe for Best Actress in a Comedy. Her husband wrote a more multidimensional role for her in *The Misfits,* which began filming in

1960 and costarred screen stars **Clark Gable** and Montgomery Clift. Unfortunately, by then Monroe's marriage to Miller had disintegrated. The couple lived apart and hardly spoke as Miller continued to work on the script while the production progressed. Monroe's health began to deteriorate, and she suffered from intense stage fright. She often showed up on the set very late and could not remember her lines.

Monroe and Miller divorced in January 1961, the same month that *The Misfits* was released. By April of 1962 Monroe was working on Twentieth Century Fox's *Something's Got to Give.* The film was plagued by many delays because of Monroe's tardiness on the set as well as a trip to New York to appear at President John Kennedy's gala birthday celebration. It was at this party that Monroe sang her now-famous sultry rendition of "Happy Birthday." Even though Monroe had gotten permission in advance for the New York trip, Fox studio executives were not happy. She was fired in June, only to return on August 1 to a wage two and one-half times her original salary.

Despite being rehired, Monroe never completed the film. In the early morning of August 5, 1962, she died in her sleep from a drug overdose. Speculation continues today as to whether her death was a suicide or an accident.

Sidney Poitier

Influential Figure in American Film
1927–

I want to make motion pictures about the dignity, nobility, the magnificence of human life."

—SIDNEY POITIER, UPON RECEIVING AN OSCAR FOR HIS ROLE IN *LILIES OF THE FIELD*

Amid thunderous applause, the seventy-five–year-old actor walked to the stage of the Kodak Theatre in Hollywood, California, on March 24, 2002. Sidney Poitier, one of the film industry's most respected actors and producers, had been awarded an honorary Oscar for his "extraordinary performances and unique presence on the screen, and for representing the motion picture industry with dignity, style, and intelligence throughout the world."

"I accept this award," Poitier said, "in memory of all the African-American actors and actresses who went before me . . . on whose shoulders I was privileged to stand. . . . My love and my thanks . . . to those audience members around the world who have placed their trust in my judgment as an actor and filmmaker."

Poitier graciously credited the actors and directors who came before him, but theater and TV audiences knew that Poitier himself was a vastly influential figure in American film history. In 1963, during the height of America's racial unrest, he was the first African American to win an Academy Award for a lead role. Later films, especially *Guess Who's Coming to Dinner* (1967) and *To Sir, with Love* (1967), helped tear down the social barriers between blacks and whites. "When the Academy honors Sidney Poitier," said Academy president Frank Pierson, "it honors itself even more."

Sidney Poitier weighed three pounds when he was born prematurely on February 20, 1927, in Miami, Florida. His parents, Bahamian farmers Evelyn and Reginald Poitier, were in America selling a crop of tomatoes and taking a brief vacation from their other children: sons Cyril, Reginald, Carl, and Cedric, and daughters Ruby and Teddy. Ten years later, when the United States placed an embargo on Bahamian produce, the Poitiers's business on Cat Island collapsed. The family moved to the Bahamian city of Nassau to live with relatives. There Sidney saw his first motion pictures—westerns starring Tom Mix, Gene Autry, and Roy Rogers. He was so entranced by the larger-than-life gunslingers that after the first movie he ran behind stage to look for the actors.

As a teen, Sidney got into mischief. At thirteen he was arrested and briefly jailed for stealing corn. Sidney felt so contrite when Reginald Poitier paid the owner of the corn with borrowed money that he vowed to stay out of trouble. When he turned fifteen, however, his parents sent him to live with his older brother Cyril's family in Miami; they believed it was the only way to save their son from delinquency.

In Florida, Sidney experienced racial prejudice for the first time. It was "all over the place like barbed wire," he remembered. In the segregated South, Poitier saw WHITE and COLORED signs posted in public restrooms, on drinking fountains, and over bus seats. He was puzzled by the net of restrictions placed on black Americans. Then, while working as a delivery person for a department store, he ran afoul of the "Jim Crow" laws by appearing at the front door of a white home (blacks were supposed to use the back door). Two days later, the Ku Klux Klan appeared at Cyril's house and demanded to see Sidney. The boy was not home, but Cyril was frightened enough to send his brother away when he returned. After a succession of similar incidents, Sidney decided to head north.

The sixteen-year-old arrived in New York City penniless, and with no friends or relatives to help him. He was homeless for a time, sleeping in bus terminals and on rooftops until he earned enough money through a series of menial jobs to rent a room in Harlem. When he lost his job and was evicted from the room, he lied about his age and was accepted into the U.S. Army, where he could stay warm and be fed and clothed.

Poitier left the army the following year, determined to enter show business. His first audition for the American Negro Theater went so badly that he took six months trying to eliminate his accent and perfect his skills. He was accepted on his second try, and shortly afterward he landed a minor role in a Broadway production of *Lysistrata.*

Success followed quickly. After a three-year tour with *Anna Lucasta,* Poitier got his first major film role in *No Way Out* (1950). His performance as a doctor treating a white bigot attracted a great deal of attention, and he obtained roles in *Cry, the Beloved Country* (1951) and *Blackboard Jungle* (1955), as well. Though Poitier was winning better roles than any other black actors were receiving at the time, he still believed they were conspicuously less prominent than those given to white actors.

After turning down several projects that he viewed as demeaning, Poitier finally earned leading-man status. His role in the 1958 film *Defiant Ones* secured his first Academy Award nomination for Best Actor. Five years later he became the first African American to win a leading-role Oscar when he won the Best Actor award for the hit film *Lilies of the Field.*

Poitier was catapulted to stardom after three more remarkable films—*To Sir, with Love* (1967), *Guess Who's Coming to Dinner* (1967), and *In the Heat of the Night* (1967). That year, a nationwide poll named him the country's most popular actor. In 1969 he teamed with **Barbra Streisand** and **Paul Newman** to form the First Artists' Production Company, designed to give the three actors financial and artistic control over their films.

Poitier spent the 1970s and 1980s directing rather than performing, although he did take roles in some of his own films, such as *Buck and the Preacher* (1972) and *Uptown Saturday Night* (1975). He also raised a family: with his first wife, Juanita, whom he married in 1952, he had four daughters, Beverly, Pamela, Sherri, and Gina. The couple separated in 1963 and later divorced. He met Joanna Shimkus while working on the 1969 movie *The Lost Man;* the couple had two daughters, Anika and Sydney, before they married in 1976.

In 1988 Poitier returned to acting with performances in *Little Nikita* and *Shoot to Kill.* He has since appeared in seven TV and feature films. He was nominated for Best Actor Emmy and Golden Globe awards for the 1991 TV movie *Separate but Equal;* he received Emmy, NAACP Image, and Screen Actors Guild award nominations for his performance in *Mandela and de Klerk* (1997). In 1999 he was the executive producer of *Free of Eden,* and the following year he won an NAACP Image Award for his performance in the TV movie *The Simple Life of Noah Dearborn* (1999). Poitier has also earned Life Achievement Awards from the American Film Institute and the Screen Actors Guild. His most recent role was in the 2001 TV movie *The Last Brickmaker in America.*

Despite continuing racial inequality in the film industry, Poitier's talent, integrity, and affable personality have won the respect and admiration of fellow actors and of fans around the world.

Audrey Hepburn

Actress and Humanitarian
1929–1993

To save a child is a blessing: to save a million is a God-given opportunity.

—AUDREY HEPBURN
ABOUT HER WORK WITH UNICEF

When people hear the name Audrey Hepburn, it undoubtedly evokes images of her memorable film and stage character portrayals, such as Holly Golightly in *Breakfast at Tiffany's* (1961) and Eliza Doolittle in *My Fair Lady* (1964). Audrey received many honors, including an Academy Award, two Tonys, the Screen Actors Guild Life Achievement Award, and the Jean Hersholt Humanitarian Award, posthumously. Perhaps best known as an actress, Audrey is also remembered as a great humanitarian. As Goodwill Ambassador for the United Nations Children's Fund (UNICEF) from 1987 until 1992, Audrey worked tirelessly for the poor, starving, suffering children in Third World countries like Ethiopia, Bangladesh, and Somalia. Though born into a world of wealth and prominence, Audrey knew all too well about hunger and hardship.

On May 4, 1929, in Brussels, Belgium, English banker John Hepburn Ruston and his wife, Dutch Baroness Ella van Heemstra, became the parents of a baby girl. Named Edda Kathleen van Heemstra Hepburn Ruston (though called Audrey), she was a shy, gentle child who loved animals and nature's peacefulness. Her parent's marriage was often turbulent and finally ended when John left the family in 1935. For the quiet six-year-old, it was devastating. "The most traumatic event in my life." "[A] tragedy from which I don't think I've ever recovered. I worshipped him and missed him terribly from the day he disappeared," said Audrey.

After John's departure, Ella sent Audrey to an exclusive girls' boarding school in London. Away from her family (Audrey had two older stepbrothers, Alexander and Ian, from Ella's previous marriage), Audrey was terribly lonely and afraid. During that time she did discover one thing that brought her joy—ballet. However, there wasn't much time for Audrey to learn dance because England had declared war on Germany in 1939 after the Nazis invaded Poland. Ella took the family to Arnhem, Holland, where she thought they would be safe from a war that would quickly consume Europe.

The Nazis occupied Holland in 1940, stripping the van Heemstras and others of their wealth and property. Relatives were murdered. The occupation robbed Audrey of a normal adolescent life. Instead of attending parties or going to the local cinema, Audrey spent her days just trying to survive. Food was scarce, and she suffered from malnutrition, surviving on turnips and tulip bulbs. Holland was liberated on Audrey's sixteenth birthday, and she and her family were able to live free again. Of that period she said, "We lost everything, of course—our houses, our possessions, our money. But we didn't give a hoot. We got through with our lives, which was all that mattered."

After the war Audrey auditioned at the Marie Lambert ballet school in London and was accepted on a scholarship. Because of her 5-foot 7-inch height and slim 110-pound weight, she also began doing some modeling work.

Though her build was good for modeling, it was not good for ballet, so Audrey channeled her energy into modeling and landing bit parts in films and on stage.

By 1951 Hepburn had appeared in minor roles in several British films including *Laughter in Paradise* and *The Lavender Hill Mob*. Her career break came while she was shooting a scene for *Monte Carlo Baby* in a hotel lobby on the French Riviera. Hepburn was spotted by the famous French writer Collette, who was casting her play *Gigi*. When she saw Hepburn, Collette knew immediately that she was perfect for the title role.

Shortly after being cast in *Gigi,* Hepburn auditioned for a movie role being cast by Hollywood director William Wyler. He found her irresistible and offered her the lead part in *Roman Holiday*. In a matter of months Hepburn found herself starring in a Broadway play and a Hollywood movie. However, at rehearsals it was obvious that Hepburn's acting needed improvement. She worked hard and her performances got better. Though *Gigi* received mixed reviews from the critics, they loved Hepburn.

When *Gigi* closed in early 1952, Hepburn began work on *Roman Holiday*. Costar Gregory Peck was completely taken with the young actress. The film opened in August 1953 to rave reviews from critics and moviegoers. Hepburn's "look," her refined style and pixielike stature, was new to the cinema. When the Academy Awards were handed out in the spring of 1954, Hepburn won the Best Actress Oscar for *Roman Holiday*.

On the personal front, Hepburn had been engaged to Yorkshire multi-millionaire James Hanson, who proposed during the premiere of *Gigi*. However, when Hepburn realized that she would have to give up her career to be Hanson's wife, she broke off the engagement. A more lasting romance blossomed when she met fellow actor Mel Ferrer at a party. There was an instant attraction between the two, and they married in 1954.

Over the next few years Hepburn appeared on stage and made several other successful films including *Sabrina* (1954), *Love in the Afternoon* (1957), and *Funny Face* (1957), a musical in which she got to glide around the floor with legendary dancer Fred Astaire. For her work on Broadway in *Ondine* (1954), as a fairy who falls in love with a knight, Hepburn won the Tony Award (the theater equivalent of the Oscar).

Though thrilled with the success of her career and happily married, Hepburn's greatest desire was to have children. She would suffer two miscarriages before finally giving birth to a son on January 17, 1960. Hepburn named her son Sean, which means "gift of God." He was baptized in the same church, and by the same pastor who married Hepburn and Ferrer in 1954.

After Sean's birth, Hepburn went back to her career, working on films, including two of her most well known—*Breakfast at Tiffany's* and *My Fair Lady*. Her portrayal of Holly Golightly earned Hepburn her fourth Oscar nomination. Unfortunately, Hepburn's marriage was failing, and she and Ferrer finally divorced in 1968. She began dating Italian psychiatrist Dr. Andrea Dotti, and the two wed in 1969. On February 8, 1970, Hepburn gave birth to her second child, a son she named Luca. After living in Rome for about a year, Hepburn returned with her children to La Paisible (the Peaceful Place), her home in Tolochenaz, Switzerland.

"Semiretired" for five years, Hepburn was coaxed into making the film *Robin and Marian* with **Sean Connery** in 1976. Only a few more film appearances followed, including *Bloodline* (1996) and *They All Laughed* (1981). Hepburn, aware for a while that Dotti had not been faithful, finally filed for divorce in 1980. On the set of *They All Laughed*, Hepburn met actor Robert Wolders. The two became great friends and remained companions for the rest of Hepburn's life.

In 1987 Hepburn began a second career, as a special Goodwill Ambassador for UNICEF, the United Nations (UN) organization that provides food, medical, and educational assistance to children all over the world who are in crisis. The appointment was particularly special for Hepburn, as she had been aided by

United Nations Relief and Rehabilitation Administration, the forerunner of UNICEF, when she was a refugee in Holland as a teenager.

On behalf of UNICEF, Hepburn attended fund-raisers and made countless trips to visit people in impoverished countries in Central America, Asia, and Africa. Hepburn continued her work for UNICEF until she became ill with colon cancer in 1992. She returned to her beloved La Paisible, where she remained until her death on January 20, 1993.

Grace Kelly

Fairy-Tale Life of Actress-Turned-Princess
1929–1982

Hollywood amuses me. Holier-than-thou for the public and unholier-than-the-devil in reality.

—GRACE KELLY

Some people dream of a fairy-tale life; Grace Kelly actually lived one. Born into one of the wealthiest families in Philadelphia, yet determined to make it on her own, she supported herself in New York while attempting to get acting jobs, and then quickly moved to California where she was almost immediately a film success, starring with all-time greats such as Gary Cooper and **Clark Gable.** As if that weren't enough, the star's beauty and elegance attracted a prince, and she became his princess wife. It seemed incredible that all of this good fortune occurred, but it was even more surprising that it occurred before the young woman had reached the age of twenty-seven.

Born on November 12, 1929, to John and Margaret Kelly, Grace Kelly was the third of four children, brought up to be strong in both athletics and academics. Her father had been an Olympic gold-medal rower and then a highly successful businessman, having inherited a brick business that he then developed into a major industry in Philadelphia.

Graduating from high school in 1947 after receiving a good education at parochial and private schools, Grace set off for the American Academy of Dramatic Arts in New York City. By 1949, after doing some modeling work and winning small television roles, she made it to the Broadway stage. Shortly thereafter, in 1951, she traveled to California and made her first Hollywood film appearance in *Fourteen Hours,* in which she had a very small part.

Only one year later Grace performed with the much admired Gary Cooper in *High Noon,* a film that is still seen as a great western and for which Gary Cooper won an Academy Award. Grace's elegance, poise, beauty, and sensuality created an almost immediate sensation with moviegoers. By 1953 she received a contract with MGM and starred with **Clark Gable** and Ava Gardner in *Mogambo,* which turned out to be quite popular and which brought her an Oscar nomination. Only two years later Grace would actually win the Best Actress award for her role in *The Country Girl,* in which she starred with Bing Crosby.

Grace's cool charm, sexual allure, and box-office magnetism drew master director **Alfred Hitchcock** to team her with powerful male leads in three of his films: *Dial M for Murder* with Ray Milland and *Rear Window* with **Jimmy Stewart,** both in 1954, and *To Catch a Thief* with Cary Grant in 1955. To this day the films are seen as masterful. Also in 1954, Grace appeared in *Green Fire* with Stewart Granger and *The Bridges at Toko-Ri* with William Holden, Fredric March, and Mickey Rooney, making her Hollywood's most popular star by the mid-1950s. Little did anyone know that while achieving stunning and fast success, Grace's movie career would be short-lived.

For Grace, beauty and poise defined not just her screen personae but her true self, and these would be part of what would appeal to one of the world's most eligible bachelors at the time, Prince Rainier of Monaco (a tiny principality on the Mediterranean), whom Grace met at the Cannes Film Festival in France in 1955. Grace returned to the United States and worked with Bing Crosby and Frank Sinatra on *High Society,* a musical comedy that was a remake of the 1940 film *The Philadelphia Story.* Her duet with Bing Crosby on the song "True Love" brought them a Gold Record. In the same year she would perform in *The Swan,* but for the blond beauty, this would be her last year in films. It proved quite ironic that *The Swan* plot revolved around a young woman engaged to a prince. Grace's second meeting with Prince Rainier, at the home of a Kelly family friend in the United States, was special enough for the two to become engaged four days later. They married on April 19, 1956, creating an abundance of media attention. After the wedding at St. Nicholas Church in Monaco, there was a garden party on the grounds of the palace. By five o'clock the bride and groom set off on their honeymoon, sailing away on the prince's yacht.

Since Grace had still been under contract with MGM, a deal was negotiated that her wedding would be filmed for the studio and shown in theaters throughout the United States. Americans would continue to keep track of Grace's every move, clamoring for news about her children: Princess Caroline, born in 1957; Prince Albert, born in 1958; and Princess Stephanie, born in 1965.

In her roles as mother and princess, Grace was not content to perform only necessary duties. She served on the board of directors of Twentieth Century Fox for some years. Additionally, Grace was president of the Red Cross in Monaco, and when they held their fund-raising ball, they received support from many U.S. stars. Grace also provided help for the La Leche League, a group founded to encourage and provide information on breast-feeding.

Rumors circulated that Grace actually had become unhappy and lonely. In 1964 she considered starring in a new Hitchcock movie, *Marnie,* but her husband declined the offer made to her when negative public opinion seemed to grow in Monaco. No matter, Americans still found the family intriguing, even as Grace grew older.

On September 14, 1982, the famed princess and her daughter Princess Stephanie were victims of a terrible car crash. While driving along a stretch of the French Riviera, Grace lost control of the car, and it rolled down an embankment. Princess Stephanie only received minor injuries, but Grace apparently had suffered a stroke. She was unconscious when rescuers got to her, and she died the next day.

Sean Connery

First Actor to Portray Spy-Hero James Bond
1930–

Everything I've done has had to be accomplished in my own cycle, my own time, on my own behalf, and with my own sweat.

—SEAN CONNERY

Over a hundred years ago famed writer Oscar Wilde (1854–1900) wrote, "All that I desire to point out is the general principle that Life imitates Art far more than Art imitates Life." For actor Sean Connery it happened in reverse. As a child in Scotland, Connery delivered milk to help supplement the family's income. One of his stops was the Fettes School in Edinburgh—the same school that novelist Ian Fleming's fictitious debonair spy James Bond attended. Twenty-one years later Connery portrayed Fleming's spy hero in the first James Bond film, *Dr. No.* The character, also known as Agent 007, became Connery's signature role.

The charismatic actor with the trademark Scottish brogue was born Thomas Sean Connery on August 25, 1930. His parents, Joe and Euphamia, were very poor, and the family lived in a tiny two-room flat in Edinburgh.

As a youngster, Thomas enjoyed playing tag and soccer. He was bigger than most of the boys and was a good fighter, so the local gang nicknamed him "Big Tam." When Thomas was eight, his parents had another child, Neil. Sean loved his role as big brother. As they grew older he and Neil became inseparable, often skipping school to fish at Union Canal.

Though attending school-full time, Thomas had two jobs by the time he was eleven. He worked in a pawnshop and at a dairy, which he preferred. He enjoyed driving the horse-drawn milk cart around town, delivering milk, and loved caring for the horses back at the stable. When Thomas turned thirteen, he quit school and went to work full-time. At sixteen he joined the Royal Navy, but was released after three years due to stomach ulcers.

Once home, Thomas had several jobs, including laying bricks, polishing coffins, modeling, and working as a lifeguard. While working as a nude model for the Edinburgh Art School, Thomas became interested in bodybuilding. He says he did it to impress the girls, but his gym mates thought he looked so good that they nominated him to represent Scotland in the 1950 Mr. Universe contest. Thomas made the nine-hour trip to London and, after flexing the muscles on his six foot two-inch body, placed third in the tall men's division. By chance a casting director was at the event and offered Thomas a part in the stage musical *South Pacific*. Though he couldn't sing or dance, Thomas accepted the offer.

It took only one rehearsal onstage for Thomas to be hooked. At that moment he decided to make acting his career. Feeling that he needed a stage name, he took his middle name plus Connery. Connery appeared in several more plays before being cast in the 1954 BBC television presentation *Requiem for a Heavyweight*. Moving on to film work, Connery made his (uncredited) film debut in *Lilacs in the Spring* in 1955. He appeared in several films over the next few years, including *A Night to Remember* (1958) and Disney's *Darby O'Gill and the Little People* (1959).

Despite his acting credits, Connery was still a relative unknown until producers Harry Saltzman and Albert Broccoli cast him as James Bond in the 1962 screen adventure *Dr. No.* Connery won the part over Cary Grant, Rex

Harrison, Trevor Howard, Patrick McGoohan, and Roger Moore, even though *Bond* author Ian Fleming hadn't envisioned him in the role. The film was a box-office hit, and the Bond role made Connery a star. Banking on the success of *Dr. No,* Connery played Bond four more times in the next five years, including *Goldfinger* (1964), which grossed $51 million and *Thunderball* (1965), which earned a whopping $63 million.

The James Bond movies were very popular, but Connery was becoming weary of playing the same character. After completing *You Only Live Twice,* Connery quit the role to spend more time with his family (he married Diane Cilento in 1962, and they had a son, Jason, in 1963) and indulge in his passion—golf. Connery would be coaxed into reprising his Bond role on two more occasions—in the 1971 box-office draw *Diamonds Are Forever,* and again in 1983's *Never Say Never Again.* (Other actors that have been cast as Agent 007 include Roger Moore, Timothy Dalton, and Pierce Brosnan.)

Though known best for his role as James Bond, Connery branched out working on other films, and was able to show his range as an actor. He has worked with some of the best directors in the motion picture industry including **Alfred Hitchcock, Steven Spielberg,** and Brian De Palma, and with some of Hollywood's biggest stars, including **Audrey Hepburn, Harrison Ford,** and **Robert De Niro.**

Connery's roles have been as varied as his costars, and his ability to play so many different characters has contributed to his longevity as an actor. From playing Harrison Ford's father in *Indiana Jones and the Last Crusade* (1989), defecting Russian sub captain Marko Ramius in *The Hunt for Red October* (1990), ex-con John Patrick Mason in *The Rock* (1996), cat burglar Robert "Mac" MacDougal in *Entrapment* (1999), to reclusive writer William Forrester in *Finding Forrester* (2000), Connery brings an intensity and lighthearted wit to all his character portrayals. Expanding his skills beyond acting, Connery starting producing films in the 1990s as well.

Life after Bond has been good for Connery. In 1987 he received a Golden Globe and an Academy Award for Best Supporting Actor, playing Irish street cop Jim Malone in *The Untouchables.* Two years later he was again nominated for a Golden Globe and an Academy Award for Best Supporting Actor for his performance in *Indiana Jones and the Last Crusade.* Despite having long abandoned the toupee to cover his thinning hair, Connery was voted *People* magazine's "Sexiest Man Alive" in 1989 and "Sexiest Man of the Century" in 1999.

Professional awards have continued to come Connery's way. In 1995 he received the Cecil B. DeMille Award for "outstanding contribution to the entertainment field." In 1999 Connery was the recipient of the twenty-second Annual Kennedy Center Honors for his lifetime contribution to arts and culture. Perhaps his most distinguished honor came in July 2000 when Queen Elizabeth II of the United Kingdom knighted him in his hometown of Edinburgh.

Sir Sean Connery has no plans to retire from making movies. In February 2002 he signed a contract with Twentieth Century Fox to star in *League of Extraordinary Gentlemen,* a period-era X-Men-type film. The agreement also made provisions for Connery to appear in possible sequels. Still, he allows time for leisure activities, playing golf or watching the Glasgow Rangers, his favorite soccer team. Connery also enjoys spending time at his home in Marbella, Spain, with second wife French artist Micheline Roquebrune, whom he married in 1975 (Connery divorced Cilento in 1973).

At a press conference in 1996 Connery joked about his age saying, "How many senior citizens do you know who are making action movies these days?" Though a grandfather, Connery feels he still has lots of roles left in him. When asked about his desires beyond acting, he replied, "More than anything else, I'd like to be an old man with a good face, like Hitchcock or Picasso."

Elizabeth Taylor

English-Born Actress and AIDS Activist
1932–

My troubles all started because I had the body of a woman and the emotions of a child.

—ELIZABETH TAYLOR

"Passion" is the name of the perfume that Elizabeth Taylor created in 1986, a description that is most fitting for the actress herself. Married eight times, the public has avidly followed her life's passions. The beautiful actress with violet eyes always seemed in need of love and attention.

It is not surprising that Elizabeth Rosemond Taylor was born to a determined mother who had been a successful actress herself and a successful father who was an art dealer with a very prosperous business. Though born in London, England, on February 27, 1932, Elizabeth, her parents (who were both American), and her younger brother, Howard, moved to America in 1939, settling in Los Angeles, California. At age ten Elizabeth signed a contract with Metro-Goldwyn-Mayer (MGM) and was cast in her first film role in *Lassie Come Home* (1943). A year later she starred opposite Mickey Rooney in the highly successful *National Velvet* (1944). During filming Elizabeth was thrown from a horse and damaged her back. The injury from the accident would plague her for the rest of her life.

By age fifteen Taylor already had been declared the most beautiful woman in the world. Taylor had already appeared in several films, and in 1949 her face adorned the cover of *Time* magazine. When she started work on what would become one of her best films, *A Place in the Sun,* she met Conrad Hilton Jr., heir to the hotel chain. She married Hilton on May 6, 1950, in an extravagant affair managed by MGM. The marriage was a disaster, barely lasting until year's end.

Taylor was not without a companion for long. On Februrary 21, 1952, nineteen year-old Taylor married the British actor Michael Wilding, who was twice her age. Before their marriage ended in 1956, the couple had two sons, Michael and Christopher. Taylor continued on with her film career, costarring with James Dean and Rock Hudson in the 1956 movie *Giant.* She fell in love with the film's producer Mike Todd. Converting to Judaism for her new beau, Taylor married Todd on February 2, 1957. In the fall the couple welcomed the birth of their daughter, Liza.

Taylor was enjoying her acting career, and received her first Oscar nomination for *Raintree County* in 1957. Tragically, less than a year later her contented life crumbled. On March 24, 1958, while flying to New York to attend a Friar's Club dinner where he was being honored, Todd was killed when the plane crashed in the mountains of New Mexico. Taylor was devastated by Todd's death. She sought the emotional support of Eddie Fisher, the famous singer, who had been Todd's best friend. Taylor became more dependent on Fisher, and he soon found himself in love with her. Though fans saw his marriage to actress Debbie Reynolds as a match made in heaven, Fisher had been unhappy for some time. Fans were outraged by news of their dissolving marriage and blamed Taylor for her part in destroying it.

During this time Taylor was filming the intensely emotional *Cat on a Hot Tin Roof,* which was released in 1958. For her performance she won her second

Oscar nomination. On May 12, 1959, Taylor married Fisher. That same year *Suddenly Last Summer* was released, bringing Taylor another Oscar nomination.

Ironically, the very role that Taylor did not want finally won her an Oscar. The film was *Butterfield 8* (1960). Playing a prostitute, Taylor was very concerned that it would harm her reputation. Some say she received the Oscar not so much for her performance but as a result of the serious illness that hit her in March 1961, shortly before the Oscars were awarded. While in England preparing for her next film, *Cleopatra,* Taylor collapsed and was rushed to the hospital. Suffering from viral pneumonia, Asian flu, and anemia, Taylor stopped breathing and was given an emergency tracheotomy. She fell into a coma but came off the critical list within a week. Her quick recovery from the near-fatal illness won over her fans once again.

Back on the set for *Cleopatra,* Taylor made an extraordinary $1 million for the work. It was during filming that she and costar Richard Burton, who was also married at the time, began an intense romance that again upset the public. After both divorced, the two were married on March 15, 1964, continuing a passionate relationship. They appeared in a number of films together, most notably the powerfully brutal *Who's Afraid of Virginia Woolf?* (1966), for which Taylor won her second Academy Award. The couple divorced in 1974, remarried in October 1975, but divorced again in July 1976.

Taylor's seventh marriage in December 1976 was to John Warner, a stately Virginian campaigning for the U.S. Senate. By 1981 the couple separated, and Taylor turned for the first time to Broadway, acting in *The Little Foxes.* She received mixed reviews but earned a Tony nomination. In 1982 Taylor divorced Senator Warner and in 1983 appeared on Broadway with her old love, Burton. They starred in *Private Lives,* which attracted public attention but received only a lukewarm response from critics.

Taylor checked herself into the Betty Ford Clinic in 1983 to overcome her dependency on alcohol. Her recovery was short-lived. In August of 1984 Taylor was devastated after the sudden death of Richard Burton. When a number of her close friends became sick from AIDS, she channeled her energies into campaigning for research into the disease. She became the cofounder and chair of the American Foundation for AIDS Research in 1985. For her work furthering AIDS research she later would receive the Jean Hersholt Humanitarian Award from the Academy of Motion Picture Arts and Sciences, as well as the French Legion of Honor Award. In 1986 Taylor ventured into the retail business with the introduction of her first perfume, "Passion," followed by "White Shoulders" in 1991. In 1993 she introduced the Elizabeth Taylor Fashion Jewelry Collection.

Despite her humanitarian and business efforts, Taylor found herself back in the Betty Ford Clinic in 1988. While there, the fifty-six year-old actress developed a close relationship with another patient, Larry Fortensky, a forty-year-old construction worker. They married in 1991. That same year she started the Elizabeth Taylor AIDS Foundation. In 1993 she was awarded the American Film Institute's Life Achievement Award. She divorced Fortensky in 1996 and in early 1997 underwent an operation to remove a benign brain tumor. In 1998 Taylor received the Screen Actors Guild Life Achievement Award, and in May 2000 Queen Elizabeth II, at Buckingham Palace, made Taylor a Dame of the British Empire.

Recently reflecting on seventy years of highs and lows, Taylor said:

> I've been so lucky all my life. Everything was handed to me. Looks. Fame. Wealth. Honors. Love. I rarely had to fight for anything. But I've paid for that luck with disasters. The death of Mike Todd and so many good friends . . . destructive addictions, broken marriages. . . . I don't regret anything about my past. I had a ball, and my relationships were great and fascinating and exciting.

Shirley MacLaine

Award-Winning Actress/Dancer and Author
of Best-Seller Out on a Limb
1934–

I think of myself as a communicator, not an entertainer. I communicate what I'm feeling. What I'm thinking. What I believe. What I don't believe.

—Shirley MacLaine

Sometime in the 1970s actress Shirley MacLaine began exploring New Age spiritualism and wrote about that journey in the 1983 best-selling book *Out On a Limb*. With the release of her ninth book, *The Camino* (2000), Shirley has continued to share what she has discovered on that journey. Often the butt of jokes from the media and recipient of a lot of eye-rolling from colleagues for revealing some of her "past life" exploits (including having been a Japanese geisha and Charlemagne's lover), MacLaine says she's not bothered by the ridicule. "I'm amused by people who think I'm a nutcase. I even help them write the jokes! I just insist that they're funny. If they're not funny, I think *that's* a humiliation."

Long before she began exploring her higher self and the metaphysical world, Shirley MacLaine was known as the girl with the curly red hair and weak ankles. Thanks to those weak ankles, her mother enrolled Shirley in ballet classes; thanks to her height (5'7" inches tall), she later scrapped ideas of becoming a ballerina and opted for a different kind of career in the theater.

She was born Shirley MacLean Beaty on April 24, 1934, in Richmond, Virginia. Her mother, Kathlyn MacLean Beaty, had been a drama teacher with aspirations of becoming an actress. When she married, she gave up those dreams to raise a family. Shirley's father, Ira, a native Virginian, was an educator who shared his knowledge of philosophy and psychology with his daughter. When Shirley was three, brother Warren Beatty was born. Both would grow up to achieve successful careers in Hollywood.

At the end of her junior year at Washington-Lee High School in Arlington, Virginia, Shirley went to New York for the summer and auditioned for a part in the revival of Rodgers and Hammerstein's *Oklahoma!* She got a part in the chorus, and from that moment on knew she would be happier in musical theater than in ballet.

When MacLaine graduated, she packed her bags and headed to New York, where in 1953 she made her Broadway debut as a chorus girl in *Me and Juliet.* Her big break came in *The Pajama Game.* When the show's star, Carol Haney, broke her ankle, understudy MacLaine took over the role and was a natural. During one performance producer Hal Wallis was in the audience. He offered MacLaine a movie contract with Paramount Pictures, and three months later she was off to Hollywood to work in her first film, with famed director **Alfred Hitchcock** on his black comedy *The Trouble With Harry* (1955). In her next feature film MacLaine portrayed an Indian princess in the now classic Jules Verne adaptation *Around the World in 80 Days* (1956).

Shortly after completing *Around the World in 80 Days,* MacLaine gave birth to a daughter on September 1, 1956. The new parents (MacLaine married producer Steve Parker in 1954; they later divorced) named her Sachi. After a two-year hiatus, MacLaine was back at work on her next film, *Some Came*

Running with singer Frank Sinatra. Her performance as a down-and-out prostitute earned MacLaine her first Academy Award nomination.

MacLaine next took on a musical role, showing off her well-trained dancer's legs, in the 1960 film *Can-Can.* That same year she appeared with "Rat Packers" Frank Sinatra, Dean Martin, Sammy Davis Jr., and Peter Lawford in the original version of *Ocean's Eleven.* MacLaine was the only "dame" member of the "Pack." She would later recount those days in her book *My Lucky Stars* (1995). She also received her second Oscar nomination for her role in director Billy Wilder's *The Apartment.*

With her success in musicals, comedies, and dramas, MacLaine was an in-demand actress. In 1963 she reteamed with Jack Lemmon to star in *Irma La Douce,* bringing MacLaine her third Academy Award nomination in five years. She convinced friend and famed choreographer Bob Fosse to direct her in the movie version of Neil Simon's Broadway musical *Sweet Charity* (1969). MacLaine had a ball portraying a dime-a-dance girl looking for a nice man to settle down with. A tune from the show, *If My Friends Could See Me Now,* became MacLaine's trademark theme song.

MacLaine made a few more films over the next few years but also became a political activist. She worked on Senator Robert Kennedy's presidential campaign and served as a Democratic Convention delegate in 1968. MacLaine had also begun to write down her thoughts during breaks in filming and added author to her list of credits with the release of her book *Don't Fall Off the Mountain* in 1970. It was the first of many books she would write on topics ranging from travel experiences to reincarnation.

MacLaine added to her film credits in 1975 by producing her first documentary, with Claudia Weill, *The Other Half of the Sky—A China Memoir.* The film was well received and earned an Oscar nomination for Best Documentary. MacLaine returned to Broadway in 1976, in the spectacular one-woman show *A Gypsy in My Soul,* and then returned to the screen in 1977. MacLaine turned in an Academy Award–nominated performance in the critically acclaimed *Turning Point,* playing a middle-aged ballet dancer who comes to regret giving up her career to become a housewife. Incredibly, the film, which acquired eleven Oscar nominations, came away with none.

After a superb performance in *Being There* with **Peter Sellers,** MacLaine spent more time discovering her inner self, further exploring the realm of reincarnation and out-of-body travel. Risking public ridicule, the gutsy MacLaine published a book in 1983 about her journey, titled *Out on a Limb.* That same year she came back to Hollywood to star in the multi-Oscar-winning film *Terms of Endearment.* Her performance as the overprotective, somewhat prickly widow Aurora Greenway won MacLaine her fourth Oscar nomination. She celebrated her twentieth anniversary in show business by finally taking home the golden statuette.

During the rest of the 1980s MacLaine divided her time between writing, lecturing on spirituality and reincarnation, and her film career. She appeared in few films, including a television movie adaptation of her book *Out on a Limb.* At the end of the decade MacLaine came back strong in two films, *Madame Sousatzka* and *Steel Magnolias.* MacLaine, as the crabby, cynical divorcée Ouiser Boudreaux, and costars **Sally Field,** Dolly Parton, Olympia Dukakis, Darryl Hannah, and **Julia Roberts** take the audience on an emotional roller-coaster ride in a film with hysterically funny moments and moments of deep sorrow.

Despite the difficulty in finding challenging parts for women "over forty," MacLaine seemed little affected. She starred in Carrie Fisher's semiauto-biographical *Postcards From the Edge* in 1990 and continued to specialize in playing eccentric, strong-willed women in such films as *Guarding Tess* (1994), *Mrs. Winterbourne* (1996), and reprising her character Aurora Greenway in the *Terms* sequel, *The Evening Star* (1996).

In 2000 MacLaine stepped behind the camera to direct her first feature film, *Bruno,* starring Gary Sinise and Kathy Bates. She teamed up with friends

Joan Collins, **Elizabeth Taylor,** and Debbie Reynolds to star in the television movie *These Old Broads,* written by Carrie Fisher. A movie to be released in 2003 is in preproduction. MacLaine keeps busy updating her own Web site, www.shirleymaclaine.com, which she launched in June 2000. The site is, as MacLaine states, "a reflection of my world; always in transition and always in search of truth."

Julie Andrews

Award-Winning Stage and Screen Star
1935–

When you start out, who knows what will happen in life. You put one foot in front of the other, and miraculous things can happen.

—JULIE ANDREWS

*I*n June 1997 Julie Andrews underwent surgery to remove a small benign polyp from her vocal cords—a routine procedure, performed on an uncommonly gifted singer. Unfortunately, something went wrong, and Julie's incredible four-octave singing voice was silenced. For a while it appeared that the damage was permanent; however, in 2000 Julie went to see a doctor who specializes in vocal restoration. Slowly, some vocal function returned.

On October 16, while hosting the PBS Great Performances special *My Favorite Broadway: The Love Songs*, Julie attempted to sing a few notes of "The Rain in Spain" with Michael Crawford. The song is from *My Fair Lady*, the show in which Julie made her Broadway debut in 1956. The audience erupted, cheering and giving her a standing ovation. It was a warm expression of love and support for Julie, a celebration of her journey back.

Named for her two grandmothers, Julia Elizabeth Wells was born in Walton-on-Thames, Surrey, England, on October 1, 1935. Her father, Ted, taught woodworking and her mother, Barbara, was a pianist at her sister's dance school. During World War II, Julie's parents separated, eventually divorcing. Barbara married Ted Andrews, a singer she met while playing piano for a variety show, and they formed their own vaudeville act.

To get closer to his new stepdaughter, Ted began giving Julie singing lessons. Incredibly, Ted discovered that her voice had perfect pitch and a four-octave vocal range. Julie joined her parents' show and changed her last name to Andrews. When the war ended in 1945, Julie went back to school but spent holidays and summers on tour with her parents. She made her first radio appearance in 1946 on the BBC show *Monday at Eight,* singing a duet with Ted. At age eleven Julie gave her first solo performance at London's Stage Door Canteen, where audience members included the queen of England and Princess Margaret.

From the 1940s to the mid-1950s, Julie made several appearances on BBC programs as well as pantomime, stage, and revue performances, including *Red Riding Hood, Humpty Dumpty, Jack and the Beanstalk,* and *Cinderella.* In 1954, when she was nineteen, Julie was cast as Polly Browne in *The Boy Friend.* She made her American debut on Broadway in *The Boy Friend* after signing a one-year contract to continue in the lead role. The show was a smash hit, and she became a star.

Julie's American television debut came in 1955, when she starred with Bing Crosby in CBS's musical version of *High Tor.* Julie achieved theater superstar status a year later when she obtained the title role of Eliza Doolittle in Lerner and Loewe's *My Fair Lady.* The show ran for two years on Broadway and then eighteen months in London.

Julie took a break in her performance schedule to get married. On May 10, 1959, Julie walked down the aisle to join her husband-to-be, costume designer Tony Walton, wearing the wedding dress he created for her. The two had met on a train ride home one night in England after Julie had finished a performance in *Humpty Dumpty.*

Continuing her stage success, Julie reunited with Lerner and Loewe in 1960 to play Queen Guinevere in *Camelot.* Attending the show one night was animation legend **Walt Disney.** He was so taken with Julie's performance that he offered her the title role in his upcoming movie musical *Mary Poppins.* Before beginning production on *Mary Poppins,* Julie took some time off to start a family. She gave birth to her daughter Emma Kate on November 27, 1962.

Starring in *Mary Poppins* was a film career breakthrough for Julie. Playing the assertive nanny to a banker's two children, she took them on a magical journey with the help of chimney sweep Bert, played by Dick Van Dyke. Memorable songs from the 1964 film included "A Spoonful of Sugar" and "Supercalifragilisticexpialidocious." Nominated for thirteen Academy Awards, the film won five, including the Best Actress Oscar for Julie.

The following year Julie Andrews agreed to do her second musical, *The Sound of Music,* a film based on the life of onetime postulant (a nun candidate) Maria Augusta Trapp. As the nanny to the seven children of Captain Georg Von Trapp, Julie truly demonstrated her range as an actress and singer. The movie's many memorable songs include "My Favorite Things," "Do, Re, Me," and "Maria." *The Sound of Music* won five Oscars, including Best Picture and Best Director, and Andrews received her second Best Actress Oscar nomination.

Though Julie was a bona fide star, she suddenly found herself somewhat typecast. Trying to extend her range as an actress, she took parts in more serious dramas, including *Torn Curtain, Star,* and *Hawaii,* though none proved to be as successful as the musicals. She also found that her career was taking her in a different direction than her husband Tony's. They divorced before the end of the decade.

On a chance meeting in 1968, Julie made the acquaintance of Blake Edwards, a very successful Hollywood film producer-director. His hits included *Breakfast at Tiffany's* and *The Pink Panther*. After the two discussed a film project, their relationship blossomed. Blake and Julie were married in the backyard garden of their home on November 12, 1969. Julie appeared in several of Edward's productions over the next three decades, including *The Tamarind Seed, 10, S.O.B., Victor/Victoria,* and *That's Life*.

One of the most successful collaborations between Andrews and Edwards was the 1982 hit *Victor/Victoria*. Julie received her third Oscar nomination for her performance as a woman pretending to be a man, who pretends to be a woman. In 1995 Edwards took the story to Broadway. In a triumphant return to the stage, Andrews received her third Tony Award nomination.

After the surgery on her throat in 1997, Julie was no longer able to perform. A published author of children's books, including her first story, *Mandy,* in 1971, Julie continued to add to her credits with *The Last of the Really Great Whangdoodles* and *Little Bo*. Inspired by her grandson, who is "crazy about trucks," Julie collaborated with her daughter Emma Walton on a series of books about a dump truck named Dumpy.

After regaining some use of her voice, Julie returned to acting. In 1999 she starred with James Garner in the television movie *One Special Night*. She then reunited with her *Sound of Music* costar Christopher Plummer to do a live television broadcast of *On Golden Pond* for CBS. In 2001 she returned to the big screen in the Walt Disney Pictures film *The Princess Diaries*. Her latest project is her most personal—she decided to sit down and write her autobiography.

Married to Blake for thirty-two years, Julie is the proud mom of five children (one by her first marriage, two by Blake's first marriage, two adopted

Vietnamese orphans) and grandmother of five. Julie Andrews has received many honors throughout her career. She has an English rose named after her, and on May 16, 2000, she was made a Dame Commander of the British Empire by Queen Elizabeth II at Buckingham Palace. In December 2001 Julie joined **Jack Nicholson,** composer Quincy Jones, pianist Van Cliburn, and opera singer Luciano Pavarotti as the latest artists honored by the Kennedy Center for the Performing Arts. Each was chosen for their "unique and extremely valuable contribution" to America's cultural life.

Dustin Hoffman

Award-Winning Leading Man of Hollywood
1937–

You should try acting, my boy. It's much easier.

—LAURENCE OLIVIER TO DUSTIN HOFFMAN, AFTER LEARNING THAT HIS COSTAR STAYED AWAKE FOR SEVERAL DAYS TO MAKE HIS *MARATHON MAN* CHARACTER SEEM EXHAUSTED

An award-winning veteran actor, Dustin Hoffman lacks what most people view as conventional good looks. One critic described him as "resembling both Sonny and Cher." Yet in his remarkable career, the immensely talented actor has managed to take on some of the most challenging roles in film history. From his performance as a handicapped street hustler in *Midnight Cowboy* to his male actor pretending to be a woman in *Tootsie* to his portrayal of an autistic adult in *Rain Man,* Hoffman has forever changed Hollywood's image of the classic leading man.

Dustin Lee Hoffman was born on August 8, 1937, in Los Angeles to furniture and set designer Harry Hoffman and his wife, amateur actress Lillian Hoffman. Dustin thought about becoming a doctor, but he discovered acting while attending Santa Monica City College. He dropped out to study at the Pasadena Playhouse Actor's Studio.

In 1958 Hoffman moved to New York City, where he worked a series of odd jobs, earned a few minor television roles, and toured in summer stock stage productions. At one point he grew so frustrated that he considered abandoning acting to become a teacher. In 1960, however, he landed a part in the off-Broadway production *Yes Is for a Very Young Man* and soon after appeared in *A Cook for Mr. General* (1961). He began studying at the Actors Studio in New York with the famed Lee Strasberg, who taught a technique known as Method Acting, in which the actor "immerses" himself in a character to give a more realistic portrayal.

Hoffman's hard work began to pay off in 1964 when he landed stage roles in *Waiting for Godot* and *The Dumbwaiter*. He quickly earned a reputation for being difficult to work with—but he also turned in exceptional performances and received excellent reviews. He won an Obie Award in 1966 for his performance in Broadway's *Journey of the Fifth Horse* and won three prestigious awards for his role in *Eh?* Director Mike Nichols was impressed enough with the young actor to cast him in his next film, *The Graduate*.

The film was a roaring success. Thirty-year-old Dustin turned in a striking portrayal of Benjamin Braddock—a disaffected college student who is seduced by a married woman and then falls in love with the woman's daughter. He earned a Best Actor Academy Award nomination and a Golden Globe Award for Most Promising Male Newcomer.

Though shy and private, Hoffman took on roles with fierce intensity, and his remarkable range astounded critics and audiences. He got a second Oscar nomination for playing handicapped street hustler Ratso Rizzo in *Midnight Cowboy* (1969). In *Little Big Man* (1970), Hoffman was an Old West Indian-fighter who aged one hundred years (thanks to latex makeup). He costarred with Steve McQueen in the 1973 prison drama *Papillon,* then obtained a third Oscar nomination for his depiction of comedian Lenny Bruce in *Lenny* (1974). Two years later he starred opposite **Robert Redford** as real-life *Washington Post* journalist Carl Bernstein in the film adaptation of *All the President's Men,* about the reporters who broke the story of the Watergate scandal. For the harrowing 1976 film *Marathon Man,* Hoffman deliberately kept himself awake for days on end, for a scene in which his character needs to be exhausted and sleepless.

Hoffman struck gold again in the 1979 movie *Kramer vs. Kramer.* He turned in a heartfelt performance as a driven career man whose wife (**Meryl Streep**) leaves him with their young son. The role won Hoffman his first Academy Award. In *Tootsie* (1982), he stretched his talents further, playing a failed actor who disguises himself as a woman to get a starring TV role. Many believed that the part was virtually unplayable; Hoffman not only played it, he received his fifth Oscar nomination.

Hoffman's stage rendition of Willy Loman in Arthur Miller's classic *Death of a Salesman* (1984) was poorly received, but his reprisal of the role for television in 1985 earned Emmy and Golden Globe Awards for him. He teamed up with colleague and friend Warren Beatty for *Ishtar* (1987), but the film was a dismal failure. Hoffman next costarred with megastar **Tom Cruise** in *Rain Man* (1988). The older actor's sensitive performance as an autistic who is also an idiot savant (a mentally challenged person with detailed knowledge of a specialized area) brought him his second Best Actor Academy Award and fourth Golden Globe.

In the late 1980s and early 1990s, Hoffman turned to relatively light-hearted roles. He costarred as **Sean Connery**'s son and Matthew Broderick's father in *Family Business,* the story of a three-generation team of high-class thieves. He was Mumbles in Warren Beatty's *Dick Tracy,* a take on the long-running comic strip. In 1991 he was gangster Dutch Schultz in *Billy Bathgate* and Captain Hook in *Hook.*

In 1992 Hoffman seemed to be reviving his Ratso Rizzo character in the unsuccessful *Hero,* playing a small-time thug who inadvertently redeems himself by performing an act of heroism. In 1995—in a role that superstar

Harrison Ford turned down—Hoffman played epidemiologist Sam Daniels in *Outbreak. Sleepers* (1996) was not well received, but Hoffman nevertheless teamed up with its director, Barry Levinson, for the 1997 film *Wag the Dog,* playing a Hollywood producer who "creates" a war using tricks of the trade. Hoffman's slick performance brought a Best Actor Oscar nomination.

After costarring in *Sphere* (1998) with Sharon Stone and Samuel L. Jackson, Hoffman returned to producing (he had produced one other film, *Straight Time* in 1978). In 1999 he produced *A Walk on the Moon, The Furies,* and the TV children's special *The Devil's Arithmetic,* for which he shared a Daytime Emmy nomination with the project's other executive producers.

A fitting tribute to Hoffman's talent came in April 1999, when he was honored by the American Film Institute (AFI) in the televised *A Salute to Dustin Hoffman,* during which he was given the AFI Life Achievement Award.

Hoffman has been married twice, to Anne Byrne (1969–1980) and to Lisa Gottsegen (1980–present). Lisa and Dustin have four children—Jacob, Max, Rebecca, and Alexandra. Dustin is also the father of Jenna from his marriage to Byrne, and Karina, Byrne's daughter from a previous marriage. A devoted parent, Hoffman has seen several of his children choose acting careers. Jacob made cameo appearances in *Rain Man* and *Hook* and has appeared in three other movies; Rebecca and Max were also in *Hook,* and Rebecca was in the 1994 TV movie *Le Nozze di Figaro;* Jenna Byrne has had roles in *Outbreak, Wag the Dog, The Wedding Singer,* and several other films.

In 2001 he announced his directorial debut: the thriller *Personal Injuries,* based on the novel by Scott Turow. The film is scheduled for release in 2003; he will also costar in and produce the film. After decades of stellar performances, Dustin Hoffman's fans have learned that they shouldn't expect "the usual" from him. Hoffman says he never stops looking forward to delving into a new and more challenging character. "The next role," he says, "is what keeps me going. I feel like I haven't done my favorite picture yet."

Jack Nicholson

One of America's Finest and Most Unusual Actors
1937–

If you get an impulse in a scene, no matter how wrong it seems, follow the impulse. It might be something and if it ain't—Take Two!

—JACK NICHOLSON

Jack Nicholson has reigned as one of America's finest actors and one of its most unusual personalities for more than forty years. His antihero film roles and trademark "shark's grin" smirk have earned him a unique spot in Hollywood.

Jack's mother, June Nilson, was a promising dancer when she met a charismatic married man. They fell in love, but when June became pregnant, she was sent to live with cousins. Born John Joseph Nicholson on April 22, 1937, in New York City, Jack returned with his mother, June, to her hometown of Neptune, New Jersey. There Jack was raised by grandparents Ethel May and John Nicholson Sr. But Jack grew up believing that June was his older sister and Ethel May and John were his parents. Not until a *Time* magazine interviewer discovered otherwise in 1974 did a stunned Nicholson learn the truth.

John Sr., a window dresser and sign maker, often took the boy to movie theaters and treated him kindly. Unfortunately, he was an alcoholic and died in 1955.

Though never a strong student, Jack loved performing in theater productions at Manasquan High School. At seventeen he traveled to California to visit his half sister, Pamela Liddicoat, and decided to stay. He took odd jobs with MGM Studios, studied acting, and earned bit parts onstage and in TV shows such as *Sea Hunt* and *Dr. Kildare.*

Nicholson's break came when director Roger Corman tapped him for the starring role in *The Cry-Baby Killer.* Next he played a masochistic dental patient in *Little Shop of Horrors* (1960) and Peter Lorre's son in *The Raven* (1963). He appeared with the legendary Boris Karloff in *The Terror* (1963) and got his first screenwriting credit for *Thunder Island.* He spent some years laboring in a string of unsuccessful movies until he was cast as the replacement for Rip Torn in *Easy Rider* (1969).

Nicholson's performance as a dropout lawyer transformed him into a top-shelf actor and earned him an Oscar nomination. After a minor role in *On a Clear Day You Can See Forever* (1970), he turned in a stellar performance in *Five Easy Pieces:* Nicholson's famous "chicken salad sandwich" scene remains a classic. The performance brought him a Best Actor Oscar nomination. By the time he starred in *Carnal Knowledge* (1971), Jack Nicholson was a full-fledged star.

Amazingly, Nicholson next turned down an array of excellent roles. He refused the role of Michael Corleone in *The Godfather* (it went to **Al Pacino**); in 1973 he declined to play Johnny Hooker in *The Sting* (**Robert Redford** landed the role). He also turned down roles in *The Great Gatsby, Apocalypse Now,* and *Coming Home.* The movies he did choose, however, were smash hits, including back-to-back Oscar-nominated performances in *The Last Detail* (1973) and *Chinatown* (1974). He won his first Oscar for the magnificently defiant mental patient Randall Patrick McMurphy in *One Flew Over the Cuckoo's Nest* (1975). Highly aware of the business side of Hollywood, he thanked **Mary Pickford,** an early actress and film innovator, for "being the first actor to get a [financial] percentage of her pictures."

Nicholson's star status freed him to take more daring projects. In 1975 he costarred with Warren Beatty in *The Fortune,* starred in the independent film *The Passenger,* and sang in the movie version of the rock opera *Tommy.* During the rest of the 1970s, however, his films were unremarkable. They included *The Last Tycoon* (1976) and *Goin' South* (1978), which he also directed.

Nicholson returned full force in 1980 in an over-the-top performance as Jack Torrance in *The Shining* (based on the Stephen King novel). Believing that the quality of the actors and directors in film projects are as important as the roles, Nicholson began choosing projects more carefully. He portrayed playwright Eugene O'Neill in *Reds* (1981) and in 1983 accepted a Best Supporting Actor Oscar for *Terms of Endearment.* Nicholson was not shy about taking credit for his choice. "When I read the part, I knew I'd win the Oscar for it," he later asserted.

Among Nicholson's best performances was the moronic hit man in *Prizzi's Honor* (1985), costarring Kathleen Turner and Anjelica Huston. Huston's father, John, directed the film and gave Nicholson a bit of advice about his character: "Remember, he's *dumb.*" In *Heartburn* (1986), he played a fictionalized version of *Washington Post* journalist Carl Bernstein, and in 1987 he earned another Oscar nomination as a barfly opposite **Meryl Streep** in *Ironweed.* Comic turns included *The Witches of Eastwick* (1987) and *Batman* (1989).

A longtime dream of Nicholson's—to produce a sequel to *Chinatown*—came true in 1990, but *The Two Jakes* was a box-office failure. He bounced back, however, in an Oscar-nominated performance for *A Few Good Men* (1992). Nicholson took home a record $5 million for his supporting role and quipped that it was "one of the few times when it was money well spent." In

1994 the American Film Institute honored him with a Life Achievement Award.

Critics noted that Nicholson had shifted away from what might be called roles that "make his feelings come through his skin." Instead, he concentrated on films that focused on middle-aged characters coming to terms with advancing old age. In *The Crossing Guard* (1995), Nicholson played a jeweler mourning the death of his daughter, killed by a hit-and-run driver. He received his third Academy Award for playing an ornery, reclusive author who falls in love with a young waitress (Helen Hunt) in *As Good As It Gets* (1997). In 2002 he was a retired police officer determined to catch a serial killer in *The Pledge*. Upcoming films at the time of writing include *About Schmidt* (2002) and *Anger Management* (2003).

Nicholson remains one of Hollywood's most innovative actors. A consummate professional, he prefers not to "cash in" on his status. "A star on a movie set is like a time bomb," he explains. "That bomb has got to be defused so people can approach it without fear."

Robert Redford

Actor, Director, Creator of Sundance Film Festival
1937–

I decided that I'd only make movies that were a mirror of my own time.

—ROBERT REDFORD

Though strikingly handsome, Robert Redford didn't want to be just another pretty face. His blond hair, chiseled features, and magnetic charisma attracted attention to him that he was not always comfortable with. Though Redford longed for recognition of his talent, he was not prepared for the attention that came with fame and celebrity status.

Charles Robert Redford Jr. was born not far from the glamour of Hollywood in Santa Monica, California, on August 18, 1937. His father, Charles, was a milkman who worked long, tiring hours; his mother, Martha, was outgoing and dynamic. Young Charles hardly knew his father because he was so seldom home, but he adored his mother.

Redford was a sensitive but scrappy kid who began to rebel as a young teen. He stole car hubcaps, and once broke into Universal Studios. Yet he showed an artistic side, demonstrating a flair for writing and drawing. Redford also loved the outdoors. As a child, Redford fell in love with nature after making a trip to Yosemite National Park. Preserving the power and beauty of the natural wilderness became one of his lifelong passions.

Redford channeled much of his restless energy into sports, winning a baseball scholarship to the University of Colorado. But he soon tired of the "win at any cost" attitude and started skipping practice. In 1955 tragedy struck when his mother died from cancer. A year later Redford dropped out of college and went to Europe. He wandered around Italy and France for a while before returning to the States in 1957.

Settling in New York City, twenty-year-old Redford might have continued his aimlessness had he not met Lola Van Wagenen, a college student living in his apartment building. Lola became a stabilizing force in Redford's life. Feeling rejuvenated, Redford enrolled at the Pratt Institute of Art. He and Lola married in September 1958 (they had four children before divorcing in 1985).

At school Redford became intrigued by set design and was encouraged to experience performing onstage. He auditioned at the American Academy of Dramatic Arts and found an inner connection. Acting allowed Redford to mask his own emotions while pretending to be someone else. It also gave him a way to release his bottled-up emotions.

Redford made his Broadway stage debut in 1959 in a small role in *Tall Story.* His performance got him an agent, and soon he was getting bigger and better parts both onstage and in television. Redford made his first movie appearance in the 1962 film *War Hunt,* where he met costars Tom Skerritt and Sidney Pollack.

Redford launched into prominence after starring in the 1963 Broadway play *Barefoot in the Park.* The show was a hit, and Redford's performance opened the way to Hollywood. He worked on several films, but they flopped at the box office. Needing a break, Redford took his family to Spain for a vacation. When he returned, he reprised his role in *Barefoot in the Park* for the big screen opposite Jane Fonda. Finally, Redford was in a film that was well received by critics and viewers alike.

Still, Redford was considered an unproven star when director George Roy Hill cast him with actor **Paul Newman** in the 1969 smash hit *Butch Cassidy and the Sundance Kid.* In his seventh movie role, Redford became an overnight sensation.

Redford struggled to balance his celebrity with maintaining his privacy. He formed his own production company, Wildwood Films, and began to bring his intelligence and passion to his own projects. Intrigued by society's increasing need to win at all costs, Redford wanted to produce a trilogy depicting that theme in the fields of sports, politics, and business. In his first attempt, *Downhill Racer,* Redford played a cocky skier more interested in individual triumph than being a team player. His next endeavor, *The Candidate,* was a dark film examining how people get elected to public office in America.

The 1970s was a prosperous decade for Redford. He agreed to star opposite **Barbra Streisand** in director Sydney Pollack's 1973 political love story *The Way We Were.* The movie was a monster hit, and Redford overcame his hesitancy about playing a romantic lead. He reteamed with director George Roy Hill and Paul Newman to make *The Sting* and solidified his appeal as a strong leading man in *The Great Gatsby* and *All the President's Men.*

In 1980 Redford moved behind the camera to direct the critically acclaimed, Oscar-winning drama *Ordinary People.* The film grabbed the top honor as Best Picture of the Year, and Redford won the Best Director Oscar. With his string of successes he began devoting less time to acting and more time to political causes, environmentalism, and founding his now-famous Sundance Institute. It is there that aspiring artists go to develop their own creative filmmaking skills. The institute is situated on 3,000 acres Redford purchased in his beloved Utah, not far from where he built a home for his family back in the 1960s. The institute's reputation has grown over the years, and thousands flock there to participate in the annual Sundance Film Festival.

Redford returned to the big screen in 1984 as a baseball player in *The*

Natural. Accepting another leading man role, Redford joined actress **Meryl Streep** in the moving story of author Isak Dinesen in *Out of Africa.* A few more films followed, as well as another turn in the director's chair in the 1988 movie *The Milagro Beanfield War.*

In the 1990s Redford again received critical acclaim for directing the aesthetically beautiful *A River Runs Through It.* The cast included Redford's friend Tom Skerritt and a blond, young Redford–looking actor named Brad Pitt. The 1993 film *Indecent Proposal* was one of Redford's biggest hits, which was followed by the third of his winning-at-any-cost trilogy, *Quiz Show,* which depicted the scandals of the TV quiz shows of the 1950s. Many critics felt it was Redford's best directorial achievement, and he received an Oscar nomination for his efforts.

After appearing in the 1996 film *Up Close and Personal,* Redford set his sights on bringing Nicholas Evans's novel *The Horse Whisperer* to the screen. Though panned by critics, it was a labor of love for Redford. In 2000 Redford directed stars Matt Damon and **Will Smith** in *The Legend of Bagger Vance,* the moving story of an aspiring golf pro who goes off to fight in World War I. Busy back on the movie set, Redford returned to the screen in two films in 2001— *The Last Castle* and *Spy Game.*

In a career that has spanned five decades, Redford has demonstrated his passion for the arts. As an honored recipient of the National Medal of the Arts in 1996, Redford said, "Art, in all its forms, feeds and nurtures the soul of a society; provokes thought and debate; causes critical thinking; and fosters understanding of things foreign to our own immediate world."

Chosen by the Board of Governors of the Motion Picture Academy to receive an honorary Oscar in 2002 for his contributions to the film industry, Robert Redford's citation reads: "Actor, Director, Producer, Creator of Sundance, inspiration to independent and innovative filmmakers everywhere."

"Lights! Camera! Action!": Directors

Anyone who has ever been privileged to direct a film also knows that although it can be like trying to write War and Peace *in a bumper car in an amusement park, when you finally get it right, there are not many joys in life that can equal the feeling.*

—STANLEY KUBRICK, DIRECTOR OF *2001: A SPACE ODYSSEY*

The film director has the one single most critical role in making a motion picture. He or she is the boss from whom everyone else takes his or her cue. It is the director who creatively interprets the script and creates the sounds and images from the written words on the page. The director takes the story off the pages and turns it into a visual reality on film. He or she does so by determining a point of view for the camera lens, which in turn helps to decide the choice of shots, where the camera(s) needs to be, and where the actors will need to move within a scene or sequence so the camera can record it on film. In bringing the story to life, a director must plan out the dramatic pace of the film, finding the right blend of sound and images to create the vision he or she has in mind. In order for the film to be successful, the director has to bring all the elements together in such a way that it maintains audience interest.

Cecil B. DeMille behind the camera

Aside from bringing a script to life, directors are responsible for both the technical and artistic aspects of the film. They work with many people who help accomplish that goal. The director works with the cast and crew, supervises scene setups and rehearsals, approves costumes and music, and communicates instructions to the staff working on the film throughout the project. Each director has their own approach to making a film.

Some directors are very hands-on, involved in many aspects, like selection of the cast, cinematography, and even the editing of the picture. Others prefer to focus on just one aspect, perhaps channeling all of their attention to ensuring that the pictorial beauty of the film is captured. Whatever his or her particular style, a director can be envisioned as an orchestra conductor, leading all of the cast and crew to bring one visual story to life in the form of a motion picture.

Throughout movie history, many directors have brought their unique vision to the creation of a film. Below are a few of the directors who have contributed their talents to the creation of some of the most memorable films produced.

D. W. Griffith (1875–1948)

Often called the father of film, Griffith was the first director to fully recognize the potential of the medium. Griffith is credited with developing the talents of some of film's earliest stars, including **Mary Pickford** and Lillian Gish. A cofounder of United Artists, some of his most acclaimed films are *Birth of a Nation* (1915), *Intolerance* (1916), and *Broken Blossoms* (1919).

Cecil B. DeMille (1881–1959)

The quintessential director, DeMille even dressed the part and carried a megaphone around on the set. A flamboyant personality, DeMille was well suited to bring such biblical spectacles to the screen such as *King of Kings* (1927), *Samson and Delilah* (1949), and *The Ten Commandments* (both the 1923 and the 1956 versions).

D. W. Griffith

John Huston (1906–1987)

The son of acting great Walter Huston and the father of actress Anjelica, the excessive living, multitalented Huston received many accolades for his acting, writing, and directing skills. Among his most recognized films are *Treasure of the Sierra Madre* (1948) and the Bogart-Hepburn classic *The African Queen* (1952).

Orson Welles (1915–1985)

Beginning in radio on the "Mercury Theatre on the Air," Welles and associate John Houseman produced the now famous Halloween prank radio broadcast *The War of the Worlds* (1938). His first film, *Citizen Kane* (1941), was considered a commercial failure, losing $150,000 at the box office. Ironically, today, *Citizen Kane* is regarded by most to be the greatest motion picture ever made.

Woody Allen (1935–)

The one-time stand-up comedian and writer has brought a unique style of directing to his films. Often the lead is a neurotic New Yorker, frequently starring Allen himself. Somehow his ridiculous gags, bizarre situations, and keen social satire translate well to the screen, making Allen one of the most successful film directors in the industry's history. Credits include *Annie Hall* (1977), *Hannah and Her Sisters* (1986), and *Crimes and Misdemeanors* (1989).

Woody Allen

Francis Ford Coppola (1939–)

One of the first of a new group of film directors in the 1960s who came to Hollywood via film school, rather than having worked his way up through various studio jobs, Coppola dreamed of being a filmmaker at age ten while bedridden with polio. He brought to the screen the trilogy gangster saga *The Godfather* (1972, 1974, 1990), launching the careers of such stars as **Al Pacino** and **Robert De Niro**.

Penny Marshall (1942–)

Despite terrific success as an actress, including her character as the lovable Laverne DeFazio in the hit sitcom *Laverne and Shirley,* Marshall moved behind the camera, directing her first film *Jumpin' Jack Flash* in 1986. She has had a string of box-office hits, including *Big* (1988), *Awakenings* (1990), *A League of Their Own* (1992), and *Riding in Cars with Boys* (2001). Marshall has the distinction of being the first female to direct a movie that grossed over $100 million (*Big*).

Martin Scorsese (1942–)

Another of the 1960s schooled filmmakers, Scorsese's trademark style includes New York settings, lead characters who struggle with inner demons, and unyielding therapeutic violence. He often works with **Robert De Niro** and has directed him in such films as the Oscar-winner *Raging Bull* (1980). His other films include the dark drama *Taxi Driver* (1976) and the film for which **Paul Newman** finally won his Oscar, *The Color of Money* (1986).

George Lucas (1944–)

Though he hasn't directed many films, his name carries some of the biggest clout in the filmmaking business. The creator of the *Star Wars* space episodic adventures and the trilogy escapades of Indiana Jones, Lucas not only brought high-energy adventure films back to the screen, he also took special effects to a truly incredible art form. *Star Wars* was the top-grossing film of all time until *Titanic* overtook the number-one spot twenty years later. His mega-success has allowed Lucas to devote much of his time to technical developments that have enhanced the movie experience in genres beyond science fiction.

Ron Howard (1954–)

He grew up on television, first as precocious Opie on *The Andy Griffith Show,* then as 1950s teen Richie Cunningham on the sitcom *Happy Days,* and then on-screen as Steve Bolander in *American Graffiti* (1973). After Howard's directorial efforts on the 1982 movie *Night Shift,* he caught the industry's attention with his next film, the mega-hit *Splash* (1984). His creative talents have brought to the screen such other memorables as *Backdraft* (1991), *Apollo 13* (1995), and his Oscar winner *A Beautiful Mind* (2001).

Al Pacino

Multi-Award-Winning Actor of Stage and Screen
1940–

The one I love is what Wallenda said . . . "Life's on the wire, the rest is just waiting." That's where life is for me. That's where it happens. And it does.

—AL PACINO ON ACTING

Passionate. Brooding. Intense. Guarded. Obsessively private. Brilliant actor. All describe eight-time Academy Award nominee Al Pacino. Sidney Lumet, who directed Pacino in his Oscar-nominated performance in *Dog Day Afternoon,* said, "He is literally incapable of doing anything fake." For Pacino, there are three reasons why he accepts a part—the director, the script, and the character. Explains Pacino, "If I relate greatly to the director, the text is pretty good and I think I can do something with the character, I might take it. Or, if I can relate greatly to the character and the text and the director are okay, I'll take it too." That's a mellower Pacino talking. There was a time when all three elements had to be great.

Alfredo James Pacino, the only child of Salvatore and Rose Pacino, was born on April 25, 1940, in New York City. When he was two, his parents divorced, so Al and his mother moved in with her parents in the South Bronx.

As a child, he was quiet and shy and sheltered by his mother, who did not allow Al out of the house alone until he began going to school. His only connection with the outside world was when Rose would take him to a feature at the local movie theater. The rest of the time he hung around with his grandfather, spending hours listening to him tell stories about what New York was like in the early 1900s.

Al began honing his acting skills back then too, reenacting scenes that he remembered from the movies he saw. Once let loose on the outside world, Al was just a regular kid; he played ball, told tall tales that he tried out on his friends, and got into the usual street mischief.

At fourteen Al saw a production of the Anton Chekhov play *The Seagull* at the Elsmere Theater in the South Bronx, and was mesmerized. He decided that perhaps he wanted to become an actor, so he transferred to the High School of Performing Arts.

By seventeen the only subject he wasn't failing was English, so he dropped out. Al drifted from job to job, and had plenty of them; he was a mail boy, a janitor, a shoe salesman, and an usher. He worked in a fruit store, a supermarket, and even moved furniture. His longest stretch in one job was working for *Commentary* magazine.

From working various jobs, Pacino saved enough money to enroll in the Herbert Berghof Studio. That's where he met Charlie Laughton, an acting teacher who introduced him to the things that surround acting, like directing and writing. Charlie became his father figure, brother, and friend. He got on the acting career path. Pacino started apprenticing, writing and directing off-off-Broadway productions.

In 1966 Pacino applied to Lee Strasberg's famed Actors Studio, where he was taught Method Acting (where you learn how to create a life for a character by using experiences and impressions from your own life). Things in Pacino's career moved quickly after that. He worked with James Earl Jones in *The Peace*

Creeps and then starred in the off-Broadway drama *The Indian Wants the Bronx,* for which he won an Obie Award for Best Actor. The following year, Pacino made his Broadway debut in *Does the Tiger Wear a Necktie?* Despite the fact that the play closed after only forty shows, Pacino received critical praise for his compelling performance as a drug addict and won his first Tony Award.

Pacino made his film debut in 1969 in *Me, Natalie,* which was a box-office flop. His next feature film was *The Panic in Needle Park* (1971). The film received mediocre reviews, but director Francis Ford Coppola took notice of Pacino's performance and cast him as Michael Corleone, the reluctant Mafia son pushed into the family business in *The Godfather.* The film's headliner cast included legendary actor **Marlon Brando** and Diane Keaton, James Caan, and Robert Duvall.

Throughout the filming, Pacino was tense, but he played the role brilliantly, transforming Michael from a quiet war hero to a cold, calculating mob boss. He got a 1972 Best Supporting Actor nomination, and suddenly was rocketed to stardom. Pacino went on a four-year run, being nominated for Oscars in 1973 for his riveting performance in *Serpico,* a New York City cop who discloses corruption in the police department; in 1974 for reprising his role in *The Godfather, Part II;* and in 1975 as a volatile bisexual who botches a bank robbery in *Dog Day Afternoon.*

Pacino made some bad choices in other films, like *Bobby Deerfield* (1977), *Cruising* (1980), and the $28-million embarrassment *Revolution* (1985). Considering himself a theater actor first, Pacino was able to balance his unsuccessful films with his rewarding work onstage. He returned to Broadway to star in *The Basic Training of Pavlo Hummel* (1977), winning his second Tony Award.

In 1979 Pacino's portrayal of a wacko lawyer in *And Justice for All* earned him a fifth Oscar nomination. He turned in an explosive performance as the chilling drug lord Tony Montana in *Scarface* (1983). As a change of pace, Pacino accepted supporting roles in the films *Dick Tracy* (1990) and *Glengarry*

Glen Ross (1992), receiving Oscar nominations for both performances. Finally, after seven unsuccessful bids for the golden statuette, Pacino won an Oscar in 1992, playing blind, disillusioned colonel Frank Slade in *Scent of a Woman.*

There have been other film projects—Pacino reunited with *Scarface* director Brian DePalma to star in *Carlito's Way.* In 1995 Pacino and **Robert De Niro** were finally teamed up in the film *Heat.* Working with notable stars Johnny Depp in *Donnie Brasco* and Keanu Reeves in *The Devil's Advocate,* Pacino is still full-throttle in a career that has spanned more than a quarter of a century.

Though Pacino may well be most associated with his gritty tough-guy portrayals, his heart is never far from the theatrical stage. "The play is the thing. That's my motivation," says Pacino. He expanded his work on the Broadway stage in front of packed houses, directing and starring in Eugene O'Neill's one-act play *Hughie.* His fascination with Shakespeare, particularly the character Richard III, prompted Pacino to direct and star in an unusual documentary-style film, entitled *Looking for Richard* (1996). In an almost frenzied search of the meaning of the English bard in everyday life, Pacino hit the streets of New York and asked people how they felt about Shakespeare, and his interpretation of the hunchbacked king Richard III. The impromptu street encounters are intermixed with a behind-the-scenes look at the casting, preparation, and rehearsals for Pacino's film project, *Richard III.*

Pacino insists that for him acting is always about the work, the process. In 2000, at age sixty, he was awarded the Cecil B. DeMille Award and was inducted into the Theater Hall of Fame. Still, he moves to his own beat, always trying new things, looking for characters that will challenge him.

Harrison Ford

Successful Actor and Star of the Star Wars *Trilogy*
1942–

I hold on to normalcy as if it were my life preserver. A normal family life, normal work relationships—they are what keep me in touch with the audience I'm trying to reach.

—HARRISON FORD

On a summer day in 2000, hiker Sarah George suddenly became ill while climbing the Tetons. A passing hiker placed an emergency call to County Sheriff Bob Zimmer, who called a resident of nearby Jackson Hole, Wyoming. The resident, megastar Harrison Ford, often volunteered for rescues. He flew his Bell 407 helicopter to pick up George. Piloting with the same deftness as his character in *Star Wars,* Ford took George to a hospital, then headed home to his eight hundred-acre ranch.

One of the most successful actors in Hollywood, Harrison Ford has seen ten of his thirty-eight films gross more than $100 million. He has worked with legendary directors George Lucas, **Steven Spielberg,** and Sydney Pollack and has shared the screen with Tommy Lee Jones, Melanie Griffith, Michelle Pfeiffer, and Brad Pitt.

Ford was born on July 13, 1942, in Chicago, Illinois, to a Catholic father and a Jewish mother. He says he had a normal childhood in a home where he felt "supported and encouraged." At school, however, Harrison was shy and reclusive. He was tormented incessantly by school bullies. Not surprisingly, he didn't do well academically. "I didn't believe in careers and thought that holding down a . . . job was a monumental task. I just wanted excitement."

Harrison went to college at Ripon, a small school in Wisconsin, but he rarely attended classes. In his junior year, however, he signed up for a drama class and was smitten from the moment he stepped onstage. Harrison decided to leave school to pursue acting. With his new wife, classmate Mary Marquardt, Harrison settled in Laguna Beach, California, where he took odd jobs and worked at the local theater. A Columbia Pictures talent scout spotted him and signed him for a $150-per-week job with the studio. But the minor TV and film roles he had were uninspiring.

After the Fords had two sons, Benjamin and Willard, Harrison took up carpentry to supplement his income. His first professional project was a $100,000 recording studio for musician Sergio Mendes. Ford eventually built a client list that included many of Hollywood's celebrities, and with a comfortable income he was able to be more selective in his choice of acting roles.

Harrison's first break came when the young director George Lucas sought actors for his film *American Graffiti* (1973). Harrison landed a small part in what became a Hollywood triumph. More important, however, was the impression he made on Lucas. A few years later the director thought of Harrison for the 1977 space thriller *Star Wars*. With its simple theme of good versus evil and its breathtaking special effects, the movie took Hollywood by storm. *Newsday* called the movie "one of the greatest adventure movies ever made."

As Hans Solo, the cocky, fortune-hunting pilot of an intergalactic spaceship, Harrison infused his own disarming wittiness and charm into the role.

"He has this great sense of spontaneity, as if every reading is his first," Lucas said of Ford's ability to create enduring characters. Harrison reprised the role in *The Empire Strikes Back* (1980) and *Return of the Jedi* (1983). The films are among the top-ten all-time highest-grossing movies.

Harrison appeared in half a dozen films, none as memorable or successful as *Star Wars,* before Lucas presented him with another career-building opportunity. He was working with **Steven Spielberg**—director of the new film, who was another creative genius in the industry—on an adventure trilogy about the exploits of archaeologist Indiana Jones. Originally, Harrison wasn't in the running at all. "Lucas hadn't considered using his Hans Solo for another heroic role," wrote *Newsweek,* "and he was the last actor interviewed for the lead." The film turned out to be pure magic for Ford: "I had the most fun I ever had with a character and with a director," he said.

Today, *Raiders of the Lost Ark* remains the twelfth highest–grossing film ever. Many, including Spielberg himself, credit Ford for the film's blockbuster appeal. He has a keen sense of what works in a scene, and made valuable contributions. For example, Harrison felt that a drawn-out sword fight between Jones and an enemy was dramatically wrong. He offered Spielberg an alternative that matched his character's cocky self-assurance: in the film Indy gives his combatant an almost dumbfounded look, then pulls out a gun and shoots him.

Harrison reprised Indiana Jones in two more films, *Indiana Jones and the Temple of Doom* (1984) and *Indiana Jones and the Last Crusade* (1989). But though his career was launched by playing masculine, witty heroes, Harrison did not want to limit himself to those roles. His 1985 portrayal of police officer John Book in *Witness* allowed him to demonstrate his range—and his brilliant performance earned him an Academy Award Best Actor nomination.

Harrison's appeal ensures that he has no shortage of roles to choose from. He has played an ex-CIA agent in two films based on Tom Clancy novels,

Patriot Games (1992) and *Clear and Present Danger* (1994); he reprised David Jansen's TV role as a wrongly accused doctor pursuing his wife's one-armed murderer in *The Fugitive* (1993). He played the president of the United States fighting international terrorists in *Air Force One* (1997).

Harrison seeks variety in his roles. Often he will take one that is just plain fun, as in *Working Girl* (1988), opposite Melanie Griffith and *Six Days, Seven Nights* (1998), costarring Anne Heche. Though not box-office blockbusters, Harrison believes that such lighthearted pictures have their own measure of success. He loves "the challenge of it, the fun of it," he says of comedies.

Ford takes his success in stride. Home and family are his priorities. His marriage to Mary Marquardt ended in 1979, a casualty of his restlessness and impatience for success. In 1983 a mellowed Ford married screenwriter Melissa Mathison. They separated in 2001. They have two children, fourteen-year-old Malcolm and eleven-year-old Georgia. Though the Wyoming ranch is his favorite place, he also spends time at his New York City apartment. Ford likes to indulge in another passion too—flying.

Harrison Ford is among a handful of stars that command $20 million per film. He believes in sharing his good fortune with others: for example, a family charitable foundation is run by one of Ford's grown sons. But Ford prefers to offer his services quietly and privately, so the foundation does not bear Ford's name.

Harrison tries to avoid the celebrity spotlight, but at times he cannot escape his fame. His footprints appear in the cement at Grauman's Chinese Theatre; his star appears on the Hollywood Walk of Fame. Perhaps his most prestigious honor was the 2000 Life Achievement Award by the American Film Institute. Ford joined film legends **Bette Davis, Elizabeth Taylor, Dustin Hoffman, Sidney Poitier, Alfred Hitchcock,** and **Steven Spielberg.** "It's a mystery to me how I happened to get invited to join that list. But I'm very flattered," he said.

Most comfortable in jeans and a T-shirt, Harrison is unlike many other film stars. He has no desire to direct or produce. He prefers the collaboration and teamwork that comes with acting. "It's a question of how I want to live my life," he explains. "Now I make one movie a year, then I go away and do other things. . . . It's a full-time job. I have a life."

Barbra Streisand

Award-Winning "Actress Who Sings"
1942–

There is a part of anybody who is worth their salt that is very insecure, a part that is lonely and sad. As emotional human beings, we have secrets and mysteries and strange feelings, and that's what comes out in [one's] work.

—BARBRA STREISAND

The Emmy Awards were postponed twice in 2001 because of the the terrorist attacks on September 11. When they were finally presented on November 4, Barbra Streisand was announced as the winner of the Emmy for Outstanding Individual Performance in a Variety or Music Program (for her show *Timeless*). But the multitalented entertainer did not go onstage to accept the award. Most watchers assumed she was not at the ceremony.

Toward the end of the program, soft music began playing while cameras focused on a dimly lit stage. A backdrop listed the names of those who perished in the September 11 attacks. Then a singer in silhouette appeared. *"When you walk through a storm, hold your head up high / And don't be afraid of the dark"* sang the unmistakable voice. By the time Streisand turned to face the audience, viewers were overwhelmed with emotion.

The award-winning entertainer, who once called herself an "actress who sings," was born Barbara Joan Streisand on April 24, 1942, in Brooklyn, New York. Barbara's father died when she was only fifteen months old, and her mother, Diana, struggled to make a living. She left Barbara and her older brother, Sheldon, with her parents while she worked.

Her mother married Louis Kind in 1950, and the family moved to Flatbush, New York. Barbara and her stepfather did not get along, and she escaped home life at the Saturday afternoon movies. Watching the glamour and opulence of Hollywood movies, Barbara fantasized about becoming a screen star herself.

Barbara was put off by the amateurish plays of her high school, but she fell in love with the theater after seeing *The Diary of Anne Frank* on Broadway. Before long, she landed odd jobs in small New York theaters, working as a stagehand and as a summer stock member. She graduated early and with honors from her Flatbush high school and immediately moved to Manhattan, where she began singing as a means to break into theater. When she signed up for a talent contest at a club called the Lion in 1960, she changed the spelling of her name to Barbra. She won the contest, landed jobs at other clubs, and developed a strong following at celebrity hangouts such as the Bon Soir and the Blue Angel.

By 1962 Streisand had been spotted by a talent scout and won a recording contract with Columbia Records. She also debuted on Broadway in *I Can Get It for You Wholesale.* Streisand earned rave reviews for her minor role—and won the New York Drama Critics' Circle Award and a Tony nomination. In 1963 she debuted on TV on the *Ed Sullivan Show* and launched a successful road tour. Streisand married fellow actor Elliott Gould on March 21, 1963; they had one child, Jason, born in 1966, also a film actor. (The couple divorced in 1971.)

In 1963 Streisand landed the role of Fanny Brice in Broadway's *Funny Girl.* When the show closed in 1964, she was a star. Her singing career was skyrocketing: she won two Grammys for *The Barbra Streisand Album* and was nominated for an Emmy and a Tony. During one week in the fall of 1964, five of her songs appeared in the Top 100 in *Cashbox* magazine.

In 1965 Streisand won five Emmys for her one-woman television special *My Name Is Barbra.* The singer was particularly pleased with the show because she had negotiated for complete creative control. After her son was born, Streisand appeared in the film version of *Funny Girl,* earning both her first Golden Globe and Academy Award (1969) in a tie with screen legend **Katharine Hepburn.** The National Association of Theatre Owners named her Star of the Year, and in 1970, just eight years into the business, she received the Star of the Decade Tony Award.

Streisand next appeared in *Hello Dolly* (1969), and *On a Clear Day You Can See Forever* and *The Owl and the Pussycat* (both 1970) before forming her own production company, Barwood Films. She starred in *What's Up, Doc?* then in the first Barwood project, *Up the Sandbox* (1972). Although *Sandbox* was not a commercial success, it received critical praise.

Teaming with heartthrob **Robert Redford** in *The Way We Were* (1973) brought Streisand a second Oscar nomination, and the title song (which she recorded) became a number-one hit. For *A Star Is Born* (1976), Streisand was executive producer and cowrote the film's theme song, "Evergreen." *Star* received five Academy Award nominations and made Streisand the first female composer to win an Oscar.

Although she continued to record solo albums, Streisand performed two duets—"You Don't Bring Me Flowers" (1978) with Neil Diamond, and "Guilty" (1980) with Barry Gibb, which captured Grammys for both singers. She fulfilled a longtime goal when she brought *Yentl,* the story of a girl passing as a Yeshiva boy in order to get an education, to the big screen in 1983. It was the first time a feature was produced, cowritten, and directed by a female who was also its star. *Yentl* won Best Picture and Best Director Golden Globes and five Oscar nominations.

In 1986 Streisand hosted a fund-raising concert, *One Voice,* for Democratic senatorial candidates. That year she also released *The Broadway Album* and earned an eighth Grammy. *The Prince of Tides* (1991), in which Streisand starred and also produced and directed, received overwhelming acclaim; its commercial success validated Streisand as a bona fide filmmaker. Though she did not receive an Oscar, she was nominated for the Directors Guild prize.

In 1992 Streisand was honored with a "Living Legend" Grammy Award. She actively campaigned for Bill Clinton and the Democrats in 1992. Two years later she delighted fans by returning to the stage after twenty-seven years. Her concert tour thrilled crowds in Los Angeles, San Francisco, New York, Washington, D.C., and London, and broke box-office records. The singer donated more than $10.25 million in profits to charities. *Barbra: The Concert,* which ran on HBO television, won two Emmys and a Peabody Award, and Streisand received a Lifetime Achievement Grammy.

The Mirror Has Two Faces (1996) marked Streisand's third triple effort as star, producer, and director. The film received two Oscar nominations. On July 1, 1998, Barbra married actor James Brolin at her Malibu home. Inspired by her new romance, she recorded a series of love songs for *A Love Like Ours* (1999) and returned to the stage in 1999—for what she said was the last time—for her *Timeless* concert tour.

In a career that spans almost half a century Streisand has forged a path of innovative music, film, and theater projects. She remains the top-selling female vocalist, with a number-one album in each of the last four decades. The recipient of countless honors, including the National Endowment for the Arts's National Medal of Arts, Streisand believes she has still more to give. Reflecting on one of her lifetime achievement awards, Streisand said, "I'd rather think of myself as a work in progress."

Robert De Niro

Regarded as One of the Greatest Actors in Modern Film
1943–

It's important not to "indicate" [in acting].
People don't try to show their feelings, they
try to hide them.

—ROBERT DE NIRO

Widely regarded as one of the greatest actors in modern film, Robert De Niro hardly seemed a candidate for Hollywood stardom when he was growing up in New York City. The acclaimed actor, director, and producer was born into a family of artists, and his favorite boyhood occupation was reading. The pale youngster was so shy and reserved that his peers nicknamed him "Bobby Milk."

Robert De Niro Jr. was born on August 17, 1943, to Robert De Niro Sr., a Greenwich Village abstract expressionist painter, and Virginia Admiral De Niro, also a painter and later the owner of a typesetting and printing business. Bobby's parents separated when he was two years old, after which he lived mostly with his mother. His first onstage role was that of the Cowardly Lion in a school production of *The Wizard of Oz.* As he grew older he got over his shyness and began associating with the street kids in his Little Italy neighborhood. He started taking drama classes at the renowned Stella Adler

Conservatory, and at sixteen he dropped out of school with the goal of becoming a professional actor.

De Niro continued his training at the prestigious Actors Studio and studied with the notable acting instructors Lee Strasberg and Luther James. He landed his first film role in Brian De Palma's *Wedding Party* (filmed in 1966 but released in 1969). The first picture of De Niro's to be released was another De Palma film, *Greetings* (1968).

De Niro appeared in nine films before his 1973 films *Bang the Drum Slowly* and *Mean Streets* drew critical and popular attention. *Mean Streets* marked the start of a longtime affiliation with director and childhood friend Martin Scorsese. De Niro burst into the limelight in 1974 in Francis Ford Coppola's *The Godfather, Part II,* playing the young Vito Corleone. To prepare for his role as the Italian-speaking don—who knows just a few words of English—De Niro learned the Sicilian dialect of the fictional character. Like its predecessor, the film was a smash hit, winning Academy Awards for Best Picture, Best Director, and Best Adapted Screenplay. De Niro himself earned his first Oscar, for Best Supporting Actor.

In 1976 De Niro rejoined Scorsese for the grimly violent film *Taxi Driver,* costarring a young actress named **Jodie Foster** as a teenage prostitute. De Niro played the intense taxi driver Travis Bickle, who becomes obsessed with protecting the youngster. His striking performance won him a Best Actor Oscar nomination. The next year he teamed with Scorsese again as a jazz musician in the musical *New York, New York.*

The actor returned to his now-trademark character—the intense brooder with an undercurrent of menace—in *The Deer Hunter* (1978), securing a second Best Actor Oscar nomination. In 1980 he took on perhaps the most challenging character of his career, gaining an astonishing sixty pounds to transform himself into heavyweight champion boxer Jake LaMotta in the film *Raging Bull.* The role garnered De Niro his first Best Actor Academy Award, and the film was nominated for eight Oscars, including Best Picture, Best Director, and Best Supporting Actor (Joe Pesci).

During the 1980s De Niro continued to show his creative range. Among his more successful pictures was *The Mission* (1986), a historical drama in which he plays a reformed persecutor of Jesuit missionaries in the eighteenth-century South American jungle. The following year, he costarred in *The Untouchables* as legendary mobster Al Capone. He also appeared in the hit action-comedy *Midnight Run* (1988) as an irascible bounty hunter determined to turn in a white-collar criminal (Charles Grodin). Other films during this period, such as the mob film *Once Upon a Time in America,* the romantic drama *Falling in Love* (both 1984), and the offbeat fantasy *Brazil* (1985) were less successful, but they demonstrated De Niro's remarkable versatility.

In 1989 De Niro converted a former Manhattan coffee factory into the TriBeCa Film Center and established the headquarters of his new production company, TriBeCa Films. The studio's first project, the 1989 film *We're No Angels,* was a huge disappointment, but the company rebounded and is still actively promoting and funding successful projects.

Aside from a few box-office failures, including Mary Shelley's *Frankenstein* (1994) and *The Fan* (1996), De Niro turned in a string of consistently fine performances during the 1990s. He received his fourth Best Actor Oscar nomination in 1990 for his portrayal of a coma patient who regains consciousness in *Awakenings.* That same year, he scored big as part of a Mafia threesome (costarring Joe Pesci and Ray Liotta) in *Goodfellas,* and he was a terrifyingly credible psychotic killer in the 1991 remake *Cape Fear,* for which he got yet another Oscar nomination. In 1993 he made his directorial debut with *A Bronx Tale* (1993); he also produced and costarred in the picture.

In the sleekly produced crime film *Heat* (1995), De Niro paired for the first time with **Al Pacino** (although both appeared in *The Godfather, Part II,* they'd had no scenes together). He produced and costarred (with **Dustin Hoffman**) in the wry comedy *Wag the Dog* (1997); he plays a Washington "spin doctor" who teams up with a Hollywood producer (Hoffman) and "produces" a fake war that distracts public attention from a presidential scandal.

De Niro had a blockbuster in the 1999 TriBeCa Films production *Analyze This,* in which he plays an angst-ridden mob leader. He gave a delightful performance as the comic-strip villain Fearless Leader in *The Adventures of Rocky and Bullwinkle* (2000) and is a menacingly charming father of the bride in *Meet the Parents.* In 2001 he costarred with Ed Burns in *15 Minutes,* and with Edward Norton, Angela Bassett, and **Marlon Brando** in *The Score.* Following the terrorist attacks of September 11, he participated in television specials honoring those who died, including *America: A Tribute to Heroes,* and *9/11,* which he hosted.

Robert De Niro's upcoming film projects include *Showtime* and *City of the Sea.* He will also reprise previous roles in *Meet the Fockers* (a sequel to *Meet the Parents*) and *Analyze That* (a sequel to *Analyze This*). Regardless of what De Niro is working on, critics and fans can be certain that he will turn in a smooth, subtle performance, as he has done throughout his career.

Cher

Multitalented Singer and Actress
1946–

I've never compromised who I am—not ever. If I've gotten anywhere in my life, it's been on my own merits.

—CHER

Cher has no illusions about fame. "Some years I'm the coolest thing that ever happened, and the next year everyone's so over me," she says frankly. Her apparent disregard for public opinion stems from a combination of great success—including an Oscar for *Moonstruck* (1988)—and widely publicized failure. Deeply loyal to her fans, the resilient, candid actress nonetheless claims to live by one simple rule. "I answer to two people: myself and my God."

Cherilyn Sarkisian was born in El Centro, California, on May 20, 1946, to Jackie Crouch and John Sarkisian. Jackie, who later changed her name to Georgia Holt, was a struggling actress who has married eight times—three times to Sarkisian. Even in grade school Cher was smitten by the glamour of show business. "I didn't know what [I] was going to be; I just wanted to be famous," she says, often practicing her "autograph" and standing in front of a mirror imagining herself onstage.

In 1961 Georgia married banker Gilbert La Piere, who adopted Cher and half sister Georgeanne and sent them to a private prep school in Encino, California. Cher adapted to her new situation with flair, entertaining class-mates with her throaty singing voice. She was intelligent and studied hard, but not until she was thirty did Cher discover that she suffers from dyslexia, a learning disorder that makes reading numbers and words difficult.

Cher dropped out of high school at sixteen and left home for Los Angeles. In a coffee shop on Hollywood Boulevard, she met twenty-eight-year-old Salvatore "Sonny" Bono, a junior assistant for record producer Phil Spector. Cher was immediately taken with Sonny. "It was like one of those bolt-out-of-the-blue moments when something inside you just says, 'From this second, you're never going to be the same again.'"

Cher got the break she longed for one day when Spector needed an extra backup singer and tapped her for the job. In 1964 Sonny and Cher performed their own unofficial marriage ceremony in Tijuana, Mexico, and soon after that they launched a professional partnership, hitting the road as "Caesar and Cleo." In 1965 they recorded Sonny's song "I Got You, Babe" under their own names, and it soared to the top of the charts. A string of Top 40 singles followed, including "The Beat Goes On" and "Bang Bang." It wasn't only their music that attracted followers. The pair dressed like hippies, with shaggy hair, bell-bottom pants, wildly patterned tops, fur vests, and knee-length boots.

As a harder kind of rock took hold in the late 1960s, Sonny and Cher's folksy music slipped out of style. Their movie *Good Times* (1967) flopped, as did their second film attempt, *Chastity* (1969). Sonny and Cher were legally married in 1969, and their daughter, Chastity, was born that year. They abandoned their hippie garb for tuxedos and designer gowns and hit the nightclub circuit.

In 1971 CBS programming director Fred Silverman offered them their own weekly variety show. *The Sonny and Cher Comedy Hour* was an instant success and stayed high in the ratings during its three-year run. Off-camera, however, the couple's marriage was deteriorating. By the show's second season they were constantly feuding and had begun publicly seeing other people. In 1975, after a bitter legal struggle, Sonny and Cher were divorced.

Cher launched a solo variety TV series that year, but by the third episode she felt overwhelmed and asked Sonny to join her professionally. Cher had married—and divorced—rock star Gregg Allman, and their child, Elijah Blue Allman, was born in July 1976. The new *Sonny and Cher Show* was canceled in August 1977. By 1979 Cher was an out-of-work single mother and decided to turn her attention to acting.

Cher turned in an earnest performance in the 1982 film *Come Back to the 5 and Dime, Jimmy Dean, Jimmy Dean.* Hollywood director Mike Nichols was so impressed that he cast her in *Silkwood* (1983). Her strong performance earned a Best Supporting Actress Oscar nomination—and stopped the snickering of doubting movie-industry gossips. For her role in *Mask* (1985), she shared the Cannes Film Festival Best Actress Award.

Cher had become what one critic called a "media myth," using her fame and flashy style to her advantage. In 1987 she was signed for three major films: *The Witches of Eastwick, Suspect,* and *Moonstruck.* Cher's childhood dream came true in 1988 when she won a Best Actress Oscar for *Moonstruck.* After twenty-five years she had at last reached the pinnacle of success.

Cher next decided to renew her singing career and signed with former boyfriend David Geffen's label, collaborating with artists like Jon Bon Jovi, Michael Bolton, and Richie Sambora. Her new "light metal" sound, coupled with her outrageous outfits, completed her transformation. Between 1987 and 1992 she had eight hit singles, including "If I Could Turn Back Time" and "Heart of Stone."

By the time she completed the film *Mermaids* (1990) and a singing tour in 1991, however, Cher was near collapse. She retreated to less grueling projects, such as her commercial endorsements of fitness centers. When she began taping infomercials for a line of hair-care products and a new home-furnishings business she'd started, critics were appalled. Cher was undaunted by the criticism. The work, although hardly prestigious, had given her a chance to rest. She made a comeback in the mid-1990s in a segment of the critically acclaimed HBO special *If These Walls Could Talk,* which she also directed. She dedicated herself to fundraising for AIDS charities and released a new album, *It's a Man's World.*

Cher was in London in January 1998 when Chastity called with devastating news: Sonny Bono, then a California congressman, had been killed in a skiing accident. A grief-stricken Cher returned to California. Although she and Sonny had traded barbs for years after their divorce, their relationship had warmed, and they'd maintained a special bond. In a tearful eulogy Cher praised Sonny as a good friend, father, and partner. In her memoir she referred to Sonny's death as "My First Tragedy."

After coming to terms with Sonny's death, Cher costarred with veteran film actresses Judi Dench, Maggie Smith, and Joan Plowright in Franco Zeffirelli's 1997 hit *Tea With Mussolini.* Audiences and critics loved her performance as a flamboyant American socialite visiting Italy under Mussolini's dictatorship. In 1999 Cher had a Top 40 hit for the first time in twenty-two years with "Strong Enough," and her 1998 album *Believe* went platinum four times. She joined top vocalists Whitney Houston, Tina Turner, and Brandy on an album called *VH1 Divas Live '99.*

Cher has cemented her celebrity status in recent years with her usual energetic and varying projects. In 2000 she used the creative freedom afforded by the Internet and released *Not.Com.mercial,* available only by download. A departure from her usual pop sound, the album includes intensely dark songs—the first she has written entirely by herself. She collected her first Grammy Award, in 2000, for the hit "Believe" and was nominated for two other Grammys, as well as an American Music Award. In 2002 Cher followed up with *Living Proof,* an album of catchy dance tunes.

Cher's impact on film, music, and pop culture has been debated for years. In a field where novelty brings fame, however, Cher has managed to reinvent herself to meet every new challenge. "You have to figure out . . . creative ways to stay vital, interested, have new dreams," she says.

Sally Field

Actress Who Rose from TV Stardom
to Major Motion Pictures
1946–

Acting is not about the glory or the glamour—
whatever that is, it's about the quiet times,
when something clearly takes over. It doesn't
last long, but oh my God, it's exquisite.

—SALLY FIELD

Like many of her female colleagues, Sally Field knows it is difficult to find good roles for "mature" women. And like them, Field does not consider retiring from acting. Instead, she keeps looking for good scripts. She may be petite (5'2") and perky—but she's a fighter with steely determination.

Alan Greisman, Field's ex-husband and friend, described her in an interview with A&E *Biography:* "She is a bit of the grit and determination she had in *Places in the Heart.* She . . . has the sense of humor that she had in the character in *Soapdish,* and she . . . has the fight of the character she played in *Norma Rae.*" That inner strength and never-give-up attitude has served Sally Field well in a business that can be very competitive and unforgiving.

In the days when she starred in *Gidget* and *The Flying Nun,* Field was concerned that she wasn't measuring up. Much of that feeling was rooted in her childhood. She was born on November 6, 1946, in Pasadena, California, to Richard and Margaret "Maggie" Field. Five years later Sally's parents divorced, and she and her older brother, Ricky, shared a single room with Maggie at her grandmother's place. Maggie, probably best known as the "screaming lady" in the sci-fi film *The Man From Planet X,* struggled to make a living as an actress herself.

After Maggie married Hollywood actor-stuntman Jock Mahoney, the Fields settled in a comfortable suburb of Los Angeles, but tensions between Sally and her stepfather began almost immediately. A handsome and charming man, Mahoney nevertheless had a dark side. He could turn mean and was often difficult to please. Stubborn and headstrong, Sally often clashed with Jock in a battle of wills that lasted through her teen years.

By the time Sally was a senior at Birmingham High, she had become an exuberant teenager—head cheerleader, member of the student council, and competitive member of the drama club. Acting had become her passion. Ironically, Jock suggested that she audition for a summer acting workshop at Columbia Studios, which led to a starring role in ABC's new sitcom *Gidget.* The bubbly eighteen-year-old debuted on September 15, 1965.

Gidget was canceled after one season, but Sally got a second crack at television success as Sister Bertrille in *The Flying Nun.* The show ran from 1967 to 1970. In 1967 she also made her film debut in *The Way West.* In September 1968 Field married her high school sweetheart, Steve Craig. During the last season of *The Flying Nun,* Field became pregnant. On November 10, 1969, she gave birth to a son, Peter. Field continued to do television work, first as a reformed junkie in *Maybe I'll Come Home in the Spring* (1970) and in another short-lived TV series, *The Girl with Something Extra.*

Soon after giving birth to son Elijah in 1972, Field filed for divorce from Craig. She hired a new agent and turned in a stunningly dramatic performance as a psychiatric patient with multiple personalities in the TV movie *Sybil,* starring opposite Joanne Woodward. Her performance achieved the 1976 Best Actress Emmy.

Field next took a role as a runaway bride in the film *Smokey and the Bandit* (1977). During filming, Field and costar Burt Reynolds fell in love. The movie was a monster hit—the highest-grossing film of the decade. While working on light comedy films with Reynolds, Field was cast by *Sybil* director Martin Ritt in *Norma Rae,* the story of a small-town union organizer. Field embraced the title role, becoming the fiery, independent woman she herself was inside. Her riveting performance nailed the 1979 Best Actress Oscar.

Field ended her relationship with Reynolds in 1981 and signed on with her school friend and well-known producer Michael Ovitz. She also formed her own company, Fogwood Productions, and began the tedious process of seeking good film scripts. After a few hit-and-miss films, including *Absence of Malice* and *Kiss Me Goodbye,* she took on a role written expressly for her by screenwriter-director Robert Benton—a widowed Depression-era farm woman in *Places in the Heart.*

Field finally felt content with her life. In 1982 she began dating producer Alan Greisman, and they married in 1984. The following spring, Field won her second Academy Award, the Best Actress Oscar for *Places in the Heart.* In her acceptance speech, a nervous Field tried to convey how she felt: "I haven't had an orthodox career and I've wanted more than anything to have your respect. The first time I didn't feel it, but this time I feel it and I can't deny the fact that you like me right now. You like me! Thank you."

The press ridiculed Field for seeming insecure and childish in her speech, but Greisman told A&E *Biography,* "The truth is it was really, really honest, in a town that can be very hurtful. The notion that you're getting acknowledgment instead of rejection is the most honest feeling you can express."

Having reached the forty-plus actress plateau, Field was keenly aware of the dwindling number of film roles available for women her age. With mature actresses acquiring less than 10 percent of Hollywood's best roles, Field began wondering whether talent was enough.

In December 1987 Field gave birth to a third son, Sam. She returned to the screen in 1988 opposite **Tom Hanks** in the disappointing *Punchline.* Aside from the sentimental hit *Steel Magnolias,* most of her films in the following years received little attention. In 1991 Field produced her first film, *Dying Young,* and two of her film roles in the mid-1990s put her right back in the spotlight. She played **Robin Williams**'s ex-wife in the hilarious *Mrs. Doubtfire* (1993) and took her first character role in the smash hit *Forrest Gump* (1994), as Gump's resolutely determined mother. Field delivered the film's most memorable lines: "Life is like a box of chocolates, Forrest. You just never know what you're gonna get."

In 1995 Field produced and starred in the TV miniseries *A Woman of Independent Means.* That year she divorced Alan Greisman, though the two remain friends. Increasingly more interested in filmmaking, Field made her directorial debut in 1998 for an episode of the miniseries *From Earth to the Moon,* for pal Tom Hanks. She also happily embraced the real-life role of grandmother when son Peter and his wife, Amy Scattergood, had a daughter, named Isabel.

In 2000 Field directed her first full-length feature film, *Beautiful,* which starred Minnie Driver as a woman who hides her sadness and insecurities by becoming a beauty queen. Field also agreed to take on a recurring guest-starring role on the hit TV show *ER,* as the bipolar mother of Abby Lockhart. The role brought Field her second Emmy.

The actress returned to series television in 2002 as the newest U.S. Supreme Court Justice in *The Court.* When asked if she hesitated to play someone old enough to be appointed to the Supreme Court, Field replied, "I'm not going to run from my age. If I do . . . I would miss all the roles that are potentially out there for women who are in their fifties."

Steven Spielberg

Influential Director and Producer
1946–

Once a month the sky falls on my head, I come to, and I see another movie I want to make.

—STEVEN SPIELBERG

Steven Spielberg was destined to direct films. While in grade school he experimented with 8 mm film and created scores of "movies," usually involving wrecks between Lionel model trains. Then he invited his friends to a screening—and charged admission while his sister sold popcorn. That childhood fascination with the "magic" of creating new worlds has stayed with Spielberg. The wide-eyed wonder he had as a child is evident in his films. It is no surprise that he is regarded as one of the most innovative directors in Hollywood history.

Born in Cincinnati, Ohio, on December 18, 1946, Steven Allan Spielberg grew up in Haddonfield, New Jersey, and Scottsdale, Arizona. At thirteen he won a prize for his 40-minute war film *Escape to Nowhere.* Three years later he earned his first filmmaking income—a hefty $100—when his 140-minute movie *Firelight*, premiered in a local movie theater. Years later Spielberg said that the movie sparked his idea for *Close Encounters of the Third Kind.*

While attending California State College (now University), Spielberg submitted a twenty-four-minute film, *Amblin,* to the Atlanta Film Festival. The film won and landed Spielberg a seven-year TV director's contract with Universal-MCA. Spielberg went on to direct episodes of *Columbo; Night Gallery; Owen Marshall, Counselor at Law;* and *Marcus Welby, M.D.* He produced his first feature-length TV movie, *Duel,* in 1971, and his skill and talent drew immediate attention in Hollywood. Three years later his first feature film, *The Sugarland Express* (1974), premiered in theaters.

Spielberg's next film, *Jaws* (1975), was a blockbuster hit and the hottest movie of that summer, grossing $260 million. The man-eating shark that stalked the waters off New England's beaches terrified audiences. Another smash hit, the science fiction film *Close Encounters of the Third Kind* (1977), brought Spielberg his first Academy Award nomination for Best Director. It received eight Oscar nominations in all. Both films, which relied on special effects, a sense of wizardry, and an element of surprise, established Spielberg as an innovative newcomer with a strong sense of his audience.

Although the director's next film, *1941* (released in 1979), was a flop, Spielberg was undaunted. He teamed up with friend George Lucas (the producer of the now-legendary first *Star Wars* film) to work on *Raiders of the Lost Ark* (1981). The film marked the first of several collaborations with Lucas. Spielberg received a second Best Director Oscar nomination for his work, and the movie's success would inspire two hit sequels, also directed by Spielberg: *Indiana Jones and the Temple of Doom* (1984) and *Indiana Jones and the Last Crusade* (1989).

In 1982 Steven Spielberg got his first producer credit for *Poltergeist.* He also produced and wrote the first film to be released under his new production studio, Amblin Entertainment, *E.T.: The Extra-Terrestrial,* a sentimental story about a boy who befriends a stranded alien, was a monster success. It became the highest-grossing film in history, with a total of nearly $400 million. *E.T.*

established Amblin Entertainment as a hallmark company. With its stamp, films released by major studios like Universal, Columbia, and Warner Bros. won greater success.

Responding to criticism that he had not produced any motion pictures for adults, Spielberg adapted Alice Walker's Pulitzer Prize–winning novel *The Color Purple* for the big screen. The film premiered in 1986, starring **Whoopi Goldberg,** Danny Glover, and Oprah Winfrey. He silenced the critics when the film got a remarkable eleven Oscar nominations; incredibly, he received none. The following year the Academy finally recognized Spielberg's contributions to the industry by presenting him with the Irving G. Thalberg Memorial Award, which goes to "creative producers whose bodies of work reflect a consistently high quality of motion picture production."

Among Spielberg's other producing credits during the 1980s were *Gremlins* (1984), *Back to the Future* (1985), *The Money Pit* (1986), *Who Framed Roger Rabbit?* (1988), and *Back to the Future Part II* (1989). A string of less-than-spectacular films, including *Empire of the Sun* (1987), *Always* (1989), and *Hook* (1991) did not deter Spielberg from creating more imaginative projects.

In 1993 Spielberg wowed audiences with the dinosaur fantasy *Jurassic Park.* Packed with spectacular special effects, *Jurassic Park* surpassed even *E. T.*'s opening-week record and grossed $100 million in just nine days. He followed with two sequels—*The Lost World: Jurassic Park* (1997) and *Jurassic Park III* (2001).

Spielberg produced and directed one of his most poignant films in 1993— the haunting black-and-white film *Schindler's List,* based on the prizewinning book by Thomas Keneally. The film told the true story of Nazi Party member Oskar Schindler (played by Liam Neeson), who ended up saving many Jewish lives. It received an astonishing twelve Academy Award nominations and won seven Oscars, including Best Picture and Best Director, Spielberg's first. With the proceeds from the film, he established the Righteous Persons Foundation, a grant-giving organization dedicated to improving Jewish life and preserving Jewish culture.

The next year Steven Spielberg teamed up with music and film industry giants David Geffen and Jeffrey Katzenberg to form the first new Hollywood movie studio in more than seventy-five years: DreamWorks SKG. The first film produced by DreamWorks was *Amistad* (1997), but it seemed overshadowed by the epic *Titanic,* which ran in theaters at the same time.

In the summer of 1998 Spielberg enjoyed even greater success with the release of *Saving Private Ryan,* a harrowingly realistic World War II epic starring **Tom Hanks.** *Private Ryan* was nominated for eleven Oscars and won five— including Spielberg's second Best Director Award. Both Hanks and Spielberg were so deeply affected by their work on the film that they donated $500,000 for the construction of a D-Day museum in New Orleans.

In addition to *Saving Private Ryan,* DreamWorks also produced such hits as *Twister* (1996), *Men in Black* (1997), *American Beauty* (1999), *Gladiator* (2000), and the animated delight *Shrek* (2001). Spielberg reteamed with Tom Hanks to produce *Band of Brothers* (2001), a critically acclaimed multipart war TV series for HBO. The director's newest projects include *Minority Report* (2002), starring Tom Cruise, and an adaptation of the best-selling book *Memoirs of a Geisha* by Arthur S. Golden.

In addition to his coveted Academy Awards, Spielberg has also collected several Golden Globe and Directors Guild Awards. He received a Life Achievement Award from the American Film Institute and numerous other honors, including a 1996 Emmy Award for the 1995 animated *Pinky and the Brain Christmas Special.*

Spielberg attributes much of his success to inspiration from his wife and children. After a brief marriage to Amy Irving in 1985 (they had one son), Spielberg became involved with actress Kate Capshaw, who costarred in *Indiana Jones and the Temple of Doom.* They were married not long after and have five children together (Capshaw also has one daughter, Jessica Capshaw, from a previous marriage).

The boy who created *Escape to Nowhere* and *Firelight* is still dreaming big. He has produced, written, and directed many of the most beloved—and highest-grossing—films in history. "If Spielberg never directed another film, his place in movie history would be secure," *Chicago Sun-Times* critic Roger Ebert has said. "No other director has been more successful at the box office. . . . No director or producer has ever put together a more popular body of work. That's why the movies we're seeing [today] are made in his image."

Glenn Close

Respected Stage and Screen Actress
1947–

I think in movies, the close-up is what it's all about. No other art form has the close-up, which basically allows the audience to look into somebody's soul.

—GLENN CLOSE IN A 1995 INTERVIEW

Glenn Close's striking good looks, patrician demeanor, and varied performances have established her as one of America's most fascinating and talented stars. In late 2000, however, the fifty-three-year-old actress announced that she was "slowing down" the pace of her acting projects. She wanted more time with her daughter, Annie (then twelve). "I'm on the cusp of age where everything is harder," explained Close. "I'm compelled to seek fewer people, less noise, less pressure, and I've worked so hard, I'm wondering when I'm going to start enjoying it."

Close's comments were an example of a reflective, intellectual personality that colors every character she has played in a career spanning more than twenty-five years. Though a respected stage actress, Close nonetheless spent many years as a relative unknown before she became the Hollywood star she is today.

Glenn Close was born on March 19, 1947, in Greenwich, Connecticut, to

William T. and Bettine Close. Her parents were members of a "salvation" movement known as Moral Re-Armament. They became so involved in the group that when Glenn was thirteen, they abandoned the town their ancestors had helped found 300 years earlier and settled in Zaire (now the Democratic Republic of the Congo), in central Africa.

The Closes might have been drawn more deeply into the cultlike organization, but William, who was a surgeon, answered a different calling. He established a medical clinic in Zaire, where the couple lived for sixteen years. The Closes sent their children—Glenn, Tina, Jesse, and Alexander—to boarding schools in Switzerland and Connecticut. The children lived with their parents when they weren't attending school.

Close says today that the experience of living in Africa was enlightening. "My parents were very idealistic," she says, "and I think they were susceptible at a certain time in their lives to the allure of a group like [Moral Re-Armament]. . . . Looking back as an adult, I'm so proud of my parents, so in awe of them—they're great humanists."

The Close children later returned to Greenwich and lived with their maternal grandmother. Glenn attended Rosemary Hall, an exclusive girls' school, where she organized a theater group with other class members. After graduating in 1965, Close joined "Up With People," a troupe of young entertainers who toured the country singing upbeat, socially conscious music. Close was also part of the trio called the Green Glenn Singers, and she wrote two songs, including the sugary "Run and Catch the Wind."

In 1970 Close enrolled in William and Mary College in Williamsburg, Virginia, where she majored in anthropology and drama. By the time she graduated in 1974, she had decided to become an actress. Her first lead role was in the play *Love for Love* (1974), with the New Phoenix Repertory Company.

For years Close worked diligently in theater and had several minor roles in TV movies, including *Rules of the Game* (1975) and *Orphan Train* (1979). In her first Broadway appearance, in *Barnum,* she was spotted by director George Roy Hill. He was so impressed with her talent that he cast her as the free-spirited mother in the 1982 film *The World According to Garp.* For her first feature-length film role Close earned her first Oscar nomination.

Close has demonstrated remarkable acting versatility. In 1983 she appeared in the box-office hit *The Big Chill,* receiving a Best Supporting Actress Oscar nomination. The following year, she won a Tony Award for her role in Broadway's *The Real Thing.* She got an Emmy nomination for her TV role as the mother of an incest victim in *Something About Amelia* (1984), and she played a lawyer who becomes romantically involved with her client in *Jagged Edge* (1985). She acquired another Oscar nomination in 1985 for her role in the baseball fable *The Natural,* starring **Robert Redford.** Her riveting portrayal of the vengeful, psychotic lover in the thriller *Fatal Attraction* (1987) shocked audiences and wowed Academy members, bringing her a fourth Oscar nomination.

As the manipulative Marquise de Merteuil in the 1988 film *Dangerous Liaisons,* Close got a second Best Actress Oscar nomination. In the film set in seventeenth-century France, Close's character convinces an ex-lover (John Malkovich) to seduce the young bride of her former husband.

The actress received two more Tony Awards for her performance in *Death and the Maiden* (1992) and for her flamboyant depiction of silent-screen star Norma Desmond in *Sunset Boulevard* (1995). During the 1990s she was involved in several television movies. She played the title role in the "Hallmark Hall of Fame" project *Sarah, Plain and Tall* (1991) and its sequel, *Skylark* (1993). Close won two Emmys (one as executive producer and one as lead actress) for *Sarah,* which drew the largest audience in the Hallmark program's forty-year history.

In 1995 Close played the title character in the controversial TV movie *Serving in Silence: The Margarethe Cammermeyer Story* (1995), which she also coproduced. Cammermeyer, a decorated colonel in the U.S. Army, admitted she was homosexual during a security clearance interview. She was discharged from the service but sued the U.S. Army over the discharge and won in federal court. The film was nominated for six Emmys and won three; Close earned an award for Outstanding Lead Actress in a Miniseries or a Special.

Close has received critical acclaim for her comic performances, too. She was First Lady Marsha Dale in the wacky *Mars Attacks!* (1996) and the hilariously wicked Cruella De Vil in Walt Disney's *101 Dalmatians* (1996). The following year she appeared as the U.S. vice president in *Air Force One,* and as the mother of a young man dying of AIDS in the TV movie *In the Gloaming.* She reprised her role as Sarah Witting in *Sarah, Plain and Tall: Winter's End* (1999) and delighted movie fans with her return as Cruella De Vil in *102 Dalmatians* (2000).

Close's nonacting pursuits include co-owning a coffee shop called Leaf and Bean and a bookstore called Poor Richard's in Bozeman, Montana. Despite her announcement in 2000 that she was pulling back from acting, the award-winning actress emphasized that slowing down did not mean stopping. "I've never turned down anything I thought was worth doing—yet," she said. She has since appeared in the TV movies *South Pacific* (2001) and *The Ballad of Lucy Whipple* (2001), for which she was executive producer. She also appeared in *The Safety of Objects* (2001). In 2003 she will appear in *Le Divorce,* based on a novel by Diane Johnson.

Close says that her parents' strong convictions have had a lasting effect on how she has lived her life. "They're people who have always felt that one should give back positively to society," she says. "They taught us that if much is given, you should give back."

Meryl Streep

Acclaimed Actress of Stage and Screen
1949–

Acting is being susceptible to what is around you and it's letting it all come in. Acting is a clearing away of everything except what you want and need—and it's wonderful in that way—and when it's right, you're lost in the moment.

—MERYL STREEP

When the Academy Award nominations were announced on February 15, 2000, it was a record-tying honor for two-time award winner Meryl Streep. This latest nomination equaled the twelve career nominations of legendary actress **Katharine Hepburn.** Streep earned the honor for her portrayal of East Harlem violin teacher Roberta Guaspari in *Music of the Heart.* Always the consummate actress, Streep studied the violin for three months so she could actually play it in the film.

What is so remarkable about Meryl Streep is that she seems to "become" her characters with such ease. She was born Mary Louise Streep on June 22, 1949, in Summit, New Jersey. Parents Harry Streep II, an advertising executive with

Merck pharmaceuticals, and Mary Louise, a freelance illustrator, nicknamed their new daughter "Meryl." Mary Louise gave birth to two more children, Harry III (affectionately called "Third") and Dana, before the family moved to the more upscale community of Bernardsville, New Jersey.

Meryl refers to her youth as awkward. She felt like a misfit and didn't think she was very likable. Always too big for her age, she wore glasses; had frizzy, mousy brown hair; and was bossy and nosy. Says Meryl, "I was an ugly little kid with a big mouth, an obnoxious show-off." Despite her shortcomings, she managed to bowl over her teachers and classmates when she sang "O Holy Night" in French at the school Christmas show. Meryl's voice had promise, and she took singing lessons from Estelle Liebling, the same teacher who coached opera diva Beverly Sills. As Meryl became more interested in boys and being popular in school, however, singing became less important. After four years she quit.

When she was fourteen, Meryl traded in the glasses for contact lenses and bleached her hair blond, completing a transformation from an ugly duckling to popular teen. She became a Bernardsville High School cheerleader, had boyfriends, and attended dances. In tenth grade Meryl auditioned for a part in the school production of *The Music Man,* and her love for acting was born.

Despite the efforts she put into her appearance and social activities to gain popularity, Meryl was also an excellent student and was accepted at Vassar College, an all-female college in Poughkeepsie, New York. At Vassar, Meryl blossomed intellectually and emotionally. She was among young women who thrived on exchanging thoughts and exploring ideas, and in sharing their hopes and dreams with one another.

Streep loved her time at Vassar. Instead of worrying about how to fit in, she could focus her attention on her studies and acting. She was a natural on the stage. When she read the part of Blanche DuBois in *A Streetcar Named*

Desire, she stunned her drama teacher, Clint Atkinson. He later called Streep "a brilliant actress. . . . There was a volcano within her. I found her acting hair-raising, almost mind-boggling."

Streep performed in a few more plays in college, continuing to reveal an ability to disappear into every character she portrayed. After college Streep joined the Green Mountain Guild, a small Vermont theater group that performed at various ski resorts. But the Guild work just wasn't challenging enough for Streep, so she enrolled in the Yale School of Drama. There Meryl found herself drawn into a whirlwind schedule, performing no fewer than forty different roles in three years.

In the fall of 1975, with a master's degree in hand, Streep headed for New York. The acting gods must have been aligned with her from the very beginning. She slept through a very important "cattle call" audition with the Theater Communications Group. However, she convinced the casting director of Joe Papp's Public Theater to give her an audition. Streep got her first professional stage role in *Trelawny of the Wells.* After seeing her perform, most critics agreed that Meryl Streep was an actress to watch. In her first year in New York, Streep received several theater award nominations and won an Outer Critics Circle Award for her performance in *27 Wagons Full of Cotton.*

In her very first film audition Streep won a small role in *Julia,* which starred Vanessa Redgrave and Jane Fonda. Her next role, in *The Deer Hunter* (1978), earned Meryl her first Academy Award nomination. The following year, Streep expanded her acting range, accepting a role in the television miniseries *Holocaust.* She won a Best Supporting Actress Emmy (television's equivalent of film's Oscar award) for her performance.

The career breakthrough role for Streep came in *Kramer vs. Kramer* (1979). She won her first Academy Award playing Joanna, **Dustin Hoffman**'s estranged wife who is suing for custody of their young son. Many believe it was

Streep's tearful performance in the courtroom scene that won her the Oscar. For the next two decades Streep's film career was nothing less than spectacular. She appeared in almost a film a year from 1978 through 1999, acquiring another Academy Award in 1982 for her astonishing performance as a Nazi concentration camp survivor in *Sophie's Choice.*

Though film roles for middle-aged women are more difficult to come by, Streep found some of the best around. In the 1995 film *The Bridges of Madison County* she showed that a woman in her forties can still be desirable and romantic. Now in her fifties, there is no sign of her slowing down. Streep made a triumphant return to the New York stage in the summer of 2001. Performing at the Delacorte Theater in Central Park, Streep starred in Anton Chekov's *The Seagull.* For Streep it was like coming home; she began her New York stage career twenty years earlier working for Joe Papp in his Shakespeare Festival. The critics raved about Streep's performance and asked the question everyone was thinking after seeing her in the show: "What took her so long to return to the stage?"

Streep completed work on two movies due out sometime in 2002—*Adaptation* and *The Hours.* Though a successful film career would be more than enough for one person to juggle, it is only one aspect of Streep's very full life. She married sculptor Don Gummer in 1978 and is busy raising four children, Streep is intent on keeping her role as mother her top priority. She still grocery shops, cooks dinner, and does housework. Says Streep, "You can't get spoiled if you do your own ironing."

Streep is very busy off the stage and screen. She is a dedicated activist, involved in issues like nuclear disarmament. She founded Mothers & Others, an organization that focuses on the use of dangerous pesticides on foods. She has loaned her voice to narrate children's books, including *The Velveteen Rabbit,* and supports charitable organizations like the Pediatric AIDS Foundation and Christopher Reeve's Celebration of Hope.

Streep has received many awards and honors over her twenty-year acting career, including the Bette Davis Lifetime Achievement Award, a star on the Hollywood Walk of Fame, and the coveted French medal of Officier in the Ordre des Arts et Des Lettres. Streep still reads through stacks of scripts looking for good parts. Happy with her life and her roles as wife, mother, activist, artist— Streep says, "I like who I am now. Other people may not. I'm comfortable. I feel freer now. I don't want growing older to matter to me."

Robin Williams

The "Tasmanian Devil of Comedy"
1952–

You're only given a little spark of madness. You mustn't lose it.

—Robin Williams

Robin Williams's high-school classmates could not have imagined how prophetic their predictions were when they voted Williams "Funniest" senior and "Most Likely to Succeed." The award-winning actor who started his professional career doing stand-up comedy routines—and who was dubbed by *Entertainment Weekly* as the "Tasmanian devil of comedy"—has become one of Hollywood's finest dramatic actors, versatile enough to play wildly funny and touchingly sincere roles.

Robin Williams was born in Chicago, Illinois, on July 21, 1952, the son of a Ford Motor Company executive. The Williamses were middle-aged when they had their son; both had grown children from previous marriages, so Robin was raised as an only child. The chubby youngster was often the butt of jokes in school as he moved from town to town with his parents. He learned to counter the hurt with a quick, biting sense of humor. He loved comic Jonathan Winters and spent hours memorizing his routines.

When Robin was a teenager, the Williamses moved permanently to Marin County, California, near San Francisco. Being settled gave Robin confidence: By the time he enrolled in Claremont Men's College to study political science, he was doing improvisational comedy in area clubs. Before long he dropped political science and became a serious actor, taking courses at nearby Marin College before heading to New York City. There, he studied at the prestigious Juilliard School and earned money performing as a mime.

After Juilliard, Williams returned to San Francisco and joined the West Coast comedy club circuit as a stand-up comic. His routine was marked by endless banter, celebrity impressions, and unpredictable flights of fancy—with so many subject detours that it was difficult to keep up. He was an instant hit.

Throughout the 1970s Robin scored a string of successes on the stand-up circuit, including one of the most important clubs—the renowned Los Angeles Comedy Store. He earned a spot on a revival of the 1960s TV show *Laugh-In* in 1977 and a guest role as the hilarious space alien Mork on *Happy Days*. The Mork character launched a spin-off sitcom, *Mork and Mindy,* costarring Pam Dawber as an "earthling" and featuring Williams's comic hero, Jonathan Winters, as an alien "colleague." Williams improvised so frequently that the show's producers gave up trying to keep him to the script and instead added deliberate gaps in the action, with the script notation "Mork can go off here."

By the time the program ended in 1982, Williams was one of America's top comics. That year he starred in his own HBO program, *An Evening with Robin Williams.* He had another cable-TV hit with *Robin Williams: Live at the Met* in 1986, and joined Billy Crystal and **Whoopi Goldberg** in the first HBO *Comic Relief* special. The funds gained from these recurring HBO events go toward helping America's homeless.

While working on *Mork and Mindy,* Williams also debuted in a feature film portraying the cartoon character Popeye (1980). Most of his early films, including

The Survivors (1983) and *The Best of Times* (1986), were disappointments, but his successes included *The World According to Garp* (1982) and *Moscow on the Hudson* (1984), which earned a Golden Globe Best Actor nomination. In 1987 he achieved star status with a spectacularly manic performance in *Good Morning, Vietnam.* Director Barry Levinson allowed latitude in scenes where Williams's brazenly sharp-tongued military deejay Adrian Cronauer performed on-air monologues—and Williams obliged. His famously funny ad-libs brought him an Oscar nomination and a Best Actor Golden Globe. Two years later he earned another Best Actor Oscar nomination for his prep-school professor in *Dead Poets Society* (1989).

Robin Williams's personal life, however, was not quite as bright as his career. In the early 1980s he became addicted to cocaine but managed to become drug free by the late 1980s. In 1988 Williams married Marcia Garces. Robin and Marcia have two children, Zelda and Cody, and they share partnership in their company, Blue Wolf Productions.

After his recovery from substance abuse Williams returned to films stronger than ever. In *Awakenings* (1990) he played a doctor treating a catatonic patient (**Robert De Niro**). In 1991 he received a third Best Actor Oscar nomination and a Golden Globe Best Actor Award for *The Fisher King* (1991), costarring Jeff Bridges. In 1992 audiences delightedly watched the fast-talking blue genie of Disney's animated *Aladdin* speak in Williams's voice. In 1993 Williams played a divorced father determined to stay in touch with his children by dressing up as an elderly female housekeeper in the smash hit *Mrs. Doubtfire,* which he coproduced.

In the mid-1990s Williams's career flagged somewhat. *Jumanji* (1995), *To Wong Foo, Thanks for Everything!, Julie Newmar* and *Nine Months* (both 1995), and *Jack* (1996) were box-office disappointments. But he scored a huge hit with *The Birdcage* (1996), a remake of *La Cage Aux Folles.* Williams costarred as a homosexual club owner opposite a riotously over-the-top Nathan Lane.

He earned his first Academy Award in 1997, for Best Supporting Actor in *Good Will Hunting.*

Williams's win brought him top billing in several films during the 1990s, including *What Dreams May Come* (1998), *Patch Adams* (1998), *Jakob the Liar* (1999, also producer), and *Bicentennial Man* (1999). Although the films were popular with audiences, they earned mixed reviews from critics. To fans during this period, it appeared that the actor had abandoned his quick-witted, sarcastic characters for gentle, almost tearfully sentimental roles. But critics who declared that the actor should return to his trademark "edgy" roles got their wish: Williams's startling and deeply disturbed characters in *Death to Smoochy, Insomnia* (costarring **Al Pacino**), and *One-Hour Photo* (all 2002) surprised and delighted viewers.

Williams has made three comedy albums and has appeared in scores of TV comedy specials, including in the HBO Comic Relief benefits. He has participated in such varied projects as *AI: Artificial Intelligence* (2001), in which he was the voice of "Dr. Know"; *America: A Tribute to Heroes* (2001), an all-star program dedicated to the victims of the September 11, 2001, terrorist attacks; and *Chuck Jones: Extremes and In-Betweens, A Life in Animation* (2000), about the famed Warner Brothers cartoon animator. After a twelve-year hiatus Williams made a triumphant return to the stage with his *Robin Williams on Broadway* stand-up show in the summer of 2002.

Whether Williams is onstage, on TV, or in the next box-office hit—whether the performance is comic or serious—fans are certain to see the entertainer's best work. "[Williams] has worked hard to have it both ways: retaining his unique persona while growing and thriving as an actor," says film critic Leonard Maltin. "And, in fact, he has succeeded, securing both critical adulation and audience loyalty in the process."

Jackie Chan

International Martial Arts Film Star
1954–

I don't do special effects. I don't do computers. . . . It's not like Superman, Batman. Everybody can be Superman . . . . But nobody can be . . . Jackie Chan!

—JACKIE CHAN

*I*n the course of his twenty plus years in film, Jackie Chan's body has taken a terrible beating. He's broken several bones in his body, including his jaw, nose, fingers, and one ankle. He calls them hazards of his job—being a stuntman-action hero. His *job* has made him an international star and a multimillionaire. Not bad for a kid who grew up poor, uneducated, and without his parents to love and nurture him.

Twelve-pound baby Jackie Chan was born Chan Kong-sang on April 7, 1954, in Hong Kong, China. His parents, Charles and Lee-lee Chan, worked for the French ambassador to Hong Kong—Charles as a cook and handyman, Lee-lee as the housekeeper. The Chans lived with their only son in a small room in the back of the ambassador's mansion. The mansion was located in a wealthy neighborhood far above crowded downtown Hong Kong.

Jackie was born in the Chinese Year of the Horse—a sign of energy, ambition, and success. As a child, Jackie had plenty of energy but lacked ambition when it came to his education. He hated school and had a disciplinary problem. After several months of this, Jackie's parents placed him in Yu Jim-yuen's China Drama Academy, located in Kowloon, on the southern peninsula of Hong Kong. Jackie was going to be trained to be a performer in the Chinese opera. Charles signed a contract with Yu Jim-yuen, leaving his son's training and care to the academy master.

Jackie spent the next decade of his life at the academy. During that time his parents moved to Australia. Before they left, Charles made Master Yu Jackie's legal guardian. Jackie's parents never knew of the brutality he endured at the academy. His bed consisted of a blanket on the hardwood floor of the practice room where he slept with all the other students. The older boys, called "Big Brothers," often hit, taunted, and terrorized the younger kids. Master Yu was also abusive, inflicting severe punishment for even the most minor infractions. Beatings were commonplace for not executing a perfect backflip maneuver or not standing completely still on one leg for several minutes. Precision and discipline were Master Yu's only concerns.

Despite his harsh environment, Jackie learned his craft well. Soon he was performing in live theater productions. He liked getting away from the academy and enjoyed performing. Besides the opera productions, Jackie also got work as an extra in motion picture films.

By the time Jackie reached his teen years, the Chinese opera mostly attracted older audiences. The younger, more energetic members of Hong Kong's society were being drawn to a more dazzling form of entertainment—action films. This medium was exciting with its choreographed death-defying stunts and martial arts fight scenes. "Brothers" began leaving the academy to work as stuntmen and coordinators for studios like Golden Harvest and the Shaw Brothers.

Golden Harvest had a contract with martial arts star Bruce Lee. Chinese-American Lee brought an energy to action films that no one had seen before. He was quick, and fought against many foes at once, instead of the traditional one-on-one encounters. Though his career was brief (he died at age thirty-three of a cerebral edema), Lee's emergence in Hong Kong cinema forever changed the way action pictures were made.

Jackie left the academy when he turned seventeen, and went to the studio lots looking for work. In those days, the more willing you were to do something dangerous, the more likely you would be hired. Jackie was willing to do just about any kind of stunt needed in a picture. Because of his academy training, Jackie could jump higher, kick harder, and hit faster than many of the other stuntmen. He enjoyed the work but was anxious to be more involved—to coordinate stunts, direct the pictures, and come up with script ideas.

Over the next few years Jackie's career was like a roller coaster. Work was never steady, and the Hong Kong film industry was in turmoil after Bruce Lee's death. Every studio tried to find a new star to replace Lee, but no one could fill his shoes. The industry was struggling, and so was Jackie, until he met the man who would change his life—Willie Chan. He had seen Willie around the studio lots, scouting films for distribution. On a chance meeting at a mutual friend's wedding, Jackie and Willie spoke briefly. Before parting, Jackie gave Willie his business card.

Not long after the wedding, Willie tracked Jackie down to offer him the lead role in a remake of Bruce Lee's blockbuster *Fists of Fury*. Eager to star in his own film, Jackie signed a contract with Lo Wei Productions, a film company owned by millionaire director Lo Wei. The film was a flop, as were the next few pictures. Jackie soon tired of trying to become the "new" Bruce Lee. He had his own style and wanted to bring his originality to the big screen. In his autobiography, *I am Jackie Chan,* Jackie explains, "Bruce was Superman, but I think that audiences want to see someone who's just a man. Like them.

Someone who wins only after making a lot of mistakes, who has a sense of humor."

While on loan to another production company, Seasonal Films, Jackie became a box-office star. He had a lot of creative input in his first project, the 1978 film *Snake in Eagle's Shadow*. To everyone's delight, it was a huge hit. Jackie's second film, *Drunken Master*, surpassed *Snake in Eagle's Shadow*, making Jackie a bona fide celebrity. Soon people were stopping him on the streets asking for his autograph, and he had more money than he had ever dreamed of.

Jackie became one of the biggest stars in Asia and was in great demand. He decided to sign with Golden Harvest because the owners Leonard Ho and Raymond Chow agreed to give Jackie complete creative control over his films. Eventually, Jackie became a star in America too, after the release of the 1994 hit *Rumble in the Bronx*. Two of his biggest hits in America to date are *Rush Hour* and *Rush Hour II*.

Today Jackie has his own production company. With the founding of the JC Group, Jackie has branched out into other businesses, owning real estate and becoming a partner in the restaurant chain Planet Hollywood. He is married and has a teenage son. He rarely sees his family because of all of his traveling and working, but is very protective of their privacy.

Jackie knows he cannot keep making action films forever, though he is still far from retiring. He has thought about moving on to producing, directing, and teaching. Says Jackie, "I'd like to be the Action Man, the guy that the studios hire to train their directors about screen combat and stunt choreography. I'd like to pass on what I know to the next generation of stars and directors." With his sense of humor and his ability to create stunts that defy the laws of gravity and human endurance, audiences worldwide will be the beneficiaries for years to come.

John Travolta

Acclaimed Actor of His Generation
1954–

I never dreamed of playing those kind of parts! I knew I could, but I didn't know they would be in my future. So I don't think you can put the curtain down on yourself.

—JOHN TRAVOLTA, ON THE ROLES HE RECEIVED
AFTER HIS 1994 COMEBACK IN *PULP FICTION*

For many years during the 1980s and early 1990s, it seemed to most Hollywood observers that the star of the wildly successful 1977 hit *Saturday Night Fever* had long since reached the pinnacle of his career. But John Travolta never gave up on himself. He fought his way back to success with a string of smash hits and today is one of the most acclaimed and beloved actors of his generation.

Born on February 18, 1954, in Englewood, New Jersey, John Travolta was the youngest of six children in an entertainment-oriented family. His father, Salvatore, was a former semipro football player and co-owner of a tire shop. His mother, Helen, was a high-school drama teacher and had been a member of a radio singing group called the Sunshine Sisters.

All except one of John's older siblings—Ellen, Sammy, Annie, Joey, and Margaret—eventually went into show business, and John himself joined an actors' group when he was twelve years old. Before long he had roles in community theater plays and dinner theater musicals—and even took tap-dancing lessons from Fred Kelly, the brother of famed Hollywood entertainer Gene Kelly. Impatient to launch his career, John dropped out of school at sixteen and moved to New York City, where he made his professional debut in the off-Broadway play *Rain.* He followed with a minor role in the touring company of *Grease,* and in 1973 he costarred in the Broadway musical *Over Here!* with the famed Andrews Sisters. He had a bit part in the film *The Devil's Rain* before being cast as Vinnie Barbarino in the TV comedy series *Welcome Back, Kotter* in 1975. Travolta's role as a handsome, slow-witted high-school student turned him into an overnight sensation; his new fame also earned him roles in the 1976 movies *The Boy in the Plastic Bubble* (for TV) and *Carrie.* He recorded three pop music albums with minor success and had a hit single, "Let Her In."

Travolta's mother in *The Boy in the Plastic Bubble* was played by actress Diana Hyland. The stage and television actress had earned an Emmy nomination for an Alcoa Premiere drama starring **Robert Redford,** and had made guest appearances on numerous TV series, including *Dr. Kildare* and *Twilight Zone.* Hyland had signed on to play Dick Van Patten's wife in the new series *Eight Is Enough* when she met Travolta; they fell in love during production, despite a seventeen-year age gap. Soon after, however, Hyland was diagnosed with cancer; in March 1977 she died in Travolta's arms.

Travolta was devastated, but he had little private time to grieve. Shortly after Hyland's death his first major movie, *Saturday Night Fever,* was released. The film was a blockbuster. Travolta got his first Academy Award nomination for his portrayal of cocky, white-suited Tony Manero. The character became a late-1970s icon, and the film's sound track fueled a disco craze.

The following year, Travolta costarred in the film version of *Grease,* which was an even bigger box-office success than *Saturday Night Fever.* By now he was making only occasional appearances on *Welcome Back, Kotter,* and he seemed poised for superstardom—but a series of poor film choices ultimately derailed his career. The 1978 movie *Moment by Moment,* costarring Travolta and Lily Tomlin, was a disastrous failure. During the 1980s he turned down plum roles in *American Gigolo* and *An Officer and a Gentleman* (both were snapped up by Richard Gere). The 1980 movie *Urban Cowboy* was a great success, and he earned critical praise for *Blowout* (1981), although audiences were unenthusiastic. Travolta took another misstep by reprising the role of Tony Manero in the 1983 sequel *Staying Alive.* It was a box-office disappointment, as was his next film, *Two of a Kind* (1983). By the time he appeared in the failed *Perfect* in 1985, critics were dismissing him as a has-been.

But the actor refused to give in to doomsayers. In 1989 he costarred with Kirstie Alley in a low-budget comedy called *Look Who's Talking* and ended up with his first smash hit in more than a decade. The movie launched two sequels, *Look Who's Talking Too* (1990) and *Look Who's Talking Now* (1993). But Hollywood pundits pointed to Travolta's two 1991 failures, *Eyes of an Angel* and *Shout,* as proof that the actor's star had once again sunk below the horizon.

John Travolta proved them spectacularly wrong. In 1994 he staged a decisive comeback in the crime film *Pulp Fiction.* Director and screenwriter Quentin Tarantino had written the character of Vincent Vega specifically for Travolta; audiences and critics were stunned and delighted by the unconventional portrayal. Travolta received a second Academy Award nomination, and within two years his fee soared from $140,000 (for *Pulp Fiction*) to $20 million. He remains deeply grateful to Tarantino for giving him a chance to renew his career. Travolta calls the director one of "the best guardian angels that the planet has to offer."

Now among the hottest actors in America, John cemented his position by delivering a long string of hits. He earned a Golden Globe Award for the

1995 movie *Get Shorty*, an adaptation of an Elmore Leonard novel; in 1996 he starred in the action thriller *Broken Arrow*, was the leading man in the touching *Phenomenon*, and played a not-so-angelic angel in *Michael*. In 1997 he costarred with Nicholas Cage in the darkly funny *Face/Off*. In 1998 he was a Bill Clinton–like political candidate in *Primary Colors* and the headstrong real-life lawyer Jan Schlichtmann in *A Civil Action*. He followed these hits with the moderately successful *The General's Daughter* (1999).

Travolta's star lost a bit of luster with the 2000 failure *Battlefield Earth: A Saga of the Year 3000*. Before it was even released, the actor drew criticism for the movie, based on a novel by L. Ron Hubbard, who founded the religious organization Scientology in 1954. Some suggested that because Travolta was a Scientologist (he has been a member since 1972), the film would be nothing more than a propaganda vehicle. Travolta insisted that he made the movie for pure fun: "Fortunately, there [are] a lot of literate people in the world who know the difference between science fiction and philosophy," he said, "and this [movie] clearly separates the two." Travolta returned to top form in 2001 with *Domestic Disturbance* and *Swordfish,* in which he starred opposite **Halle Berry.** The movie *Basic* will be released in 2003.

John married actress Kelly Preston in September 1991; the following year they had a son, Jett, and in 2000 they had a daughter, Ella Bleu. Travolta and Preston named their son after John's love for flying—when not working, he's often piloting his private jet. John also wrote a children's book about aviation, *Propeller One-Way Night Coach: A Fable for All Ages* (1997). In April 2002 Rob Morrow (of TV's *Northern Exposure*) began directing an IMAX film based on the book. The movie, mostly animated, will feature Travolta in live-action scenes and in the narration.

Denzel Washington

Recipient of the 2002 Oscar for Best Actor
1954–

Life has taught me to just try and be the best that I can be, and I thank the Academy for saying to me that on this given night I was the best that I could be.

—DENZEL WASHINGTON,
IN HIS ACCEPTANCE SPEECH FOR THE
2002 BEST ACTOR ACADEMY AWARD

Ironically, the role for which Denzel Washington won his first Oscar for Best Actor was not one of his "trademark" role-model characters. In the 2001 film *Training Day,* he turned in a striking performance as a narcotics detective who is corrupt beyond redemption.

When asked whether it would bother him to receive an Oscar for an evil character, Washington said, "No, that means I did my job. . . . I make the best movie I can every time." That matter-of-fact attitude is the main reason for Washington's long-running success in Hollywood—an attitude that has also earned him the respect of his peers and the acclaim of critics and fans.

Denzel Washington was born on December 28, 1954, in Mount Vernon, New York, the second of three children born to Denzel and Lennis Washington. His father was a Pentecostal minister and his mother, a beautician. From age eleven Denzel earned his own money working part-time at a local barbershop. He hung out at the Mt. Vernon Boys Club, where he played football and basketball. When Denzel was fourteen, his parents separated, and they sent him to boarding school. After graduating from Oakland Academy in 1972, he enrolled in Fordham University; he dropped out briefly but returned the following year and pursued a dual major in drama and journalism.

In 1977, just before he received his bachelor's degree from Fordham, Washington secured his first professional acting role in the TV movie *Wilma*. After graduation he headed for San Francisco, California, where he had been accepted by the prestigious American Conservatory Theater (ACT). Within the year Washington decided that ACT was not a good fit for him, and he returned to New York, where he kept busy in theater productions, including *The Mighty Gents, One Tiger to a Hill,* and *Coriolanus.* He landed another TV movie role in *Flesh and Blood.*

In 1981 he portrayed black activist Malcolm X in *When the Chickens Come Home to Roost.* He won an Obie Award for his striking performance in *A Soldier's Play.* Though his first feature film, *Carbon Copy,* was a box-office disappointment, he began gaining critical notice. He caught the eye of TV producer Bruce Paltrow, and in 1982 he landed his biggest job thus far: the role of Dr. Phillip Chandler on the TV series *St. Elsewhere.* At the time, Washington was more interested in making feature films, but he decided to take the job for the money. *St. Elsewhere* was a critical and popular success, running for six seasons and picking up twelve Emmy Awards.

The steady income Washington earned from *St. Elsewhere* allowed him the freedom to pursue other goals. In 1982 he married Pauletta Pearson, whom he had been seeing since they met on the set of *Wilma.* In 1984 he starred in the feature film version of *A Soldier's Story.* Denzel and Pauletta's first child, a son named John David, was born in 1985.

By 1986 Denzel Washington was a familiar name in Hollywood. Director Richard Attenborough saw Washington's performance in *A Soldier's Story* and cast him as murdered South African activist Steven Biko in *Cry Freedom.* Washington's portrayal brought him an Oscar nomination for Best Supporting Actor.

In 1988 the Washingtons had another child, Katia. When the *St. Elsewhere* job ended, he took on three roles, including that of a black Civil War infantry-man in the movie *Glory.* Washington won Academy and Golden Globe Awards for Best Supporting Actor for his emotional performance.

Washington's newfound fame prompted Hollywood's leading African-American director, **Spike Lee,** to cast Washington in the role of jazz trumpeter Bleek Gillam in *Mo' Better Blues* (1990). The same year it premiered, the actor formed Mundy Lane production company. In 1991 Pauletta gave birth to twins, whom the couple named Olivia and Malcolm.

Washington was acclaimed in his next two films, 1992's *Mississippi Masala* and *Malcolm X.* He received Best Actor Academy Award and Golden Globe nominations; an MTV Movie Award for Best Actor *(Malcolm X);* Chicago, Boston, and New York Film Critics Best Actor Awards *(Malcolm X);* and an NAACP Image Award for Best Actor *(Mississippi Masala).*

In 1993 he costarred with **Julia Roberts** in *The Pelican Brief* and with **Tom Hanks** in *Philadelphia;* he got high praise for both performances. "It's doubtful whether there's a smarter leading man working today," raved *Entertainment Weekly* of his nuanced performances. "The actor shuts the doors of his face and gets us wondering how he'll react."

Washington was now earning about $8 million per film and had the power to create his own schedule and maintain control over his work. In 1995 he coproduced and starred in *Devil in a Blue Dress* and turned in a powerful performance as Lieutenant Commander Ron Hunter in *Crimson Tide*. Washington won an NAACP Best Actor Award for his role.

Washington's salary soared to $10 million when he played Lieutenant Commander Nathaniel Serling in *Courage Under Fire* (1996), costarring Meg Ryan and Lou Diamond Phillips. It was the highest salary ever paid to an African American in a dramatic role. Despite rumors of an Academy Award nomination for his portrayal, Washington was not tapped. But he was unfazed. "My concern is raising the standard of work, not complaining about someone not voting for me."

Washington took on an entirely different role in the 1996 film *The Preacher's Wife* (a remake of 1947's *The Bishop's Wife*): he is an angel sent to earth to help a preacher and his wife (played by Whitney Houston) build a church but gets involved with their lives. In 1998 he starred in three hit films, *Fallen, He Got Game,* and the controversial *The Siege*. The peak of his achievements that year was planting his handprints in the cement at Grauman's Chinese Theatre.

Washington's colleagues admire him for the exacting way he prepares for roles. His investigative approach worked well in his 1999 role as a quadriplegic examiner in *The Bone Collector*. He followed that performance with his starring role in *The Hurricane,* the real-life story of Rubin "Hurricane" Carter, a boxer wrongly imprisoned for murder. The portrayal brought a Golden Globe Best Actor Award and an NAACP Image Award.

Following the release of *Training Day* (2001), Washington starred in the 2002 film *John Q,* playing the title role of the distraught father of a desperately ill boy whose insurance company will not allow him to receive proper medical care. The film grossed nearly $24 million in its opening weekend and earned Washington the first Actor of the Year Award ever granted by the American Film Institute.

Washington's first effort at film directing, *The Antwone Fisher Story,* was released in 2002. The movie is based on the autobiography *Finding Fish*. The book "reads like a great work of fiction," says Denzel. "[His] journey is truly a triumph of the spirit, the story of a boy . . . who goes on to remarkable success beyond most of our dreams."

Denzel Washington tries to remain grounded about his own achievements. "I try to be ego-less, if there is such a thing," he says. "I try to stay humble and hungry . . . just hungry [enough] to be good at my job. A little hunger is good for you."

Can Oscar Become Color-Blind?

*O*n the evening of March 24, 2002, the Academy of Motion Picture Arts and Sciences held its annual Oscar gala event. Every Oscar show has had its share of excitement since the Academy began handing out the golden statuettes in 1928, but the seventy-fourth annual awards had a particularly heightened anticipation about it.

It was a night when former Oscar winner **Sidney Poitier** told the audience how different Hollywood is now than it was on the night he won his Oscar in 1964. He had the distinction of being the only black to win an Oscar in the Best Actor/Actress categories. The 2002 Oscars had three black nominees— **Halle Berry, Denzel Washington**, and **Will Smith.** Poitier spoke after being honored with a special Oscar for his contributions to the film industry; it was fitting that Washington and Berry would join him in making history by winning their own Oscars.

The five-time Oscar-nominated Washington (who already had a Best Supporting Oscar for his role in *Glory*) became the second black actor to win

Denzel Washington and Halle Berry celebrate upon receiving their Oscars.

the golden statuette in a lead role. Halle Berry's Oscar was the first-ever won by a black actress in a lead role. Many felt it was a long time in coming. To understand just how enormous their wins were, you have to take a look back through the award's history.

Only one other time in the Academy's history have three black performers been nominated in the lead-acting categories. It happened in 1973, when Diana Ross was nominated for her performance in *Lady Sings the Blues*, and Cicely Tyson and Paul Winfield won their nominations for their roles in *Sounder*. None won that night.

One reason for such limited nominations is that statistics are against minority performers to begin with. Only 9 percent of the 5,700 members of the Academy of Motion Picture Arts and Sciences are black. With such a small representation of the total acting body, there are fewer blacks working in feature films than whites.

In all, blacks have earned a total of thirty-four Oscar nominations. It all began with **Hattie McDaniel,** the take-charge mammy in *Gone With the Wind.* She was the first black ever nominated for an Academy Award, and the first black to win one, though it was in a supporting role.

For most blacks working in the film industry, acting meant playing menial roles. The racial attitudes about blacks in the early days of the film business were not that much different from those felt by most of white America around the country. Racial prejudice and discrimination, particularly in the South, raged on. Public facilities like water fountains and rest rooms were segregated; blacks were prohibited from dining in certain restaurants and from staying in certain hotels. Many jobs available for blacks were entry-level or unskilled labor positions such as dishwasher, house servant, janitor, maid, farmworker, and so forth.

The Hollywood film industry was dominated and run by whites. Whites filled most of the jobs involved with making films, such as studio bosses, writers, directors, and casting agents. Lead roles were written for whites; the only roles for blacks were subservient character or bit parts. It was not surprising that the first Oscar was awarded for that type of role. It *was* surprising to many that Hattie McDaniel won over such other nominees as Olivia de Havilland, Edna May Oliver, and Geraldine Fitzgerald. It was ten years before a black actor would receive another Academy Award nomination. Except for a special Oscar given to James Baskett in 1948 for his part as Uncle Remus in Disney's *Song of the South,* it was twenty-four years before another black actor was awarded an Oscar.

In the 1950s only three black actors were nominated for Oscars. In 1950 Ethel Waters received a Best Supporting Actress nomination for her role in *Pinky;* in 1955 Dorothy Dandridge became the first black to receive a Best Actress nomination for *Carmen Jones.* Young black star Sidney Poitier earned the first Best Actor nomination in 1959 for *The Defiant Ones.* It took him another five years to win one—in 1964, for his brilliant performance in *Lilies of the Field.*

The 1970s were not much better. Besides the trio nominations of 1973, only James Earl Jones and Diahann Carroll received nominations. The 1980s, however, proved to be much more promising for black actors in Hollywood. A great many talented blacks were beginning to get more opportunities in feature films. Blacks got nine Academy Award nominations, and Louis Gossett Jr. won the first Best Supporting Actor Oscar for his role in the 1983 movie *An Officer and a Gentleman.*

In the 1990s two 2-time nominees, **Whoopi Goldberg** and Denzel Washington, hit gold, each winning Best Supporting Oscars. Until the 2002 Academy Awards, only one more Oscar statuette was awarded to blacks—Cuba Gooding Jr. won a Supporting Oscar in 1997 for his role in *Jerry Maguire.* Since 1929, of the 278 acting Oscars awarded, only 6 were awarded to black performers before the 2002 Academy Awards.

Other black actors began to get recognition for their work, including Morgan Freeman, Laurence Fishburn, and Angela Bassett. Freeman has received two Oscar nominations—for *Driving Miss Daisy* and *The Shawshank Redemption.* Fishburn and Bassett earned Best Actor and Actress nominations in 1993 for their portrayals of Ike and Tina Turner in *What's Love Got to Do with It.*

It is not just in front of the cameras where blacks seem to be gaining little recognition. Black directors have not fared well either. Only one, John Singleton, has received a best director nomination, while **Spike Lee,** who's made such well-known films as *Do the Right Thing* and *Malcolm X,* has yet to receive a director's nomination.

There are many factors involved in winning an Academy Award, and race may not be as large an issue as some have claimed. Morgan Freeman, arguably one of the finest actors in the industry today, could easily have won an Oscar for his role in *Driving Miss Daisy.* But to say so means that winner Daniel Day-Lewis shouldn't have won for *My Left Foot.* Freeman turned in a brilliant performance as a convict in *The Shawshank Redemption.* But to say he should have won means that winner **Tom Hanks** shouldn't have won for his performance in *Forrest Gump.* How then do you choose?

With Berry's and Washington's wins in the top Oscar category in 2002, many are hopeful that Hollywood is finally getting in step with the cultural diversity in America. After becoming the first "woman of color" to win the Best Actress Oscar, Berry said, "I don't really know how it will transform the industry, but . . . it [may] instill hope in other people of color." In an article that appeared in the *Chicago Daily Herald* on Oscar night 2002, reporter Teresa Mask spoke to seventeen-year-old black performing arts student Delma White about her professional hopes and expectations. White told her, "I hope I will have a certain charisma that allows people to look past the color of my skin and look through to my talent."

Whoopi Goldberg

Multi-Award-Winning Actress and Humanitarian
1955–

I was raised to believe that I could become part of the fabric of this country no matter what it was I wanted to do.

—Whoopi Goldberg

Like most Americans, Whoopi Goldberg was deeply shaken by the terrorist attacks of September 11, 2001. And like most comics, Goldberg wasn't sure anymore whether there was a place for comedy in America.

Barely a month after the attacks, however, Goldberg appeared in Washington, D.C., to receive the Kennedy Center's Mark Twain Prize for American Humor. Comedians Chris Rock, Alan King, Wanda Sykes, **Robin Williams,** and Billy Crystal shared stories and "roasted" Goldberg before an appreciative audience. At the end of the evening, Goldberg addressed the audience:

> This evening almost didn't happen. I was not sure this was appropriate after September 11. . . . [But] I realized that on behalf of all those folks I spent time with in New York, these things *are* important. We must pick ourselves up by our bootstrings and laugh. . . . I'm not

embarrassed now—I feel like a firefighter or a policeman. As an American, that's what I have to offer: Dirty jokes and bad language.

Whoopi Goldberg was born Caryn Johnson in New York City on November 13, 1955. She lived in the Eliot-Chelsea housing projects with her mother, Emma, and older brother, Clyde (Whoopi's father, Robert, abandoned the family when Caryn was an infant). The Johnsons were poor, but Whoopi always felt a strong sense of security.

Whoopi remembers being enchanted by traveling acting troupes, who drove into town and set up stages on the street. "The truck would open and magic things would be coming out of it. . . . It was like the circus coming to town, and on those nights our little neighborhood was the center of the . . . universe." At eight she joined the Helena Rubenstein Children's Theater.

In school, however, Whoopi's teachers labeled her a "slow learner." It turned out that she suffered from dyslexia, a learning disability in which a person perceives letters, numbers, and words in reverse or out of order. Feeling awkward and out of place, Whoopi dropped out of school in ninth grade. The youngster had also begun trying drugs. Realizing she needed to get her life together, Whoopi checked herself into a rehabilitation program. Today, she avidly campaigns against drug use. She knows from firsthand experience that drugs are deadly to one's health and well-being.

After rehab, Whoopi started going on auditions and took bit parts in off-Broadway plays. She married and had a girl, Alexandra, born in May 1974. Although her marriage failed, Whoopi continued to focus on her goal of becoming a performer. In 1975 she settled in San Diego with Alexandra. With a limited education she had difficulty finding work, but she landed several odd jobs and earned a beautician's license. She got a job doing hair and makeup for corpses at a funeral home.

At times Whoopi was forced to go on welfare, but she never let it defeat her. She joined the San Diego Repertory Theater and worked with Spontaneous Combustion, an improvisational group. She created her stage name and began to hone her stand-up skills. In 1980 she moved to Berkeley and took up with the Blake Street Hawkeyes acting troupe. Whoopi developed a one-woman act called *The Spook Show,* earning rave reviews for her remarkable ability to "inhabit" the various characters she had created. (Among the most memorable was Fontaine, a bigmouthed recovering addict.) Director Mike Nichols saw her show, and in 1984 he took the revised program to Broadway, where Goldberg won the Drama Desk and Theater World Awards.

Goldberg's film breakthrough came when **Steven Spielberg** cast her in *The Color Purple.* Her moving portrayal of Celie brought her a 1985 Academy Award nomination. The following year she starred in the action-comedy *Jumpin' Jack Flash* and began her long-term association with **Robin Williams** and Billy Crystal, raising money for the homeless in the HBO special *Comic Relief.* Six more broadcasts followed, raising more than $35 million in all.

Goldberg accepted a recurring role as wise bartender Guinan on the television series *Star Trek: The Next Generation.* She also appeared as a Jamaican nanny in the film *Clara's Heart* (1988). In 1990 she costarred in the TV series *Bagdad Café* with Jean Stapleton and appeared with Sissy Spacek in *The Long Walk Home.* But not until the 1990 hit *Ghost* did she earn industry acclaim. As psychic con artist Oda Mae Brown, Goldberg won the Best Supporting Actress Oscar—only the second black actress in history to do so.

After that, it seemed Whoopi Goldberg was everywhere. She wrote a children's book, *Alice;* produced two comedy specials, *Tales From the Whoop: Hot Rod Brown, Class Clown,* and *Whoopi Goldberg: Chez Whoopi* (both 1991); starred in the smash hit *Sister Act* (1992); launched her own company, One Ho Productions; and hosted a late-night syndicated talk show. In 1992 she became the first female host of the Grammy Awards and appeared in a benefit concert with Gloria Estefan to raise funds for the victims of Hurricane Andrew. She also won her first Emmy Award, for her role in *Star Trek: The Next Generation.*

Goldberg turned in solid performances in *Corrina, Corrina* (1994), *Boys on the Side* and *Moonlight and Valentino* (both 1995), and *Ghosts of Mississippi* (1996). In 1994 she became the first black and the first woman to emcee the Academy Awards show. She was invited to host the show again in 1996, 1998, and 2002. In 1997 Goldberg returned to Broadway, replacing Nathan Lane in *A Funny Thing Happened on the Way to the Forum,* and published *Book,* a quirky record of her personal spin on a variety of subjects. She appeared in two novel-to-film projects, *How Stella Got Her Groove Back* (1998) and *The Deep End of the Ocean* (1999).

In 1998 Goldberg resurrected *Hollywood Squares* (she occupied "center square") that her company coproduced with Moffitt-Lee. *Strong Medicine,* a series no one initially wanted, enjoys high ratings on Lifetime. One Ho also produces features—including the TV movie *Call Me Claus,* in which Goldberg also starred—for Turner Network Television. The movie was rated the second-highest cable movie of 2001. Upcoming projects include *The Mao Game* and *The Piano Man's Daughter.* Goldberg's company is also coproducing the well-received Broadway show *Thoroughly Modern Millie* in 2002.

Caryn Johnson has come a long way from her troubled youth. She has received several NAACP Image Awards, in addition to a Grammy, an Oscar, an Emmy, and Golden Globes. In 1997 she shared the Governor's Award from the Academy of Television Arts and Sciences with Billy Crystal and Robin Williams. In 1995 imprints of her hands, feet, and trademark braids were added to Grauman's Chinese Theatre. She recently earned a star on the Hollywood Walk of Fame.

Goldberg works tirelessly on behalf of children, the homeless, AIDS victims, and substance abuse victims. In a town that likes to pigeonhole people, the versatile star is impossible to classify. That's the way she likes it. "My philosophy: Do what you can do, get as much done as you can."

Bruce Willis

Regular Guy Turned Actor
1955–

I do my work as an actor. I enjoy trying to entertain people. It's a good job, now more than ever.

—Bruce Willis

Bursting across the screen, tough cop Bruce Willis fires a gun at a bunch of bad guys in the action film *Die Hard*. He's the same actor who plays a sensitive child psychologist trying to help a young boy who sees dead people in the haunting thriller *The Sixth Sense*. The characters Willis has portrayed demonstrate his versatility as an actor. It is all the more remarkable because Willis had a terrible stutter until he discovered the magic of being onstage.

The man who would grow up to be a mega–film star was born Walter Bruce Willis on March 19, 1955. His parents, David and Marlene, met while his father was stationed in Germany. They later married, and Walter was born in Idar-Oberstein, West Germany. When Walter was two, David moved the family back to the States to his hometown of Carney's Point, New Jersey.

As a youth, Walter spent his free time knocking around with his friends. The guys were typical of the blue-collar environment—loud, tough, tight-knit, and brash. Unfortunately, life at home was not pleasant; Walter's parents were having marital problems, and it affected Walter and his younger siblings, Florence, Robert, and David. The difficulties at home may have contributed to Walter's developing a stutter. He was rather shy until he hit his teen years. Then Walter made some changes. He dropped his first name and just went by Bruce. To get beyond his stuttering, he became the class clown and resident practical joker at Penns Grove High School. He also participated in some school stage productions.

When Bruce was sixteen, his parents divorced. After finishing high school, Bruce had no real direction for his life. He bounced from one job to another, teaching himself how to play the harmonica along the way. Soon he was tending bar at the local clubs, playing music with some bands, and hanging out with his friends.

Bruce might have continued his aimlessness if he hadn't run into his former high-school Latin teacher, Grace Dilks. She had seen him in some of the school's productions and thought that despite his speech problem he had great potential as an actor. Dilks convinced Bruce to enroll at Montclair State College, which was known to have a very good performing arts program. After only eighteen months of schooling, the ever-impatient Willis felt he was ready to begin looking for professional work.

Willis headed off to New York City. When not auditioning, he worked at Café Central, where he tended bar and mingled with the clientele. Café Central attracted a mix of celebrities and wannabes in the music and acting fields, the perfect place for Willis to make friends and connections in the entertainment industry.

During this time Willis began dating Sheri Rivera, an aspiring writer. Sheri asked an actor's agent to come to see Willis in Sam Shepard's play *Fool for Love*. The agent was so impressed by Willis's performance that he signed him as a client. That summer Willis decided to take a trip to Los Angeles (L.A.) to attend the 1984 Olympics. Willis figured while he was out there he could check out some acting opportunities. The trip changed his life.

While in L.A., Willis auditioned for a starring role in a new ABC series titled *Moonlighting*. More than 3,000 men in a dozen cities had auditioned for the role of cocky, suave private investigator David Addison. It didn't take long for writer-producer Glenn Gordon Caron to realize Willis was exactly the actor he was looking for.

Moonlighting debuted in the fall of 1985 and took off like a rocket. The edgy love-hate chemistry between Willis and costar Cybil Shepherd's characters and Willis's unusual direct discussions with the audience made the show a hit. In the show's third season Willis earned both a Best Actor Golden Globe and a Best Actor Emmy Award.

When *Moonlighting* was canceled in 1990, Willis fell back into his old partying ways. Despite his wild reputation or perhaps because of it, Willis was a much-sought-after actor. In 1987 he had starred opposite Kim Basinger in *Blind Date,* followed by a funky western called *Sunset* (1988). It was Willis's next film that made him a film star. Cast as New York City police detective John McClane in the action thriller *Die Hard* (1988), Willis was paid a phenomenal $5 million dollars. There were a few conditions, however. He had to agree to stop the wild partying while working on the film and start attending Alcoholics Anonymous meetings.

There was also a new woman in Willis's life—Demi Moore. Moore had already gone through her wild partying days, and became an anchor for Willis, helping him through his own recovery. After dating for just three months, the couple married in November 1987. A lot had happened to Willis in the last half of the 1980s.

Willis and Moore became one of Hollywood's "power couples." With other "star" partners, Willis and Moore opened a chain of Planet Hollywood restaurants. In order to raise their kids away from the limelight, Willis and

Moore bought a home in Hailey, Idaho. Their first child, Rumer Glenn, was born on August 16, 1988. Two sisters soon followed—Scout Larue on July 20, 1991, and Tallulah Belle on February 3, 1994. Fatherhood means everything to Willis, and he is determined to instill in his own children the love and intimacy that was absent in his own childhood.

During the 1990s Willis and Moore continued to pursue their film careers. Willis reprised his McClane role in *Die Hard 2: Die Harder* and *Die Hard 3: Die Hard with a Vengeance.* Not wanting to fall into the typecast action-hero role, Willis took on different types of parts. He was the voice of baby Mikey in *Look Who's Talking;* the nerdy doctor in the black comedy *Death Becomes Her;* a prisoner sent back in time to discover the cause of a deadly virus in *12 Monkeys;* and a corrupt boxer in *Pulp Fiction.*

As he had at the end of the 1980s, Willis found himself riding another career crest when he starred in the 1999 drama-mystery *The Sixth Sense.* One critic called his performance "a triumph of subtlety." Once again Willis demonstrated his willingness to take on a different type of role to prove his versatility as an actor. He has shown through his body of work that he can do comedy, play the action hero, and be a serious dramatic actor too.

At age forty-seven Willis shows no signs of losing his box-office appeal. He welcomed in the new millennium with three more film hits, *Unbreakable, Bandits,* and *Hart's War.* He also won his second Emmy for his guest role in the TV comedy hit *Friends.* Though Willis's career is steady, his personal life has had some downs. In the summer of 1998 Willis and Moore decided to divorce. Nevertheless, Willis has remained close with Moore and his daughters, and they go out as a family as often as possible.

Willis appears finally to have it all together—as an actor, a father, and a grown man. In his own assessment Willis says, "I'm really just a regular guy who has had an incredibly blessed life. Everyday I work at not taking this fame thing seriously."

Tom Hanks

Versatile Actor and Director
1956–

[Movie] characters remind us that we're part of a greater humanity, and that we can actually affect the world by the choices we make once we leave the theater.

—TOM HANKS

Tom Hanks is one of the most talented and likable personalities in Hollywood. A devoted husband and father and a dedicated actor, he has a reputation for taking on challenging parts, those that one director calls "the most self-less role[s]." Indeed, Hanks considers himself fortunate to be an actor.

Thomas J. Hanks was born in Concord, California, on July 9, 1956, to Amos and Janet Hanks. A former navy machinist, Amos was a cook who met Janet when she was a waitress. Their first child, Sandra, was born in 1951; Lawrence (1953), Tom, and James (1961) followed. But by 1961 the Hanks's marriage had dissolved. Janet took James to Oakland; Amos chased jobs in Nevada and California with the older children. Life grew more bewildering when Amos remarried twice. "By the time I was ten I had had three mothers, five grammar schools, and ten houses," Tom recalls.

Tom settled into each new situation determined to find new friends. He became the class clown in every school. In Oakland he developed an interest in the U.S. space program. He used a length of garden hose as a breathing tube and weighted himself down in a swimming pool to see what being an Apollo astronaut was like.

In high school Hanks developed another passion: acting. No one dreamed when he earned the school "Oscar" for his performance in *South Pacific* that he would be accepting the real thing twenty years later. Hanks studied theater at a community college in Hayward, California, where he met Vincent Dowling, who was recruiting actors for the Great Lakes Shakespeare Festival.

In 1978 Hanks turned in an award-winning performance in the Cleveland production of *Two Gentlemen of Verona.* Bolstered by success, he headed for New York City with fellow actress Samantha Lewes, whom he'd met in college. Their son, Colin, was born shortly after they arrived. Hanks was the lead in Riverside Shakespeare Theater's *The Mandrake* (1979) and snagged a film role in *He Knows You're Alone* (1980) before winning ABC's Talent Development Program award. The prize was a $50,000 TV contract. Hanks played opposite Peter Scolari in *Bosom Buddies,* a sitcom about aspiring admen who dress in drag to get housing in a women's residence hall.

After *Bosom Buddies* was canceled in 1982, Tom made numerous TV guest appearances. On the set of *Happy Days* he met Ron Howard, who cast him opposite Daryl Hannah in *Splash* (1983). The movie positioned Hanks to become a major star. In the next two years he starred in five movies, including *The Money Pit* and *Nothing in Common.* Audiences and critics were charmed by the affable young actor.

Tom and Samantha had a second child, Elizabeth, in 1982, but they parted ways a few years later. Hanks next filmed *Volunteers,* costarring with Rita Wilson. The two hit it off and began dating; in April 1988 they were married.

Hanks's next two films, *Dragnet* and *Punchline,* did not do well. But his inspired performance in the 1988 movie *Big*—about a boy who wants to be an adult and wakes up the next morning to find out that his wish has come true—earned him a Best Actor Golden Globe and a Best Actor Oscar nomination. Although the next few projects, including *Turner & Hooch* (1989) and *Joe Versus the Volcano* (1990), were moderate successes, the badly miscast *Bonfire of the Vanities* (1990) was a massive failure. Deeply disappointed, Hanks took time off for his family (he and Rita had a son, Chester, in 1990).

In 1992 Hanks took on the role of a drunken ex-baseball star in Penny Marshall's *A League of Their Own.* To look the part of the cantankerous Jimmy Dugan, Hanks gained twenty pounds. He didn't want to confuse this part with the amiable leading man he usually played. "[I]t opened up a lot of avenues for me," he said of the character. *League* was a huge success, bringing in more than $100 million.

After costarring with Meg Ryan in *Sleepless in Seattle* (1993), Hanks accepted a vastly different project: gay attorney and AIDS sufferer Andrew Beckett in *Philadelphia.* It was the first big-budget film to feature a homosexual character in a lead role and the first to tackle the devastating impact of AIDS. Hanks's sensitive and powerful performance won an Oscar for Best Actor. In an emotional acceptance speech he spoke eloquently about the millions who had died of AIDS complications. "[T]he streets of heaven are too crowded with angels," he said. "They number a thousand for each of the red ribbons we wear here tonight. They finally rest in the warm embrace of the gracious creator of us all."

In 1994 Hanks transformed himself into the slow-witted title character of *Forrest Gump* and delivered another blockbuster performance. *Gump* became the fifth-highest-grossing film ever. Hanks himself became only the second actor to earn back-to-back Best Actor Oscars. As astronaut Jim Lovell in *Apollo 13* (1995), costarring Kevin Bacon and Bill Paxton, Hanks delighted in portraying a real-life American hero, an opportunity he saw as "every little boy's dream come true." The movie got a handful of Academy Award nominations and two Oscars. He next charmed audiences with the voice-over for Woody the Cowboy in the enormously popular computer-animated *Toy Story*. Hanks has described this project as one of his most difficult.

Tom worked the other side of the camera in 1996, directing and cowriting *That Thing You Do!* He took time off to be with his family—especially son Truman, born in 1995. Hanks then teamed up with Ron Howard again to direct and write the extraordinary twelve-part documentary TV miniseries *From the Earth to the Moon* (1998).

Hanks astounded fans as part of an ensemble cast in *Saving Private Ryan* (1998). The opening scene—a harrowing reenactment of Allied troops landing in Normandy on D-Day—has been hailed as the most realistic war scene in film history. Like the film's directors and producers, Hanks aimed to show "not the balletic play-violence of an action picture, but the terrible impact of real bullets." He wanted to honor the sacrifices of his parents' generation. The film sent audiences out of theaters weeping—and received five Academy Awards. Hanks and director Spielberg donated $500,000 to build a D-Day museum in New Orleans. Hanks received the U.S. Navy's Distinguished Public Service Award—the service's highest civilian honor—for his work.

Hanks rejoined Meg Ryan in *You've Got Mail* (1998), starred in *The Green Mile* (1999), and reprised the voice of Woody in *Toy Story 2* (1999). He joined Spielberg again for the HBO miniseries *Band of Brothers* (2001). In 2002 he departed once more from his traditional "good guy" persona as a gangster in *Road to Perdition*.

Despite enormous success, Tom Hanks remains by all accounts a "regular guy." His outlook stems from the belief that he is just doing his job, albeit with great enthusiasm. "[T]he only thing that really exists is the connection the audience has with a movie," he has said. "No actor has control of that. All you can control is your own passion for doing the work in the first place."

Spike Lee

Influential African American Director
1957–

What's the difference between Holly-wood characters and my characters? Mine are real.

—Spike Lee

"I have a big problem with Norman Jewison directing *The Autobiography of Malcolm X*. That disturbs me deeply. It's wrong with a capital W. Blacks have to control these films. Malcolm X is one of our most treasured heroes. To let a non–African-American do it is a travesty." This is what Spike Lee told the *New York Times* when Warner Brothers announced its plans for the retelling of the life of the famous civil rights leader. Lee's remarks sparked attention and controversy once again. He was bold and direct, not only with his words but with his approach. For in typical Spike Lee fashion, when he heard about the plans for Jewison to direct the film, he didn't approach Warner Brothers with his pitch that the directing job should go to him instead; he went directly to the media with a statement that he knew would be not just heard but echoed and reechoed as others responded. In the 1980s he had become the most recognized black American filmmaker, intent on portraying the true grit of the African American experience—whether by taking on tough, controversial topics in his films or with his own tongue when speaking to the media.

Born on March 20, 1957, in Atlanta, Georgia, as Shelton Jackson Lee, the future filmmaker was nicknamed "Spike" by his mother, Jacquelyn, because of his toughness. His father, Bill Lee, was a jazz musician; later he would write the scores for many of his son's movies. The family moved to Brooklyn, New York, in 1959. When it came time for college, Lee chose Morehouse College, the black school that his grandfather and father had both attended, majoring in communications. This was followed by graduate work in film at New York University.

Lee graduated from NYU in 1982. At the same time that he was employed at cleaning and shipping film for a movie distribution house in 1984, he was scavenging for money for his own first film after graduation. Determined, Lee worked with others on preproduction for the film but finally stopped the project due to lack of sufficient funds, even though more than $100,000 had been raised.

Lee's next venture began a year later with a severely restricted budget of $175,000 that put him in excessive debt. He wrote, produced, directed, edited, and costarred in his film *She's Gotta Have It*. It was a black-and-white work that was filmed in just one location with a small cast and edited in Lee's apartment on rented equipment. Island Pictures agreed to distribute it, and the film drew large crowds of blacks as well as unanticipated art-house groupies, grossing more than $7 million. An easy comedy, it confronted stereotypical male/female relationships and machismo. The film also brought Lee an array of fans for his role as the comic figure Mars Blackmon, who would later appear in Nike television commercials but never again in a movie. As for the critics, they responded nearly equally with both sharp critiques and hardy applause. Yet despite the naysayers, the film prompted the birth of more realistic filmmaking by and about blacks, which came to be termed "New Jack Cinema."

By 1988 Lee's *School Daze* was released, a musical comedy that confronted what Lee called the black caste system: Within the black community itself people are discriminated against based on the lightness or darkness of their skin as well as other physical attributes. Island Pictures pulled out of the project, but within two days, Lee negotiated a deal with Columbia Pictures. Again, the film did well at the box office, but it provoked quite a stir within the black community.

Lee next confronted racism in *Do the Right Thing* (1989). This was the beginning of a new relationship between Lee and Universal Pictures, which grossed more than $30 million from the film. The work was highly praised by many critics, although some feared that it would incite violence due to its ending's seeming ambiguity. It was awarded the Los Angeles Film Critics Awards for picture, director, and screenplay and was nominated for the Academy Award for Best Screenplay.

Lee's next work, *Mo' Better Blues* (1990), focused on relationships and the obsessiveness of a black jazz artist. While the film starred **Denzel Washington**, it drew only a moderate number of moviegoers, lukewarm reviews, and criticism for its shallow female roles and some stereotyped characters. Shortly following in 1991 was Lee's *Jungle Fever,* which focused on an interracial relationship. It fared well at the box office and inspired mixed reviews.

Lee's most sweeping undertaking so far has been his epic *Malcolm X,* also starring Denzel Washington. Once Lee was given the job of directing it, some African Americans responded negatively, claiming that Lee was more concerned with fattening his own wallet than adequately portraying the complicated Malcolm X. Aside from this problem, Lee had to contend with what he saw as a severely inadequate budget from Warner Brothers. Lee had asked them for $40 million, and when he was offered only $20 million, he set about gathering the money from other sources, some of which were famous black celebrities such as Oprah Winfrey, Bill Cosby, and Michael Jordan. Extensive publicity created what was called Malcolm-mania and a good draw at the box office when the film was released in 1992, but not much critical acclaim.

After the Academy Awards of 1993, Lee bowed out of public view, granting no interviews. In October he married Tanya Lynette Lewis, a lawyer from Washington, D.C.

Contrasting the expansiveness of *Malcolm X* were Lee's next undertakings. *Crooklyn,* released in 1994, was cowritten by Lee's siblings and was a comedy focusing on their childhood memories of Brooklyn. It was personal rather than political, revealing more dimension to the radical filmmaker, yet receiving a mixed response from reviewers and only a mediocre showing by filmgoers. Lee's first child, a daughter named Satchel after the baseball player Satchel Paige, was born in 1994. His next film, *Clockers,* was released in 1995 and received notable acclaim. Some critics cited it as Lee's best work, although it appealed to only small audiences. *Get on the Bus* (1996), *Girl 6* (1996), and *4 Little Girls* (1997) followed, with *4 Little Girls* receiving an Academy Award nomination for best documentary.

Lee remained in the public eye from other ventures as well. He opened a store, Spike's Joint, in Brooklyn in the late 1980s; it sells items that promote his movies, with some of them being available as much as a year ahead of a film's release. He also directed music videos for artists such as Tracy Chapman and Public Enemy and established a music division of his film production company. In 1997 his son, Jackson, was born. In 1998 he released *He Got Game* with Disney's Touchstone Pictures. It was his first film to open in the number-one position in the box-office rankings. Starring Denzel Washington once again, it received kudos from the critics. Still with much energy to spare, Lee wrote, produced, directed, and starred in *Summer of Sam* (1999) and soon after directed *The Original Kings of Comedy* (2000). He teaches at both New York University and Harvard.

Tom Cruise

Acclaimed Modern-Day Actor
1962–

I feel very fortunate . . . to be able to do what I love and love what I do. It's been a great journey for me, and I never take it for granted.

—TOM CRUISE, ON HIS FILM CAREER

*L*ike most others, Tom Cruise was stunned and saddened by the terrorist attacks on the United States on September 11, 2001. "There really are no words," he told an interviewer a few weeks later. He praised the people of New York and Washington who had found a way to keep going despite fear and uncertainty. "I've been telling people, '[do] random acts of kindness.' . . . Be there for each other. Reach out. We'll get through this."

That strength and determination are typical of the actor, who that year confronted constant questions about his divorce from Nicole Kidman. He had developed his positive attitude during a childhood in which he struggled with an undiagnosed learning disorder and was constantly the new kid on the block.

Thomas Cruise Mapother IV was born on July 3, 1962, in Syracuse, New York, to Thomas Mapother III, an electrical engineer, and Mary Lee Pfeiffer

Mapother, a teacher. Tom had two older sisters, Lee Anne and Marian, and a younger sister, Cass. Tom's father spent little time with his family. His job with General Electric required him to move every eighteen months or so. When young Tom started school, the Mapothers lived in Ottawa, Canada. He struggled to make friends and was frustrated with his schoolwork.

Tom suffered from a learning disorder called dyslexia, in which a person sees a printed word as a jumble of letters or sees the letters reversed. Scientists believe dyslexia is caused by a combination of neurological, physiological, and genetic factors. Tom Cruise seems to have inherited dyslexia: his mother and sisters also have it.

In 1974 Tom Mapother left his family, and Mary Lee moved with her children to Louisville, Kentucky. She received no child support, so she was forced to work three jobs. Cruise remembers that his mother was always upbeat: "For her, the cup was always half full. Always. And I loved her for it."

Mary Lee remarried four years later and moved her family to Glen Ridge, New Jersey. Tom, now sixteen, was in his third high school. He found comfort and acceptance in sports—he was on the football, basketball, lacrosse, tennis, baseball, and wrestling teams. While he recuperated from a knee injury, a choir teacher suggested he try out for the school musical. Tom took the advice and won the lead role of Nathan Detroit in *Guys and Dolls.* When he heard the applause for the opening night's performance, Tom realized he wanted to be an actor.

After graduation Tom moved to New York City, dropped his last name, and waited tables while he auditioned. He told himself he had ten years to succeed in show business. He didn't have to wait that long; a few months later he landed a bit part in *Endless Love,* starring Brooke Shields.

The following year, Tom obtained a role in *Taps,* starring Sean Penn. Critics praised Cruise's performance but were disappointed with his next movie, *Losin' It.* Cruise learned to be more careful about choosing film roles. He accepted a minor role and low pay for the opportunity to work with director Francis Ford Coppola in *The Outsiders* (1983). Tom landed his first lead role in *Risky Business* (1983). The film was a huge hit, earning $63 million. In the movie *Top Gun* (1986), however, Cruise truly achieved fame. Tom's performance as a brash, "hotdogging" pilot established him as one of the biggest stars of his generation.

Cruise now had a "signature" character: the cocky, young go-getter. He played the same character-type opposite Paul Newman in *The Color of Money* (1987), in *Cocktail* (1988), and opposite **Dustin Hoffman** in *Rain Man* (1988). Now among the hottest Hollywood stars, Cruise's fee per movie rose to $5 million.

In 1989 Cruise detoured from his usual character type and accepted a challenging true-life role as handicapped Vietnam veteran Ron Kovic in *Born on the Fourth of July.* His powerful performance won him a Best Actor Oscar nomination. Kovic himself was so pleased with Cruise's portrayal that he gave Cruise the Bronze Star he'd earned in combat. "I told him it was for his heroic performance," Kovic said.

On the set of his next film, *Days of Thunder* (1990), Cruise's life took an unexpected turn: he fell in love with his costar, Nicole Kidman and married her on Christmas Eve. Although the pair was obviously in love in real life, their on-screen chemistry in the 1991 film *Far and Away* was weak, and the movie was panned.

Cruise bounced back in the 1992 film *A Few Good Men.* In an all-star cast that included Kevin Bacon, Demi Moore, and **Jack Nicholson**, Cruise played a military lawyer. *A Few Good Men* earned $102 million and garnered four Academy Award nominations, including Best Picture. Cruise received a Golden Globe Award for his performance.

In 1993 Tom Cruise fulfilled a treasured dream. He and his wife adopted a baby girl, Isabella Jane Kidman Cruise. "Becoming a father is the greatest thing that has ever happened to me," said Cruise. "I have longed for a child for so long. I look at her and thank God . . . for giving me such a precious gift." The couple adopted a second child, a boy they named Connor Antony, in 1995.

Cruise next starred in the 1996 blockbuster *Mission: Impossible,* a takeoff on the popular 1960s TV series. That year he also starred in *Jerry Maguire* (1996), the tale of a slick sports agent that Cruise believed was "really a love story . . . from a male perspective." That performance brought a second Academy Award nomination for Cruise.

Following two offbeat movies in 1999—*Eyes Wide Shut,* directed by Stanley Kubrick and costarring his wife, Nicole Kidman, and *Magnolia*—Cruise reprised his *Mission: Impossible* role in a sequel released in 2000. Future projects include a Steven Spielberg science fiction thriller called *Minority Report* and a remake of the 1975 cult classic *Death Race 2000.*

In 2001, after nearly ten years of marriage, Cruise filed for divorce from Kidman. The two separately attended the premiere of *The Others,* their last project together. A few months later Cruise caused a media fuss when he appeared publicly with his *Vanilla Sky* costar, Penelope Cruz.

Cruise is known for his kindness and generosity and is well liked in the Hollywood community. On September 21, 2001, he joined a host of celebrities in a telethon to raise money for victims of the September 11 attacks. The actor was "awestruck" by the courage and compassion of those who died. He believes that those are qualities the rest of the world will do well to emulate. "We are at a crossroads," he said, "and we have to do whatever we can to make the world better. I feel very, *very* strongly about that."

Jodie Foster

Multitalented Actor, Producer, and Director
1962–

This is not a business that is kind to women, but it needs them. The female pioneers have to be 10 times better than a man. Maybe someday there will be an old-girl network.

—JODIE FOSTER,
ON THE HOLLYWOOD FILM INDUSTRY

Jodie Foster's career began when she was three years old and her mother could not find a baby-sitter. Brandy Foster had divorced her husband, Lucius Fisher Foster III, while pregnant with her fourth child. After she gave birth to Alicia Christian ("Jodie") on November 19, 1962, Brandy realized that the few hundred dollars of alimony she received monthly was not enough to support her family.

Fortunately, a friend named Josephine Hill invited Brandy and her four children—Cindy, Connie, Buddy, and the infant Jodie—to move into her home. Before long, the Foster children were calling Brandy's friend "Aunt Jo" and treating her son, Chris, as though he were another sibling. After a neighbor spoke about her son's appearances in TV commercials, Brandy decided to take her son, Buddy, to audition as well. Before long, the boy was earning $25,000 a year. The income allowed Brandy to buy a comfortable family home in Hollywood.

But on the day of Buddy's audition for a Coppertone suntan lotion ad, Brandy found herself without a baby-sitter and took three-year-old Jodie along. As Buddy auditioned, Jodie began mimicking her adored older brother. The charmed executives hired her on the spot.

Over the next two years, Jodie appeared in scores of commercials. She claims she had a great time. "Most kids, all they have is school," she said in 1991. "[Acting] spared me from being a regular everyday kid slob." Buddy and Jodie were also successful in TV series roles. Buddy had a four-year run in *Mayberry, R.F.D.,* which ran until 1972; Jodie got a part in one of the show's episodes when she was seven years old. A string of TV roles followed on programs such as *The Courtship of Eddie's Father, Gunsmoke, Bonanza,* and *Julia.* She even received the title role in a pilot called *My Sister Hank* (the series never aired).

Brandy Foster made it clear to her show business children that they were no better than their peers. "All of us were in it together," Jodie remembers. "My mom worked, we all did. Just to survive." Brandy also introduced her children to a variety of cultural experiences. She served international dishes, watched foreign films with her children, and collected and taught them about antique furniture. Jodie believes that this atmosphere helped her become a well-rounded and open-minded adult.

Jodie made excellent grades in school, even with career demands. On the set she juggled homework and acting with the poise of an adult. "She was just right there, just whatever was needed," says director John Badham. That dedication was sorely tested during her first feature film, *Napoleon and Samantha* (1972). While on location in Oregon, eight-year-old Jodie was mauled by one of the lions working with the actors. The alarmed trainer managed to get the animal to drop the child, and she was rushed to the hospital for shots and stitches. She was back to work in ten days.

In 1972 Brandy enrolled Jodie in the exclusive Lycée Français. By the time Jodie graduated as valedictorian in 1980, she was a rising star in Hollywood. She'd made twelve films, including an enormously controversial role as a twelve-year-old prostitute in *Taxi Driver* (1976), and *Bugsy Malone* (1976), which was named Best Film at the Cannes Film Festival. She also received a Golden Globe Award for her role in the 1977 Disney movie *Freaky Friday* and earned Best Newcomer and Best Supporting Actress awards from the British Academy of Film and Television Arts (BAFTA) for *Bugsy Malone* and *Taxi Driver.*

Foster enrolled in Yale University in September 1980. After the media attention of Hollywood, she was relieved to blend in with the academic crowd. But her attempt at anonymity was shattered on March 30, 1981, when a man named John Hinckley Jr. fired at President Ronald Reagan as he left a Washington, D.C., hotel. The assassination attempt was disturbing enough, but the story that emerged afterward was shocking. Among Hinckley's possessions was an unmailed letter to Jodie Foster, declaring that he was going to kill the president to win her affection.

Foster was devastated. She admitted to reporters and investigators that she'd received unsolicited letters from the disturbed young man but stressed that none of them suggested Hinckley would resort to violence. Although she was poised throughout the media frenzy, the incident shook her to the core. She realized the high price of being a celebrity—and she refused to become a victim of her own fame. "If they wanted weakness," she said of the media, "I wasn't about to give it to them."

Foster took a few film roles while at Yale, notably *The Hotel New Hampshire* (1984), in which she costarred with Rob Lowe and Nastassja Kinski. After she graduated in 1985, however, her next films were disappointments. Not until 1988, when she starred as rape victim Sarah Tobias in *The Accused,* did Foster regain her momentum. Her remarkable and harrowing performance earned her a Best Actress Academy Award.

Three years later Foster won a second Best Actress Oscar for playing FBI agent Clarice Starling in the film version of Thomas Harris's best-seller *The Silence of the Lambs* (1991). Foster costarred with Anthony Hopkins, whose chilling portrayal of serial killer Hannibal the Cannibal brought him the Best Actor Oscar. (The film was named Best Picture.) That year she also donned the director's hat with *Little Man Tate,* in which she costarred.

In 1992 Foster founded her own production company, Egg Pictures, and produced the company's first project in 1994. *Nell* was the story of a backwoods woman who speaks a mysterious language and has lived in isolation since birth. Foster found the title role distinctly challenging. "You have a woman who wears her emotions on the outside," she explained. "I . . . spend my whole life wearing my emotions on the inside." The movie received mixed reviews, but Foster got an Academy Award nomination.

Her second Egg Pictures project, *Home for the Holidays* (1995), was a hilariously touching comedy about a dysfunctional family, starring Holly Hunter. Foster returned to acting in 1997 with *Contact,* in which she played a pragmatic astronomer who discovers radio communications from alien life forms.

In 1998 Foster surprised fans and friends when she announced that she was pregnant. She refused to name the father, explaining that she would raise her child alone. Charles Foster was born on July 20; Jodie proudly declared motherhood "the biggest adventure of my life." After costarring with Chow Yun-Fat in *Anna and the King* (1999), she was executive producer of *Waking the Dead* (2000) and produced *The Dangerous Lives of Altar Boys* (2002). She also starred in the thriller *Panic Room* (2002).

Jodie Foster still strives to lead a private, normal life. Those who know her say that the key to her success is talent and intelligence, but also self-discipline. Foster agrees. "You must have self-knowledge and an understanding of your limits," she once said when describing her work. "[B]y quelling her fears and confronting her enemies," one interviewer wrote, Jodie Foster becomes "something no other American actress of our time has embodied with such consistency and aplomb: a hero."

Julia Roberts

One of the Most Beloved Actresses in Hollywood
1967–

You can be true to the character all you want, but you've got to go home with yourself.

—JULIA ROBERTS

Had Julia Roberts followed up on her childhood dream, film enthusiasts might never have known such captivating characters as Darby Shaw *(The Pelican Brief)*, Vivian Ward *(Pretty Woman)*, or Shelby Eatenton Latcherie *(Steel Magnolias)*. Nor might such real-life characters as Erin Brockovich (in the film by the same name) be quite as memorable. Julia Roberts's childhood dream was to be a veterinarian. To the delight of her fans, who have made Julia Roberts one of the most beloved actresses in Hollywood, her dream never came true.

Julie Fiona Roberts was born to Betty and Walter ("Rob") Roberts on October 28, 1967, in Smyrna, Georgia. Betty was a church secretary, and Rob was a vacuum-cleaner salesman. Julie had two older siblings: Eric, born in 1956, and Lisa, born in 1965 (a half-sister, Nancy Motes, was born in 1976).

When Julie was four, Rob and Betty divorced. After Julie graduated from Campbell High School in 1985, she moved to New York City to live with her sister Lisa. She launched a modeling career and began getting small acting parts. In 1986 Julia (who had changed her first name from Julie because there was another actress by that name) made her film debut in *Blood Red.* Her brother, Eric, already an established actor, was starring in the movie.

Julia landed her first major film role in 1988, appearing with Liam Neeson in *Satisfaction.* She was next cast as one of a trio of restless, small-town pizza shop girls in *Mystic Pizza* (1988). Julia's good looks and bright smile quickly drew attention, and she became part of the ensemble cast of *Steel Magnolias* (1989), costarring with **Shirley MacLaine, Sally Field,** Dolly Parton, and Daryl Hannah. Roberts's striking portrayal of a diabetic young mother earned her an Academy Award nomination for Best Supporting Actress.

The character that vaulted Roberts to superstardom, however, was an unlikely one: in 1990 she played a Hollywood prostitute who falls in love with one of her clients, a millionaire business executive (Richard Gere), in *Pretty Woman* (1990). The highest-earning movie of 1990, *Pretty Woman* garnered more than $100 million, and it made Roberts an international star. She won a Golden Globe Award and obtained another Academy Award nomination.

Her next few films, however, were disappointments. In 1990 she costarred with Kiefer Sutherland in *Flatliners,* and in 1991 she played a wife being stalked by a possessive husband in *Sleeping with the Enemy* (1991). Other unsuccessful movies followed: **Steven Spielberg**'s *Hook* (1991), with **Dustin Hoffman**; *Dying Young* (1991); and Robert Altman's *The Player* (1992).

Roberts fared better in the 1993 film *The Pelican Brief,* based on the best-seller of the same name by John Grisham. The actress played Darby Shaw, a law student who teams with investigative reporter Gray Grantham (**Denzel Washington**) to untangle a huge tobacco-industry conspiracy. Her next three films, *Prêt-à-Porter* [*Ready to Wear* (1994)], *Something to Talk About* (1995), and *Everyone Says I Love You* (1996) were relatively successful, although some critics believed Roberts's energetic style was squandered.

In 1996 Roberts tried her hand at historical films. She held the title role in the thriller *Mary Reilly* (opposite John Malkovich playing Dr. Henry Jekyll and Mr. Edward Hyde) and played Kitty Kiernan in *Michael Collins,* a tale about the controversial Irish revolutionary (starring Liam Neeson). *Mary Reilly* pleased most audiences despite its grim atmosphere, but it collected mixed reviews.

Roberts regained her superstar status in 1997 when she appeared in the hit comedy *My Best Friend's Wedding.* The film, in which she costarred with Cameron Diaz and Dermot Mulroney, returned Roberts to box-office gold by earning more than $100 million—the first of her movies to do so since *Pretty Woman.* She made two more movies, *Conspiracy Theory* (1997) and *Stepmom* (1998), before starring in two smash hits: the romantic comedies *Notting Hill* and *Runaway Bride* (both 1999). In the latter Roberts reunited with *Pretty Woman* costar Richard Gere and director Garry Marshall—a combination that was even more successful than it had been the first time. *Runaway Bride* earned $300 million in the United States alone.

Julia Roberts was now not only one of the most popular actresses in America, but she was also one of the most bankable. In 2000 she received a record $20 million—the highest salary ever paid to a screen actress—to star in *Erin Brockovich.* The film, about a true-life legal secretary who discovers and exposes a major environmental scandal in a California power company, was hugely popular and received glowing critical reviews. For her performance in the title role, Roberts won the coveted Academy Award for Best Actress, as well as many other prestigious Best Actress honors, including a Golden Globe and a British Academy Award. She received her seventh People's Choice Award for Favorite Motion Picture Actress, as well as the London Film Critics Circle Award.

In 2001 Roberts returned to her most successful film vehicle, the romantic comedy. She starred with Brad Pitt in the crime caper *The Mexican* and with John Cusack, Catherine Zeta-Jones, and Billy Crystal in *America's Sweethearts*. She also played Contessa "Tess" Ocean as part of an all-star cast that included George Clooney, Brad Pitt, Matt Damon, Andy Garcia, and Carl Reiner in *Ocean's Eleven*. The film, which one critic called "a criminally stylish return to cool," was a remake of the popular 1960 movie starring Frank Sinatra, Dean Martin, Sammy Davis Jr., and Angie Dickinson. The actress's upcoming films include *Full Frontal* and *Confessions of a Dangerous Mind*. She will also appear in *Mona Lisa Smile*, scheduled for release in 2003.

Roberts divides her free time between her ranch in Taos, New Mexico, and her home in New York City. Her continuing appeal is evident in the many noncritical awards she has garnered. She has won a string of People's Choice Awards and has been named one of E!'s "Top 20 Entertainers." She was twice included in *People* magazine's list of the "50 Most Beautiful People in the World." Active in charity work, especially with the UNICEF organization, Roberts has made a number of goodwill visits to countries such as Haiti and India.

Calling herself an "utterly average total geek," she explains that despite the glamour and stardom, she is in many ways very much like her fans. "I sit on the [movie] set and knit," she says. "I love to go to movies and I eat tons of popcorn. . . . I love my soap operas. . . . I'm the Hoover [vacuum] at the dinner table. . . . If there's thirty people in a room, I'll be one of the top-three kookiest. I have a tendency to just say anything and not edit myself."

Halle Berry

First African American Woman to Win
the Best Actress Oscar
1968–

I had to learn who I was and not to look to other people to validate me. I couldn't allow [what] the press was saying about me to color how I felt about myself. . . . I'm more in control of who I am. I know who I am—and that's what's important.

—HALLE BERRY

When Russell Crowe announced Halle Berry as the winner of the Best Actress Oscar for her role in *Monster's Ball* in March 2002, the actress was stunned. Tears of joy flowed down her face as she walked to the stage. She knew this was a historic moment. Until that night, no black actress in Academy Awards history had ever won the Best Actress Oscar.

The biracial daughter of Jerome and Judith Barry, Halle decided early on that she would not waste time figuring out whether she should be black or white. She considered herself black. Born on August 14, 1968, Halle lived with her parents and older sister, Heidi, in Cleveland, Ohio.

When Halle was four, her father left them, and Halle's mother moved her children to the white suburb of Bedford. Halle tried to fit in but was often treated differently because of her skin color. She sought acceptance by excelling at schoolwork and participating in extracurricular activities. In high school she was the newspaper editor, class president, cheerleader captain, a member of the honor society, and the first black student in that school's history to be prom queen.

Halle attended Cuyahoga Community College for broadcast journalism. She entered several beauty pageants and, in 1985, was named Miss Teen All-American and was first runner-up in the Miss USA Pageant. In 1986 she became the first African American to represent the United States at the Miss World Pageant.

Halle left college and retired from pageant competition to pursue modeling and to study acting in Chicago, Illinois. In a 2002 interview with *Movieline* she said, "[Modeling] was very shallow in many ways, because it perpetuated my physical self a lot more than I ever wanted to; but . . . I gained a lot of confidence." In 1989 Halle moved to New York City, where she landed her first acting job on the TV series *Living Dolls*. She followed with a season-long role in the TV show *Knotts Landing*. In 1991 director **Spike Lee** asked her to audition for his feature film *Jungle Fever*. Halle gained a reputation of "living her role" as Samuel L. Jackson's crack-addicted girlfriend when she showed up for filming without having bathed for days.

Positive reviews for Halle's performance in *Jungle Fever* led to more film opportunities. She got a supporting role in *The Last Boy Scout*, starring **Bruce Willis,** and portrayed Eddie Murphy's love interest in *Boomerang*. More substantial roles followed for Halle, including *Losing Isaiah*, in which she played a former drug addict trying to regain custody of her son.

Berry's first starring role was in the 1996 airplane hijack thriller *Executive Decision*. In the 1998 film *Why Do Fools Fall in Love?* Halle played one of three women claiming to be the wife of a deceased rock star. Her next role was as the street-savvy woman who takes up with Warren Beatty in his political comedy *Bulworth*.

Halle next fulfilled a personal and professional dream not only of producing a film but also of taking on a role she had longed for—that of Dorothy Dandridge, the first black woman ever to earn a Best Actress Academy Award nomination. Dandridge knew that Hollywood roles for black women were almost nonexistent in the 1950s. "If I were white," she once said, "I could capture the world." Critics applauded Berry's absorbing portrayal of Dandridge's struggle to succeed in *Introducing Dorothy Dandridge*. Berry received a number of awards, including a Golden Globe and an Emmy.

Berry's personal life was difficult during this period. She was involved with a man—whom she has never identified—who struck her in the head during an argument. She lost 80 percent of her hearing in one ear from the blow. In February 2000 Berry had another problem. At about 2:00 A.M., she slammed her Chevy Blazer into another car at an intersection not far from her home. Dazed, cut, and bleeding from a gash on her forehead, Berry left the scene.

The gash required twenty stitches, and today Halle remembers nothing about the accident. She later pleaded "no contest" to a hit-and-run misdemeanor charge. She was fined $13,000, placed on three years' probation, and ordered to serve 200 hours of community service.

Of course the publicity surrounding the accident was damaging. Berry thought her career was ruined and that she was losing everything she had worked so hard to achieve. But none of that happened. She began going to psychotherapy sessions. She met singer-musician Eric Benet. On January 19, 2001, Halle and Eric married.

Having found personal happiness, Berry had the confidence to take professional risks. As **John Travolta**'s sexy cohort in *Swordfish,* she faced her first nude scene. Though it was nerve-racking, it was also cathartic. Berry felt confident enough to pursue other roles she might not have considered. She fought to land the role of emotionally shattered Leticia Musgrove, a woman coping with an obese son and a husband on death row in *Monster's Ball*. Teamed with Billy Bob Thornton, who plays her husband's executioner, Berry was confronted with her toughest on-screen challenge—an explicit sex scene. "If I hadn't done *Swordfish,* I would never have had the confidence to do [*Monster's Ball*]," she said.

The film and its stars earned stellar reviews. *Inside Out Film* wrote, "Berry's performance is raw and real, and so vulnerable the movie turns voyeuristic." *Blackfilm.com* wrote, "The heart and soul of the film is Berry. She holds the film together with her strength and believability in the character she plays."

Berry received numerous awards for *Monster's Ball,* including the Screen Actor's Guild Award and the coveted Best Actress Oscar. "This moment is so much bigger than me," she declared in her acceptance speech. "This moment is for Dorothy Dandridge, Lena Horne, Diahann Carroll. It's for all the women who stand behind me . . . and it's for every faceless woman of color that now has a chance because the door has been opened tonight."

Of the character that won her the Oscar, Berry said, "She's so much like me in many ways. I've been to the brink. . . . Luckily, [although] in my life I've suffered great pain, [I've been in] a lot of more tragic . . . situations that I've been able to rise above and grow through."

Will Smith

Rapper and Actor
1968–

The bottom line with me is fun. I enjoy life, I enjoy people. And people—black, white, Asian, or alien—enjoy that energy.

—WILL SMITH

At eighteen, Will Smith was a millionaire. Two years later, in 1990, he was broke and owed the federal government millions of dollars in taxes. While he had money, he enjoyed every minute of it—perhaps too much. In one year he had spent $800,000. "Being able to buy anything you want makes you a little crazy," he admitted. Smith realized he had strayed from the values his parents instilled in him. It was time, he said, to "get it all together."

Willard C. Smith Jr. was born on September 25, 1968, in Philadelphia, Pennsylvania, to Willard C. Smith Sr. and Caroline Smith. He was the second of Willard and Caroline's four children; he had an older sister, Pam, and younger twin siblings, Harry and Ellen. As a child Will learned about and admired the celebrities who had come from his West Philadelphia neighborhood, including basketball great Wilt Chamberlain and NASA astronaut Guion Bluford. He loved Dr. Seuss books for their rhyming stanzas; as an adult he attributed his love for rap music to Seuss's books. "If you listen to them a certain way, books like *Green Eggs and Ham* and *Hop on Pop* sound a lot like hip-hop," he explained.

When Will was twelve, a band called the Sugar Hill Gang released *Rapper's Delight*. It was a new form of music, and like many other American music fans, Will was captivated with its unique sound and rhythm. He began practicing rap and started spinning records at neighborhood parties. Before he got to high school, he gained a citywide reputation as a rap deejay.

At Overbrook High School, Will did well but was a bit of a class clown. He enjoyed entertaining people and making them laugh. He was nicknamed "Prince" for his persuasive way of talking himself out of trouble. Rap had become his passion, and in 1986, although he was accepted at the Massachusetts Institute of Technology, Will decided to postpone college and pursue a music career.

At a party one night Will was introduced to rapper and deejay Jazzy Jeff (Jeff Townes). The two performed an impromptu set together, with Jeff cutting the records and Will rapping. They felt instant chemistry; before long they were working together as "Jazzy Jeff and the Fresh Prince." Their first single, "Girls Ain't Nothing but Trouble," was a smash hit, selling 100,000 copies in the United States and hitting England's Top 20.

The duo was quickly contracted to record an album for Jive Records. *Rock the House* catapulted Jazzy Jeff and the Fresh Prince into the national spotlight. Their second LP, *He's the DJ, I'm the Rapper*, went platinum (more than 1 million copies sold) and earned industry and popular acclaim. The two enjoyed their success immensely—but it turned to trouble when Will went broke.

The young performer refused to panic. Instead, he decided to change his freewheeling spending habits, and he returned to work more determined than ever. Jazzy Jeff and the Fresh Prince released three more albums, including *Homebase,* from which the single "Summertime" won a 1991 Grammy.

By this time Will was ready to branch out, so when producers Quincy Jones and Benny Medina offered him a chance at a TV series, he took it. Loosely based on Medina's life, the *Fresh Prince of Bel-Air* traced the exploits of an inner-city kid who is placed with a well-to-do family in Beverly Hills, California. The sitcom, which debuted in September 1990, was a perfect fit for Will. Viewers were charmed by his title character, and the show was an instant hit.

Fresh Prince of Bel-Air ran for six years. In that time, Will had married and had a son, Willard C. "Trey" Smith III, born in 1992. He had appeared in several feature films, including *Made in America, Six Degrees of Separation,* and *Bad Boys,* opposite stars such as **Whoopi Goldberg,** Donald Sutherland, and Martin Lawrence. Will decided it was time to move on from *Fresh Prince.* "I did a whole lot of living in that time," he said. "[But] my life experiences are so far advanced beyond the character's life experiences." In May 1996 Will and the rest of the sitcom cast bid farewell to their viewers in a one-hour special.

Less than two months later Will headlined in the action film *Independence Day.* It had taken him five years to become a rap star and three to become a TV star—but with *Independence Day* he leaped from aspiring young actor to international star. Audiences jammed theaters to see fighter pilot Captain Steven Hiller and company (Harry Connick Jr., Jeff Goldblum, and Randy Quaid) attack aliens trying to destroy Earth. The film's dazzling special effects and nonstop action made it a smash hit. "I don't know when I have enjoyed a movie as much as Independence Day," said one critic enthusiastically. "[It] achieves what so many films can't, a balance between action, humor, and character."

Smith's performance brought even more high praise. "At 27, he's got one of the most impressively varied resumes in young Hollywood," wrote *Newsweek* of the young celebrity. "With *Independence Day,* he goes from big star to really, really big star." Smith had earned the accolades—he had prepared for his role by practicing in a flight simulator and training with real soldiers at a U.S. military base.

Director **Steven Spielberg** was so impressed with Smith's *Independence Day* performance that he sought him out to star in his next film, *Men in Black* (1997). Smith played Agent J, a secret government operative hired to keep a watchful eye on the aliens that lived on Earth. With Agent K (Oscar-winner Tommy Lee Jones), Smith's character made sure that no humans ever learned that aliens lived among them. (The two sported dark suits and sunglasses, giving the film its title.)

Will had a great time. Jones, usually a "serious" guy, had the cast and crew in hysterics with his deadpan delivery and comedic timing. "*Men in Black* is the wryest, sharpest, most entertaining special-effects film in recent memory," said one enthusiastic critic. Smith earned $5 million for his role. He also recorded the title song, which he performed the following year—dressed in a Philadelphia Phillies jersey—at the Grammy Awards. The song won Smith a third Grammy.

Smith released two solo albums in the late 1990s, *Big Willie Style* and *Willenium,* and obtained a fourth Grammy for the single "Gettin' Jiggy Wit It." He starred in *Enemy of the State* and *Wild Wild West,* and after a heartwarming performance in *The Legend of Bagger Vance* (2000), he gained thirty-five pounds and toned up his body to play boxing legend Muhammad Ali in *Ali.* Smith not only looked the part, he had studied hours of footage to learn the nuances of the boxer's famous personality. The performance won Smith his first Academy Award nomination, for Best Actor. In 2002 Smith reunited with Tommy Lee Jones for *Men in Black II.*

Smith now commands $20 million per film, but he has never again spent beyond his means. In 1997 he married actress Jada Pinkett (his first marriage ended in 1995). A son, Jaden Christopher, arrived in 1998; daughter Willow Camille Reign Smith was born in 2000. Still going strong in a success-filled career, Smith has found his most vital role: family man, husband, and father.

Gwyneth Paltrow

Highly Acclaimed Award-Winning Actress
1972–

I don't look at other actresses and think, 'I wish I had that life.' Because I now realize how thoroughly uninteresting an actor's life can be. They don't read the paper, they don't take the subway, they don't go to museums.

—GWYNETH PALTROW

First eyed by the public as the willowy blond girlfriend of heartthrob Brad Pitt, Gwyneth Paltrow soon proved she was more than just a tagalong beauty. For at the young age of twenty-six she won the Academy Award for Best Actress for her part as the exuberantly in love and determined Viola in the highly acclaimed film *Shakespeare in Love.* The talented Paltrow was now admired for her skill as well as her elegant looks.

Born on September 28, 1972, Gwyneth Kate and her younger brother, Jake, lived charmed early years as the children of Tony Award–winning actress Blythe Danner and the late producer-director Bruce Paltrow of *St. Elsewhere* fame. While they were Los Angeles inhabitants, their summers were spent in Massachusetts's Berkshire Mountains at the acclaimed Williamstown Theater, where Danner performed. At a young age Gwyneth was intrigued with acting and got her first part at Williamstown at the age of five.

While still young, Gwyneth visited many movie sets, which added to her interest in acting. Her parents made sure Gwyneth also learned as much about the nonacting world as she could, encouraging exploration of cultural pursuits and a variety of activities. Though both parents had careers, the Paltrow family was very close and remains that way today. Gwyneth felt that her mother put her family ahead of her career, and she feels the same way about her own career and family relationships. Gwyneth is known as someone who is generous with friends, many of whom she has remained close to for years.

The Paltrow family moved to Manhattan when Gwyneth was eleven, and she was enrolled in the distinguished all-girls Spence School. She acted in some plays and also joined Triple Trio, a singing group that had no musical accompaniment. Her voice was said to be the best in the bunch, yet she remained more interested in acting. Gwyneth headed back to the West Coast in 1990, enrolling at the University of California at Santa Barbara, where she studied art history. Yet her time there was short-lived. In the summer of 1991 she costarred with her mother in the play *Picnic* at the Williamstown Theater. Receiving strong reviews for her role, Gwyneth decided to pursue acting full time.

In 1991 Paltrow appeared in her first film, a small role in *Shout* starring **John Travolta.** Connections helped Paltrow early on in her career. When she heard that the family's good friend **Steven Spielberg** was still searching for a Wendy to act in his Peter Pan movie *Hook* (1991), she easily convinced him to give her the part. In 1992 she tried television, costarring in the miniseries *Cruel Doubt.* After she was cast in the miniseries, she found that her mother would be costarring as well. Though pleased to be working with her mother again, Paltrow was also concerned about people thinking she was getting parts because of her family ties rather than her own talent.

By 1993 Paltrow had small but significant roles in the films *Malice,* with Alec Baldwin and Nicole Kidman, and *Flesh and Bone,* with James Caan. By 1995 she had gotten the opportunity to demonstrate her talent, appearing in such films as *Jefferson in Paris, Moonlight and Valentino,* and *Seven.* While working on *Seven,* Paltrow and her costar Brad Pitt fell in love. The couple quickly became one of Hollywood's hottest pairs. They became engaged in December 1996 but broke up the following year. Paltrow said they could not envision working on a good marriage and strong careers at the same time.

Paltrow was seen as a rising star, but was not getting much work. Her real opportunity came when she starred in Jane Austen's *Emma* (1996) and started a partnership with Miramax films that landed her the title "first lady of Miramax." Concerned about being typecast, Paltrow then took on the role of a prostitute in *Hard Eight* and played Pip's unrequited love in *Great Expectations.*

Seeing independent films as more suited to her, Paltrow then acted in *Sliding Doors* before starring in her most critically acclaimed role in the seven-time Academy Award–winner *Shakespeare in Love.* During the year leading up to the 1999 Academy Awards, the actress had been working on her next movie, *The Talented Mr. Ripley,* in Italy. This was at a time when Paltrow longed to be near her family, as her father was seriously ill with cancer and her paternal grandfather was very sick as well. While quite distressed, the actress was intent on maintaining professionalism and remained devoted to her work. Paltrow revealed her worries only to director John Madden. In 1999, after winning the Academy Award for her role in *Shakespeare in Love,* Paltrow took a complete break, staying in bed for ten days.

Ironically her next role was in a movie entitled *Bounce,* which she agreed to star in only a month later. She costarred with Ben Affleck. Following this film, which Paltrow felt was more important for Affleck's career than her own, she costarred in the comedy *Duets,* which her father directed. She made a cameo appearance in her friend and screenwriter Caroline Doyle's independent film *Intern* and costarred as an overweight woman in *Shallow Hal,* donning a special suit that made her appear about 200 pounds heavier. Just after finishing the filming, Paltrow showed her thin, long naked body in *Harper's Bazaar.*

Drew Barrymore

*Former Child Star and Current Day Popular Film Actress
1975–*

I didn't want to be considered another Hollywood tragedy. . . . If I've learned anything, it's [that it is] always better to tell the truth. And by doing so, maybe it will help other kids not to end up like me.

—Drew Barrymore, in 1989

One night in February 2001 Drew Barrymore and Tom Green awoke to the sound of Drew's dog, Flossie, barking furiously. Their Beverly Hills house was in flames from an electrical malfunction. Although Barrymore and Green escaped unharmed, thanks to Flossie, Drew's home was destroyed.

The actress later said she felt grateful for the experience. "It was time to start over," she explained. " [I was holding on to] things that made me know I had an identity I didn't have growing up. . . . I believe it happen[ed] for spiritual reasons."

That Barrymore saw spiritual opportunity in the disaster was a testament to her resiliency. The former child star endured a lonely youth, abusive and neglectful parents, alcoholism, drug abuse, and a suicide attempt—all before she was fifteen, and all under the constant glare of celebrity. Clearly, the fire that destroyed Drew's home was not the first time she'd lost everything.

When Drew Blythe Barrymore was born on February 22, 1975, in Culver City, California, her parents, John Drew Barrymore Jr. and Ildyko Jaid Mako, had already separated. John had a history of alcoholism, drug abuse, and violence. One day while she was pregnant, Jaid left him. With a baby to support, she kept an intense schedule of waitressing and auditioning and relied heavily on baby-sitters.

When Drew was eleven months old, Jaid took her to an audition for a dog food commercial. Drew got the part after a puppy bit her—and she laughed. In 1978 she appeared in the TV movie *Suddenly, Love.* "Somehow, at that age, she understood what it was all about," Jaid remembers.

Nearly always alone with strangers, Drew was lonely and sad. Her earliest memory of her father was a visit in which he was very drunk. Drew claims that her desire to act came from a hunger to feel loved: "I was the girl who didn't think anyone loved her, which only inspired me to try to be accepted even more." The bustle of the movie set made her feel like part of a family.

In 1981 Jaid read Drew a script about an alien who is discovered and sheltered by a boy named Elliot. That story was *E.T.: The Extra-Terrestrial,* directed by **Steven Spielberg,** who remembered Drew from a previous audition. Spielberg loved Drew's charm and imagination, and Drew saw Spielberg as a father figure. She got the part of Gertie, Elliot's younger sister.

E.T. was a smash hit—and it changed Drew's life forever. "[P]eople asked for autographs. They stared. They knew my name. . . . They wanted to touch me. . . . [I]t frightened me," she remembers. Reporters surrounded her. She rode in limousines, attended photo shoots, and was interviewed constantly. She appeared on *The Tonight Show* and was the youngest guest-host of *Saturday Night Live.* She was seven years old.

Not until the *E.T.* publicity did Drew learn that she came from a "royal family" of actors. Her grandfather John Barrymore, his brother Lionel, and his sister Ethel had been critically acclaimed actors. All three battled alcoholism, and John had four disastrous marriages. One of John's children was John Jr., Drew's father. Anxious to live up to the Barrymore name, Drew felt added pressure to succeed.

After starring in the films *Irreconcilable Differences* and *Firestarter* (both 1984), Drew had her first taste of alcohol during a "wrap" party for *Firestarter*. Her mother took her daughter to bars that Drew was legally too young to enter. When Drew's movies did poorly, she started getting rejected at auditions. She was too old for children's roles and too young for teen roles. Her grades dropped; she neglected her appearance. She felt a staggering sense of rejection.

Drew's refuge became the bars she attended with her mother. Jaid even threw her daughter a festive tenth birthday party—at a nightclub. At twelve, Drew drank regularly and smoked cigarettes and marijuana. She hung out with rebellious older kids at school and began to resent Jaid for having taken advantage of her fame. Worried about her weight, Drew wrongly believed that abusing cocaine, as her friends did, would help her stay thin. Almost instantly, she was addicted.

One night after a harrowing argument, Jaid checked Drew into a rehabilitation center for drug abusers. But she removed her twelve days later: she did not want Drew to lose her role in *Far From Home*. The rehab center assigned a counselor to travel with Drew on location. A consummate professional, Drew had never abused drugs while working—but now she also remained sober during time off.

Nervous and edgy after returning from a trip to New York for an audition, Drew slipped up and went on a drug binge. She stole her mother's credit card and car, intending to run away to Hawaii. Instead, she crashed into two cars and was arrested by rehab agents.

Drew used her rehab stay to understand her behavior and regain confidence. She told her story to *People* magazine and appeared in an *ABC Afterschool*

Special about teens in recovery. But after being "clean" for six months, she slipped up again and smoked marijuana. Publicizing her drug use had made staying clean more difficult. She began using drugs regularly and felt ashamed of hiding it.

In 1989 fourteen-year-old Drew moved into her own apartment. She sank into depression and was near breakdown when her father called to ask her for money. Drew refused him, but the guilt sent her on a drug binge. Then her mother announced she was taking a trip—with Drew's ex-boyfriend. Completely distraught, Barrymore tried to take her own life. She awoke in a hospital, where she'd been taken after her roommate found her. She entered rehab again. This time she truly wanted to get better.

Drew moved in with musician David Crosby and his wife, Jan Dance, both former addicts. "I felt she had been dealt a short deck," said Crosby. "I didn't want to see her go down the tubes." Drew regained control of her life. She published an autobiography, *Little Girl Lost* (1990), and enthusiastically returned to acting. She costarred in the 1992 TV series *2000 Malibu Road* and starred in *Poison Ivy* that year. She appeared in seven more films before 1994, including *Guncrazy,* for which she earned a Golden Globe nomination.

Barrymore continued her winning streak with *Boys on the Side,* and *Batman Forever* (both 1995), and *Scream* and *Everyone Says I Love You* (both 1996). She made five films from 1997 to 1998, including *The Wedding Singer* and *Ever After.* She also launched Flower Films Production Company and produced *Never Been Kissed* (1999), in which she starred. Among her three 2001 films was the well-received *Riding in Cars with Boys;* she also costarred in and produced *Charlie's Angels* (2002).

Drew Barrymore's personal life has been tumultuous. In December 2001 Drew's much publicized six-month marriage to comedian Tom Green ended. But Barrymore remains determined to succeed. "My goals are simple: to stay sober and live a good life," she once wrote. "All I can do is the best I can."

"Quiet on the Set"

The experience of making a movie is better and more important than the film itself.

—JOHN HUSTON, DIRECTOR/SCREENWRITER

When you watch a movie, you probably don't think about how it was made or how many people it took to create it. But have you ever stayed in the theater after the end of a movie to read the credits? If so, you have seen hundreds of names listed next to job titles you may not even recognize. It takes months of work and countless behind-the-scenes people to make a single movie.

Movies are stories, fact or fiction, told by the actors. They are the most recognizable people in the moviemaking process. What actors say comes from a script—the written form of the story. Without many other workers—for example, those who assemble the "living room" where a scene is taking place, or those who place microphones to pick up the actors' voices—there would be no movie at all.

There are three main steps in moviemaking: preproduction, production and filming, and postproduction. Each phase requires scores of people with specific expertise. When everything comes together just right, a motion picture is created.

Preproduction

The life of a film begins with an idea written down as a script, which details the story, the setting (where and when the story takes place), and the dialogue. This is the job of a **screenwriter**. Sometimes a script is adapted from an existing book or play.

Although movies are meant to entertain, moviemaking is a business—and an expensive one at that. The **executive producer** oversees the nontechnical aspects of filmmaking. He or she handles business and legal issues, raises funds, and hires key personnel. The executive producer also arranges for distributors—a studio or production company—to bring the completed film to **exhibitors** (companies that represent movie theaters).

The **casting director** auditions and selects performers for speaking roles. Once a script has been approved and the actors chosen, decisions about location, sets, and costuming are made. A **concept artist** prepares sketches based on the script to help the producer, director, and film crew members visualize what the movie will look like. If a film is shot outside a studio, a **location manager** scouts areas to find the best place to film. The **costume designer** conceives the style of clothing actors will wear based on the story's setting. For example, Russell Crowe needed much different clothing for *Gladiator* from what **Tom Hanks** needed for *Apollo 13*.

Production and Filming

Once a script is ready for production, a crew is hired to create the film. The **director** is the principal artist on a movie set, the creative drive behind the process. The director must describe to the actors the way a scene should be played. On the set during filming, he or she yells "Action," "Cut," and "That's a wrap."

A great deal of equipment goes into making a film: booms, microphones, lights, props, cables, dollies, and cameras. Sets are constructed and decorated

A crew films a movie during the production stage of moviemaking.

with furniture, draperies, rugs, paintings, appliances, and other objects. Before shooting begins, technicians prepare the set. The **cable operator** handles the sound-related cables, which must be carefully laid out and taped to the floor.

The **grip** is an all-around handyman whose job usually requires physical labor, such as erecting scaffolding. A **dolly grip** has similar responsibilities but mainly lays down dolly tracks (rails that guide cameras in tracking shots). The **key grip** is the head grip and oversees all electricians on set. The **gaffer,** or chief lighting technician, oversees lighting electricians. The gaffer coordinates with the director of photography to make sure lights are properly placed. A **boom operator** runs the machinery that allows a microphone to dangle off-camera above the actors' heads and pick up dialogue.

When film production begins, the **director of photography** (cinematographer or camera operator) supervises the lighting, selection of film stock and camera lenses, and filming. An **assistant director** works closely with the director to be sure the film stays on schedule. Additional duties include preparing the call sheet (a list of which actors are required for which scenes and when they are needed), tracking down actors who are not where they should be, and preparing the set when the director is ready to shoot. (The assistant is the one who yells, "Quiet on the set!")

Many other jobs go into filmmaking. A **makeup artist** prepares actors' faces between scenes. A **loader** keeps the cameras loaded with film. A **script supervisor** ensures that everything looks the same from one shot to the next. This is particularly helpful when scenes are shot out of sequence; for example, if an actor puts down a cup of coffee on a table to answer the phone, the cup must still be on that table when the actor goes to retrieve it.

Sometimes a script requires an actor to do something dangerous, such as being "rescued" from the water by a helicopter. If an actor doesn't feel qualified or comfortable doing this, a specialist, or **stunt performer,** will take his or her place. A **stunt coordinator** choreographs the scene so that it looks realistic and is safely performed.

Postproduction

When filming is complete, a movie is far from finished. Much of the technical work is done during postproduction. A two-hour movie may have hundreds of thousands of feet of film. The **film editor** assembles the footage to produce a cohesive story. A skilled editor can make a good picture better; a poor editor might make a great picture mediocre.

A film editor puts footage together to create the final version of a movie.

The editor takes the best shots from each scene and assembles them in sequence—a "rough cut." Next, the editor locates exact places in the film to cut into and out of shots. The film is next precisely cut and assembled into a "final cut." Finally, an engineer called the **sound mixer** creates the sound track and adds Foleys (sound effects). From that, an "answer print" is made, combining images and sound with the placement of an optical track along one edge of the final print.

No motion picture is complete without music. Imagine watching Elliot and his friends take off into the air on their bicycles without hearing the orchestra build in the motion picture *E.T.: The Extraterrestrial.* Music enhances or sets the mood for each scene and for the film as a whole. Without realizing it, each viewer has an emotional reaction to the background music in a film. The **music composer**'s job is to write the score, hire musicians to perform it, and record the result. Film music not only enhances the audience's experience, but it also provides additional revenue for the film when released as a CD soundtrack.

At last the film is ready to be released to theaters. Publicity and marketing personnel make sure the movie is well advertised. Publicity can be as simple as an advertisement in a newspaper, or it can be as dazzling as a full-blown campaign of TV and radio commercials, posters, advance screenings, and tie-in merchandise such as mugs, key chains, action figures, and marketing plans with fast-food restaurants and toy stores.

The next time you go to the movies, think about everyone who worked on it—even the ones you never see and who only have their names credited at the end of the picture. Without them, you would never be at the theater in the first place!

Mentionables

Ben Affleck (1972–)

Affleck appeared in the PBS program *The Voyage of the Mimi* at eight years old. He landed minor TV parts during his high-school years, then costarred with Brendan Fraser and best friend Matt Damon in *School Ties* (1992), his first feature film. He and Damon cowrote and played in *Good Will Hunting* (1997), winning Golden Globe and Academy Awards for Best Original Screenplay. Affleck appeared in the blockbuster *Armageddon* and the award-winning *Shakespeare in Love* (both 1998). In the summer of 2001 he was in the epic *Pearl Harbor*.

Lionel, Ethel, and John Barrymore (1878–1954) (1879–1959) (1882–1942)

The legendary "Flying Barrymores" were the most famous of a family of stage actors going back several generations. Ethel was one of the legends of her time, a beautiful and highly talented stage actress. Internationally renowned, she was the woman for whom the term "glamour girl" was coined. Lionel, her older brother, was noted as a consummate character actor; his credits include fifteen "Dr. Kildare" movies and hateful Mr. Potter in the classic *It's a Wonderful Life* (1946). John, the youngest Barrymore, was perhaps the most famous, earning the nickname the "Great Profile" for his striking good looks and dashing demeanor. He became a matinee idol after transforming himself from a Shakespearean stage actor to a film star.

Mel Brooks (1926–)

Actor, director, and producer Mel Brooks is known for his intense drive for success and his over-the-top personality. His boisterous brand of humor is best seen in films such as *The Producers* (1967), *Young Frankenstein* (1974), *Blazing Saddles* (1974), and *History of the World Part 1* (1980). In 2001 he produced a Broadway version of *The Producers,* starring Nathan Lane and Matthew Broderick; it won a record-breaking twelve Tony Awards.

Richard Burton (1925–1984)

This brilliant actor received seven Oscar nominations in his thirty-two-year career. He is probably most remembered for his on-screen role as Marc Antony in *Cleopatra* and his off-screen romance with costar Elizabeth Taylor.

James Cagney (1899–1986)

One of the original vaudeville greats, Cagney burst into stardom in the 1931 gangster movie *The Public Enemy*. Short in stature but spirited and outgoing, he enjoyed a long reign as one of Hollywood's most-sought-after stars, appearing in hits such as *Angels with Dirty Faces* (1938), *White Heat* (1949), and *Mister Roberts* (1955); in 1942 he won an Oscar for his effervescent performance in *Yankee Doodle Dandy.*

Michael Caine (1933–)

Born and raised in South London's slums, Maurice Joseph Micklewhite Jr. began his career in regional theaters and adopted the stage name Michael Caine after the 1954 film *The Caine Mutiny*. A prolific actor, Caine has appeared in more than 100 films in a career that spans half a decade, including *Alfie* (1966), *Sleuth* (1972), and *Educating Rita* (1983), for which he received Oscar nominations, and *Hannah and Her Sisters* (1986) and *Cider House Rules*

(1999), which brought him Oscars for Best Supporting Actor. Also an author and restaurateur, Caine was knighted in 2000 by Queen Elizabeth II.

Russell Crowe (1964–)

The New Zealand–born, brash "bad boy" of motion pictures was six when he appeared in his first TV movie, and played bit parts throughout his childhood in Australia and New Zealand. His first feature film was *Blood Oath* (released in the United States as *Prisoners of the Sun*) in 1990; he debuted in America in *The Quick and the Dead* in 1995. Crowe's breakthrough role came in the 1997 hit *L.A. Confidential.* He became a Hollywood superstar with his leading role in *Gladiator* (2000), which earned a Best Actor Oscar for Crowe. He then starred in *A Beautiful Mind* (2001), which won him his third Best Actor nomination in as many years.

James Dean (1931–1955)

Although Dean made only three films, *Rebel Without a Cause* (1955), *East of Eden* (1955), and *Giant* (1956), he became a cult star after they were released. The promising but haunted young actor was twenty-four years old when he died in a car accident.

Michael Douglas (1944–)

The son of famed screen actor Kirk Douglas, Michael Douglas launched his career in the 1970s with a role on the TV series *The Streets of San Francisco.* He produced the Oscar-winning film *One Flew Over the Cuckoo's Nest* and obtained roles in films such as *The China Syndrome* (1979, which he also produced), *Romancing the Stone* (1984, also produced by him), *Fatal Attraction* (1987), *Basic Instinct* (1992), and *The Wonder Boys* (2000). Douglas won a Best Actor Academy Award for *Wall Street* (1987).

Clint Eastwood (1930–)

Eastwood's first film, *Revenge of the Creature* (1955), appeared a year after he moved to Los Angeles, California, to become a film star. He gained fame with his TV role in *Rawhide* (1959–1967) and appeared in three "spaghetti westerns" directed by Sergio Leone and filmed in Italy. He also played "Dirty Harry" in five films from 1971 to 1988. *Unforgiven* (1992), which Eastwood also directed and produced, won the Best Picture Oscar.

Jane Fonda (1937–)

A member of an acting family that includes father, Henry Fonda; brother, Peter; and niece, Bridget, this Academy Award–winning actress and political activist launched her film career with "sex goddess" roles before taking on more serious, politically oriented parts. Among her best-known films are *Barefoot in the Park* (1967), *They Shoot Horses, Don't They?* (1969), *Julia* (1977), and *The China Syndrome* (1979). Nominated for six Academy Awards, Fonda has won two for Best Actress, for *Klute* (1971) and *Coming Home* (1978).

Morgan Freeman (1937–)

A veteran character actor, director, writer, and producer, Morgan Freeman earned early fame as "Easy Reader" in the hit PBS show *The Electric Company*. He turned in Academy Award–nominated performances in *Street Smart* (1987), *Driving Miss Daisy* (1989), for which he also won the Golden Globe for Best Actor, and *The Shawshank Redemption* (1994). Among his best films are *Glory* (1989), *Unforgiven* (1992), *Amistad* and *Kiss the Girls* (both 1997), and *The Sum of All Fears* (2002).

Judy Garland (1922–1969)

Born Frances Ethel Gumm, Judy Garland is best known for her legendary singing voice and the classic *The Wizard of Oz* (1939). She was fourteen when her "star quality" led MGM film mogul Louis B. Mayer to give her a film contract, and she costarred with Mickey Rooney in a string of "Andy Hardy" films. Garland classics include *Meet Me in St. Louis* (1944) and *A Star Is Born* (1955). She appeared in scores of TV specials and had her own program, *The Judy Garland Show* (1963–1964). Among the more than twelve albums and 100 singles she recorded was *Judy at Carnegie Hall* (1961), a five-time Grammy winner.

Mel Gibson (1956–   )

The sixth of eleven children, Gibson moved from New York to Australia after the Vietnam War began. In 1979 he appeared in *Mad Max,* an international smash hit; he reprised the role in *Mad Max 2* (*The Road Warrior* in the United States, 1981) and *Mad Max: Beyond the Thunderdome* (1985). Gibson next scored big with the blockbuster series of *Lethal Weapon* films (1987–1998), costarring with Danny Glover. His 1995 film *Braveheart* won five Oscars, including Best Picture. His most recent films were 2000's *The Patriot* and *What Women Want.* Gibson has seven children with Robyn Moore; they were married in 1980.

Sir Alec Guinness (1914–2000)

Alec Guinness de Cuffe appeared in John Gielgud's *Hamlet* and *Romeo and Juliet,* and in another production of *Hamlet* (1936–1937) as Laurence Olivier's understudy. His earliest films include *Great Expectations* (1946) and *Oliver Twist* (1948). Adept at comedy, he starred in *The Lavender Hill Mob* (1951) and *The Swan* (1956). He won a Best Actor Oscar for *The Bridge on the River Kwai* (1957) and a Best Actor Tony for *Dylan* (1964). Guinness is best known by younger moviegoers as Ben (Obi-Wan) Kenobi in the blockbuster hit *Star Wars* (1977); he reprised the role in *The Empire Strikes Back* (1980) and *Return of the Jedi* (1983). Knighted by Queen Elizabeth II and awarded an honorary Oscar for lifetime achievement, Guinness performed well into the 1990s.

Gene Hackman (1930–   )

Eugene Alden Hackman studied at the renowned Pasadena Playhouse along with Dustin Hoffman; his stage debut was in New York in 1958. In 1971 Hackman earned an Oscar for *The French Connection,* which was followed by a string of hits, including *The Poseidon Adventure* (1972) and *Superman* (1978). He won a second Oscar for *Unforgiven* in 1992. Among his more recent films are *Crimson Tide* and *Get Shorty* (both 1995), *Enemy of the State* (1998), and *Behind Enemy Lines* (2001).

Sir Anthony Hopkins (1937–   )

A graduate of the prestigious Royal Academy of Dramatic Art in London, Hopkins is thought of today as a film actor, although he was for many decades a stage performer. He made his film debut in *The Lion in Winter* (1968). He is perhaps best known today for his chilling portrayal of serial killer Hannibal "the Cannibal" Lecter in *The Silence of the Lambs* (1991) and the sequel, *Hannibal* (2001). Knighted by Queen Elizabeth II in 1993, Hopkins stunned British fans when he became an American citizen in April 2000.

James Earl Jones (1931–   )

The son of a former prizefighter and actor, Jones suffered from a severe stuttering problem as a child and took up acting to overcome it. He made his Broadway debut in 1957; two years later he won a Tony Award for his starring role in *The Great White Hope,* and he earned an Academy Award in 1971 in a reprise of the role. He is perhaps best known as the resonant and menacing voice of Darth Vader in the *Star Wars* films and the regal voice of King Mufasa in the 1994 animated Disney film *The Lion King.*

Tommy Lee Jones (1946–   )

Texas-born Tommy Lee Jones is a Harvard graduate and veteran of the New York theater. He launched his film career with a bit part in *Love Story* (1970).

Jones's first starring role was in *Jackson County Jail* (1976). He received an Oscar nomination for his role in *JFK* (1991). Jones won his first Academy Award for his supporting role in *The Fugitive* (1993). In 1997 he costarred with Will Smith in the blockbuster *Men in Black*. His most recent films include *Rules of Engagement* and *Space Cowboys* (both 2000) and *Men in Black II* (2002).

Diane Keaton (1946–   )

Keaton first gained recognition costarring with Woody Allen in the Broadway production of *Play It Again, Sam* (1969). She went on to appear in numerous Allen films, including *Annie Hall* (1977), for which she won an Academy Award for Best Actress. She was nominated for two other Best Actress Oscars for her performances in *Reds* (1981) and *Marvin's Room* (1996). She debuted as a feature-film director with *Unstrung Heroes* (1995). Among her other best-known films are *The Godfather* (1972) and *The First Wives Club* (1996).

Sir Ben Kingsley (1943–   )

For his stunning performance as Indian nationalist leader Mohandas Gandhi in the 1982 film *Gandhi,* British-born Kingsley was awarded the Best Actor Oscar. Other memorable performances include his role as gangster Meyer Lansky in *Bugsy* and as the soft-spoken Jewish accountant Itzak Stern in the Steven Spielberg multi-award-winner *Schindler's List.* He was knighted by Queen Elizabeth II in 2001.

Jack Lemmon (1925–2001)

Highly regarded stage and film actor Jack Lemmon earned praise for both comic and dramatic films, including *Mister Roberts* (1955); *The Odd Couple* (1968), costarring with frequent sidekick Walter Matthau; and *Glengarry Glen Ross* (1992).

Marx Brothers

This remarkably talented team of film, vaudeville, and Broadway comedians included Chico (born Leonard, 1886–1961), Harpo (born Adolph, a.k.a. Arthur, 1887–1964), and Groucho (born Julius Henry, 1890–1977). Early in their career, the three also teamed with brothers Gummo (born Milton, 1893–1977) and Zeppo (born Herbert, 1901–1979). Known for their hilarious wordplay and slapstick visual comedy, the groundbreaking Marx Brothers appeared in scores of successful comedies, including *Animal Crackers* (1930), *Duck Soup* (1933), *A Night at the Opera* (1935), and *A Night in Casablanca* (1946). Groucho, the wiggly-browed ringleader, also had a hit TV quiz show, *You Bet Your Life* (1950–1961), and appeared without his brothers in *Copacabana* (1947), *A Girl in Every Port* (1952), and *Skidoo* (1968).

Walter Matthau (1920–2000)

Born Walter Matuschanskayasky in New York City, this veteran comic actor debuted on Broadway in 1948 and launched his film career ten years later with *The Kentuckian* (1958). He costarred in the stage version of the Neil Simon hit *The Odd Couple* (1965) and reprised the role in the 1967 film version. Matthau's many films with fellow actor Jack Lemmon as sidekick include *Grumpy Old Men* (1993) and *The Grass Harp* (1996), directed by his son, film director Charles Matthau.

Rita Moreno (1931–)

Perhaps best known for her debut film role in *West Side Story*, this remarkably versatile entertainer has won an Oscar, a Tony, an Emmy, and a Grammy. Other film credits include *Carnal Knowledge* (1971) and *The Ritz* (1976), and she was an original cast member of the classic children's TV program *The Electric Company*.

Peter O'Toole (1932–)

A native of Ireland, O'Toole began his career with the Royal Shakespeare Theatre in Stratford-on-Avon, England, before earning international fame for his portrayal of T. E. Lawrence in *Lawrence of Arabia* (1962). He has earned seven Oscar nominations for his performances in films such as *Bequeath* (1964), *The Lion in Winter* (1968), *Goodbye, Mr. Chips* (1969), and *My Favorite Year* (1982). He published a memoir, *Loitering with Intent,* in 1992, and he continues performing in independent films.

Anthony Quinn (1915–2001)

Born Antonio Quiñones in Mexico, this Irish-Mexican film star earned two Oscars for *Viva Zapata!* (1952) and *Lust for Life* (1956) and two additional nominations for *Wild Is the Wind* (1957) and *Zorba the Greek* (1964). His long career in both American and European films brought him international fame; among his later films are *Last Action Hero* (1993) and *A Walk in the Clouds* (1995).

Meg Ryan (1961–)

Meg Ryan has played the romantic lead in *When Harry Met Sally* (1989), *Sleepless in Seattle* (1993), and *City of Angels* (1998) and has also taken on dramatic roles in *When a Man Loves a Woman* (1994) and *Courage Under Fire* (1996).

Kevin Spacey (1959–)

Originally a stage actor, Kevin Spacey won a Tony Award for *Lost in Yonkers* (1991) before turning to films. He is best known for playing quirky, eccentric characters in films such as *The Usual Suspects* (1995), for which he received a Best Supporting Actor Academy Award; *American Beauty* (1999), which won him a Best Actor Oscar; and *K-PAX* (2001).

Sissy Spacek (1949–   )

Mother of actress Schuyler Fisk and cousin of actor Rip Torn, Spacek reached the height of her career during the 1980s. She received an Academy Award for her starring role in *Coal Miner's Daughter* (1980) and earned four additional Oscar nominations for *Carrie* (1976), *Missing* (1982), *The River* (1984), and *Crimes of the Heart* (1986). In 2001 she earned a Golden Globe Award and a sixth Oscar nomination for the independent film *In the Bedroom,* which received five Oscar nominations; she will appear in the 2002 film *Tuck Everlasting.*

Jessica Tandy (1909–1994)

A talented and versatile actress, British-born Jessica Tandy won the first of many Tony Awards as the original Blanche DuBois in the 1948 Broadway production of *A Streetcar Named Desire.* She was also an accomplished screen actress: she got a Best Actress Academy Award for *Driving Miss Daisy* (1989) and an Oscar nomination for *Fried Green Tomatoes* (1992). She sometimes paired with her husband, Hume Cronyn, as in the *The Gin Game* (1984). Most fans were not aware that the actress was also a lawyer, having earned her degree in 1974.

Shirley Temple (1928–   )

A precocious child star, Shirley Temple made her film debut before she was four years old. When she was six, she appeared in nine feature films, including *Little Miss Marker* (1934), for which she earned a special Academy Award. One of the most popular—and highly paid—stars of her time, Temple launched scores of brand-name products with her curly hair and twinkling eyes. Unsuccessful as an adult actress, Temple retired from films and entered government service. In 1969 she became a U.S. representative to the United Nations (1969). She has also served as ambassador to Ghana (1974–1975), White

House chief of protocol (1976–1977), and ambassador to Czechoslovakia (1989–1992).

Emma Thompson (1959–)

This British actress debuted onstage in London while still attending Cambridge University. She debuted on film in the comedy *Me and My Girl* (1983) and costarred with Kenneth Branagh on BBC-TV's *Fortunes of War,* earning a BAFTA (the British equivalent of an Oscar). In 1989 she costarred in *Henry V,* which was directed by Branagh, whom she married that year (they separated in 1995). Among her finest films are *Much Ado About Nothing* (1993); *Howards End* (1992), for which she earned an Oscar; *Remains of the Day* (1993); and *Sense and Sensibility,* which earned her another BAFTA.

Spencer Tracy (1900–1967)

Often cast as the stylish, authoritative tough guy, Tracy turned in such subtle performances that he was nicknamed "the Prince of Underplayers." One of Hollywood's top stars by the 1950s, he received nine Academy Award nominations and two Oscars. He made more than forty films, including *Captains Courageous* (1937), *Boys Town* (1938), *Father of the Bride* (1950), *Pat and Mike* (1952), *Inherit the Wind* (1960), and his last film, *Guess Who's Coming to Dinner* (1967).

John Wayne (1907–1979)

Born Marion Michael Morrison in Winterset, Iowa, John Wayne earned fame playing tough, can-do western heroes in films such as *Stagecoach* (1939) and *She Wore a Yellow Ribbon* (1949). He appeared in more than seventy-five films, of which he directed two: *The Alamo* (1960) and *The Green Berets* (1968). His most memorable characters include the Oscar-winning lawman in *True Grit* (1969) and the Oscar-nominated marine in *Sands of Iwo Jima* (1949).

Organizations and Online Sites

Academy of Motion Picture Arts and Sciences
Academy Foundation
8949 Wilshire Boulevard
Beverly Hills, CA 90211–1972

The American Film Institute
The John F. Kennedy Center for the Performing Arts
2700 F Street, NW
Washington, DC 20566

The American Film Institute
2021 North Western Avenue
Los Angeles, CA 90027

Directors Guild of America
Los Angeles Headquarters
7920 Sunset Boulevard
Los Angeles, CA 90046

The John F. Kennedy Center for the Performing Arts
2700 F Street, NW
Washington, DC 20566

Screen Actors Guild
National Office and Hollywood Office
5757 Wilshire Boulevard
Los Angeles, CA 90036–3600

Web Sites

Academy of Motion Picture Arts and Sciences, official site
http://wwwdb.oscars.org/

Alfred Hitchcock Site:
Lopez-Guzman, Patricio, "Alfred Hitchcock: Master of Suspense"
http://nextdch.mty.itesm.mx/~plopezg/Kaplan/Hitchcock.html

American Film Institute home page
http://www.afi.com

Annenberg/CPB-Cinema: How Are Hollywood Films Made?
http://www.learner.org/exhibits/cinema/acting2.html

Arts and Entertainment Biography
http://www.biography.com

Directors Guild of America
http://www.dga.org/

International Movie Data Base
http://www.imdb.com

The Kennedy Center of Performing Arts
http://www.kennedy-center.org

Motion Picture Industry: Behind the Scenes
http://library.thinkquest.org/10015/data/info/reference

Screen Actors Guild
http://www.sag.org/index_flat.html

For Further Reading

Aronson, Virginia. *Drew Barrymore.* Philadelphia: Chelsea House Publishers, 2000.

Bergman, Carol. *Sidney Poitier.* New York: Chelsea House Publishers, 1988.

Biography Today: Profiles of People of Interest to Young Readers (Harrison Ford). Omnigraphics, Vol. 6, No. 3, September 1997.

Biography Today: Profiles of People of Interest to Young Readers (Brad Pitt). Omnigraphics, Vol. 7, No. 3, September 1998.

Brady, Kathleen. *People Profiles: John Travolta.* New York: Time, 2000.

Caper, William. *Whoopi Goldberg.* New Jersey: Enslow Publishers, 1999.

Chan, Jackie, with Jeff Yang. *I Am Jackie Chan: My Life in Action.* New York: Ballantine Books, 1998.

Ferber, Elizabeth. *Steven Spielberg.* Philadelphia: Chelsea House Publishers, 1997.

Forster, Evan. "Meryl Streep: A Star in Any Language," *Biography,* September 1998, p. 68.

Gaines, Ann Graham. *Whoopi Goldberg.* Philadelphia: Chelsea House Publishers, 1999.

Gifford, Denis. *Chaplin*. New York: Doubleday & Company, 1974.

Hill, Anne E. *Denzel Washington*. Philadelphia: Chelsea House Publishers, 1999.

Lee, Linda. *People Profiles: Tom Hanks*. New York: Time, 1999.

"Legends: Harrison Ford." *People Weekly* 25th Anniversary Issue, March 15–22, 1999.

Lowenstein, Stephen. *My First Movie: Twenty Celebrated Directors Talk About Their First Film*. New York: Pantheon Books, 2001.

Marcovitz, Hal. *Robin Williams*. Philadelphia: Chelsea House Publishers, 2000.

Maychick, Diana. *Meryl Streep: Reluctant Superstar*. New York: St. Martin's Press, 1984.

Meyers, Jeffrey. *Bogart: A Life in Hollywood*. New York: Fromm International, 1999.

Mills, Bart. "Harrison Ford: Rugged Romantic," *Biography*, October 1999, p. 48.

Parker, John. *Sean Connery*. Chicago: Contemporary Books, 1993.

Proferes, Nicholas. *Film Directing Fundamentals: From Script to Screen*. Burlington, MA: Focal Press, 2001.

Smurthwaite, Nick. *The Meryl Streep Story*. New York: Beaufort Books, 1984.

Surcouf, Elizabeth Gillen. *Grace Kelly, American Princess*. Minneapolis: Lerner Publications Company, 1992.

Index

Numbers in *italics* represent illustrations.

Photo Credits

Photographs © 2003: AP/Wide World Photos: cover bottom left, 202 (Kevork Djansezian), 232 (Damian Dovarganes), cover bottom center, 176, 208 (Mark J. Terrill), 249 (Tannis Toohey/Canadian Press), 46; Corbis Images: 136, 194, 224 (AFP), 18, 26, 58, 74, 87, 92, 105, 127, 145, 146 (Bettmann), 261 (Dean Conger), 253 (Rufus F. Folkks), 147, 181 (Mitchell Gerber), back cover bottom right, 31, 41 (Hulton-Deutsch Collection), 101, 132, 140 (Douglas Kirkland), 163 (LGI), 159 (Pacha), 122 (Roger Ressmeyer), cover top right, back cover top right, 150, 154, 167, 172, 198, 212, 228, 237, 241, 245 (Reuters Newmedia Inc.), 114 (Rafael Roa), 259 (Paul A. Souders), 110 (Underwood & Underwood), 118; Hulton|Archive/Getty Images: 66, 70, 190, 216; Kobal Collection /Picture Desk: cover top left, 78, 97; Photofest: cover bottom right, 50 (MGM), 62 (RKO), 84 (VistaVision), back cover left center, 220 (Warner Brothers), back cover bottom left, back cover top center, back cover top left, cover top center, 1, 9, 14, 22, 37, 54, 185.

Copyright extends to corresponding image on Contents page

About the Author

*J*udy L. Hasday, a native of Philadelphia, Pennsylvania, received her B.A. in communications and her Ed.M. in instructional technologies from Temple University. Ms. Hasday has written many books for young adults, including the 1999 New York Public Library award-winner *James Earl Jones*. Her *Extraordinary Women Athletes*, published in 2000, received a National Social Studies Council award. Her recent works include the story of the 1999 shooting at Columbine High School and a biography of actress Meryl Streep.